# THE KENTUCKY TRAGEDY

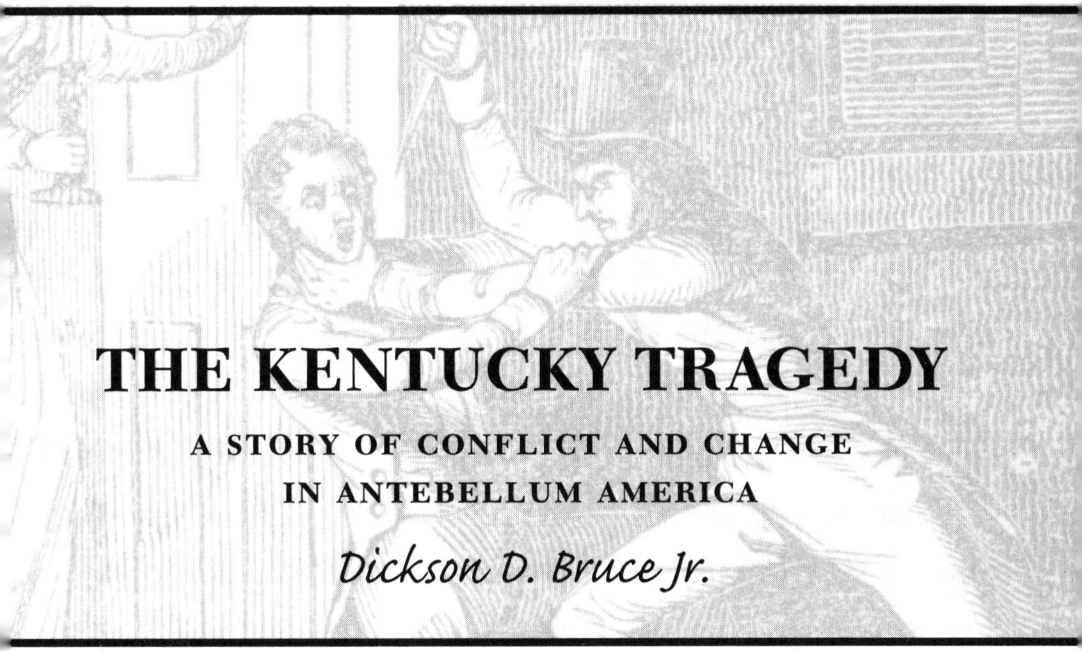

# THE KENTUCKY TRAGEDY

## A STORY OF CONFLICT AND CHANGE IN ANTEBELLUM AMERICA

Dickson D. Bruce Jr.

LOUISIANA STATE UNIVERSITY PRESS
BATON ROUGE

PUBLISHED BY LOUISIANA STATE UNIVERSITY PRESS

Manufactured in the United States of America
FIRST PRINTING

DESIGNER: *Amanda McDonald Scallan*
TYPEFACE: *New Caledonia*
TYPESETTER: *G & S Typesetters, Inc.*
PRINTER AND BINDER: *Edwards Brothers*

Library of Congress Cataloging-in-Publication Data

Bruce, Dickson D., 1946–
The Kentucky tragedy : a story of conflict and change in antebellum America / Dickson D. Bruce, Jr.
p. cm.
Includes bibliographical references and index.
ISBN-13: 978-0-8071-3173-2
ISBN-10: 0-8071-3173-3 (cloth : alk. paper)
1. Murder—Kentucky—Case studies. 2. Sharp, Solomon P., 1781–1825. 3. Beauchamp, Jereboam O., d. 1826. 4. Kentucky—Civilization—19th cetury. 5. Social conflict—Kentucky—History—19th century. I. Title.
HV6533.K4B78 2006
364.152′309769432—dc22 2005033271

The paper in this book meets the guidelines for permanence and durability of the Committee on Production Guidelines for Book Longevity of the Council on Library Resources. ♾

*For Mary, again*

# CONTENTS

## ACKNOWLEDGMENTS

I am grateful to many individuals and institutions for their assistance in completing this study. In the course of conducting research for the book, I visited a number of libraries and archives. These include the Houghton Library at Harvard, the Filson Historical Society in Louisville, the Kentucky History Center and the Kentucky Department for Libraries and Archives (special thanks to James Prichard) in Frankfort, the libraries of the University of Kentucky, and the Library Company of Philadelphia (with thanks to Phil Lapsansky). Grants from the School of Humanities at the University of California, Irvine, helped to defray the cost of some of this research.

I am also grateful to Mrs. Dorothy Steers of the Simpson County History Center in Franklin, Kentucky, for making a number of important archival and other sources available to me. And, of course, thanks to the interlibrary loan staff at the University of California, Irvine, for their invaluable support. Finally, I should note my appreciation to Clayton Lewis of the William L. Clements Library, University of Michigan, and to Raymond Wemmlinger of the Hampden-Booth Theatre Library at The Players, New York, for helping me to obtain some otherwise very obscure illustrations.

I also received valuable comments on this study at various stages of its development. Portions first saw light as conference papers, and I am grateful to such scholars as John Mayfield, David Moltke-Hansen, Kieran Quinlan, and Bertram Wyatt-Brown for remarks and suggestions that have significantly influenced this final product. The manuscript itself benefited from readings by Emily Bruce, Alice Fahs, and Birte Pfleger, as well as the two anonymous readers for the Press. I am particularly indebted to Johanna Shields for her discerning evaluation of the work, and for comments that were both critical—in the best sense of the word—and encouraging.

Finally, and as always, my thanks to my wife, Mary, for her continuing patience and support.

# THE KENTUCKY TRAGEDY

# INTRODUCTION

Any survey of antebellum America from at least the 1820s to the coming of the Civil War is likely to portray a society marked by extraordinary tensions and anxieties. These tensions and anxieties were the products of a series of interconnected changes in American political, social, and cultural life. Such changes included the emergence of a democratic, partisan politics, as well as a sectional politics of unprecedented virulence—a sectional politics that ultimately erupted into the nation's bloodiest war. They included the growth of an individualistic, competitive market economy that reached into every aspect of the nation's cultural as well as economic life, reshaping social relations and redefining social bonds. And they included developments in thinking about social and individual identity that subtly but powerfully reinforced the challenges such changes posed.

This was a period, moreover, when traditional moral and spiritual verities appeared to be less and less helpful to people confronting an increasingly complicated world. The antebellum era was a time of intellectual as well as social and political ferment. A secularizing age—almost despite itself—it was the setting for transformative, troubling, intensely materialistic reconceptualizations of human nature, centering particularly on ways of thinking about the body and the mind. Pioneered in a developing psychology that increasingly identified human motivations and feelings with organic processes located in the brain, these redefinitions quickly advanced beyond the arcane worlds of scientific inquiry and philosophical thought to shape antebellum thought and culture in sometimes surprising but inescapable ways. As a number of historians have shown, this materialism prompted new modes of thought, and concern, that came to be reflected in ideas about everything from sexuality to criminality, from diet to death.[1] When antebellum Americans thought about themselves, about their lives and their deaths, they were faced with their own materiality to an extent that was both unprecedented and difficult to evade.

At the beginning of the era, a set of events occurred in Kentucky that, for the next thirty-five years, served to reveal how compelling these uncertainties and anxieties were for people confronting the changing American world, and how they sought to come to terms with the changes they faced. These events were known as "the Kentucky Tragedy," and related to the murder of Colonel Solomon P. Sharp, one of Kentucky's leading politicians, by Jereboam Beauchamp, a young lawyer, in Frankfort in November 1825.

From the beginning, the episode entailed great controversy, but, to summarize the story briefly, it seems to have originated in allegations that, about six years earlier, Sharp had seduced one Ann Cooke. He had, it was said, used his status and his wiles to persuade her to have sex with him, resulting in the birth of a stillborn child. In the intervening period Beauchamp had married Cooke and, during the summer of 1825, had become incensed when rumors regarding the seduction had again been circulated. In his anger, reinforced by hers, he had wreaked his violent retribution upon Sharp.

But the full "Tragedy" was yet to unfold. Arrested, Beauchamp was ultimately tried, found guilty, and sentenced to die. As he awaited his execution, his wife joined him in his cell, where, at some point, they began to plot suicide. Shortly before Beauchamp's scheduled death, they put their plans into action, taking doses of laudanum Ann Beauchamp had brought into the cell. The laudanum failed to work, but, undeterred, on the morning of the execution the two took a dagger she had kept concealed and stabbed themselves. Her wounds were mortal; his were not. After some medical attention, he was taken out to die. They were buried, as they had requested, in a single grave.

Not surprisingly, these events attracted, and continued to attract, a great deal of attention. Documents related to the events, including a report of the trial and a "confession" purportedly written by Beauchamp himself, were published within weeks of the Beauchamps' deaths. These documents were republished throughout the antebellum period. Scholarly editions of some of the documents have appeared as recently as the 1960s.[2] Historians have explored and analyzed the Tragedy in works ranging from L. F. Johnson's brief account in his pioneering survey of Kentucky murders and trials to a book-length study published by the great Kentucky historian J. Winston Coleman in 1950. More recently, its events have been examined in the thorough investigations of

J. W. Cooke extending from the late 1980s through the 1990s.[3] All have stressed the complexity of the case; all have recognized its significance for illuminating the often violent, unsettled world of 1820s Kentucky.

Kentucky could be a violent place in the 1820s. It was a place where people gave credence to a strict and bloody code of honor that, among other things, provided little room for despoiling a woman's character, as Sharp was said to have done, and virtually demanded the kind of violent retribution Beauchamp exacted. Thus, to a great extent, the code served to frame how people understood the Beauchamp-Sharp affair at the time, and how they have continued to interpret its significance.[4] As the Tragedy unfolded, its participants and their contemporaries both celebrated and worried about honor's fundamental bases, raising issues that continue to illuminate what that notoriously multifaceted social and cultural ideal was about, as we shall see.

But the Kentucky Tragedy had so many levels and complications to it that it quickly became an episode about much more than honor. Even in Kentucky at the time people drew parallels between its events and a variety of traditions of thought and culture, particularly traditions of sentimentalism and sentimental fiction that dated back to the mid-eighteenth century. In keeping with those traditions, people assigned to the Tragedy a significance that was more than immediate, viewing it as, among other things, an object lesson in the dangers posed by seduction, anger, and pride.

Such apparent parallels undoubtedly contributed to the fact that, for the rest of the antebellum era, novelists, poets, and playwrights frequently found in the Kentucky Tragedy a source for literary inspiration. These included the prominent—Edgar Allan Poe, Charlotte Barnes, and William Gilmore Simms, for example—and those whose fame was less far reaching: Thomas Holley Chivers and Mary E. MacMichael. Their efforts are not unknown to scholars, who have provided important studies of the individual works these writers created, as well as valuable overviews, classically by Willard Rouse Jillson and, on a much larger scale, by Jack Surrency.[5] Based on what these scholars have said about the kinds of adaptations various authors made when taking on the Kentucky story, it is obvious what a rich source for literary re-creation and re-elaboration those authors found the Tragedy to be as they sought to make the tale their own.

These literary renditions of the Kentucky Tragedy provide real insight into the cultural life of antebellum America. The most important of them began to appear in the mid-1830s and continued through the 1850s, as the era's key social, intellectual, and cultural developments advanced far beyond where they were in the 1820s, when Sharp and the Beauchamps met their deaths. The continuing power of the story is testimony to its continuing relevance, and it is difficult to think of any other single episode from the era that inspired more literary effort and for such a long period of time. At the same time, authors tailored and retailored their accounts in ways that took it well beyond the rowdy western context in which the story had its birth. It was in this that they also revealed and built on the story's resonance with the changing antebellum world, with its many and deep anxieties and uncertainties.

The Kentucky Tragedy, however it was told, was a sensational story. It was one of many such stories that had an appeal for audiences apparently thirsty for sensational tales. Historians have long recognized the power of the sensational during the antebellum period. Murder novels, stories, and dramas were everywhere, and, since the pioneering work of David Brion Davis in the 1950s, the extent of their cultural and sociological relevance has been widely appreciated.[6] American writers found in tales of violence and murder a powerful way to encapsulate the difficulties they encountered in the face of changing ideas about gender, changing notions of class and the crises of urbanization, and changing conceptions of human motivation. They could, and often did, turn to "real life" crimes for their sources; crimes, as such, became grist for the mill of a sensationalistic, popular, and seemingly unrestrained press.[7] They could—and often did—exercise their imaginations, creating gothic fantasies of violence and death. Historians have been able to mine this rich tradition of popular and literary sensationalism to portray more fully the world in which it took shape.[8]

Nevertheless, if stories of the Kentucky Tragedy participated in this larger sensationalist literary environment, they did so in a very special way. Not only did the Tragedy inspire more treatments than any other single episode from the period, but as writers took hold of the tale, they also found in it a breadth of allusion that few of its counterparts appear to have matched. Many of the more popular stories of the era, the murder of New York prostitute Helen Jewett, for example, or that of Mary Rogers, were closely tied to the urban world in which they occurred, and maintained their urban resonance in whatever form they appeared.[9] Virtually every writer inspired by the Kentucky Tragedy made clear that she or he was after bigger game, exploring the wellsprings of jealousy, violence, betrayal, and heroism. Again, the Kentucky Tragedy, whatever its western origins, was never treated as a story only about the West—something made clear by such writers as Poe and Barnes, who dramatically shifted its setting to Renaissance Italy. The motives and emotions it portrayed could, from the perspective of its antebellum American re-creators, affect people anywhere.

And, in important ways, it must be acknowledged that the Kentucky Tragedy had a resonance that went well beyond the world of antebellum America. Nineteenth-century readers would have recognized echoes of stories that date back to long before their time (as modern readers will recognize echoes of stories dating to the present day). There are echoes of stories coming from many parts of the world, not just antebellum America. The equation of heroism with violence—found in virtually every treatment of the Tragedy, from the purportedly factual to the most elaborately fictional—is as timeless as anything can be said to be.[10] The Tragedy's appeal is, in some sense, a reminder that little in antebellum America was *sui generis*. The era's cultural and intellectual development was tied to influences as far reaching over time and space as they ever had been, and as they continue to be.

Still, the nineteenth-century tellings and retellings of the Kentucky Tragedy were strongly marked by antebellum concerns. Highly conventionalized, the various versions of the Kentucky events turned the principals into types that, however seemingly universal, were also embedded in the literary repertoire of the day. The course of events was selectively rendered, or even significantly modified, to cohere with dominant literary and cultural standards—and to get rid of any inconsistencies between the Kentucky prototypes and popular antebellum ideals.

The following account of the Kentucky Tragedy focuses on this process of selection and adaptation, citing the conventions various writers relied on to construct their stories, identifying what they chose to detail and, no less important, what they chose to change or leave out, and analyzing why it matters. Such a focus indicates just how germane the various renditions of the Tragedy were to antebellum life, including the extent to which they simultaneously depended on and revealed significant cultural anxieties, and how they expressed and defined for their readers and audiences what seems to have been a pervasive discontent.

As an effort to provide both an account of the Tragedy's events and an exploration of their literary transformations, this particular version of the Kentucky Tragedy moves in several directions. It begins, in the first two chapters, with a survey of what happened in 1820s Kentucky and of the responses, popular and literary, the events provoked. This account of Sharp's murder and its aftermath is presented in a straightforward, almost "minimalist" way. Much of the surviving documentation is both biased and self-serving, and these chapters seek to present the least disputable facts of the case, the facts about which we can have the greatest confidence. Drawing on contemporary newspapers, legal documents, and the existing scholarship, this account cannot avoid its share of pitfalls; even the chronology of events is not entirely certain (and the more one looks, the less certain that chronology appears). But such a bare bones account is useful, even necessary, if one is to make clear the extent and significance of subsequent representations and adaptations, even those that began to take shape at almost the moment of Sharp's death.

The next three chapters move back and forth from events to literature (in the process filling in the starkly rendered account with which we begin) in an effort to explore more fully what the Kentucky Tragedy could mean. Organized topically, these latter chapters indicate, first, that the Kentucky Tragedy became compelling because it did enable people to confront the powerful social, cultural, and intellectual questions that plagued antebellum America and then suggest why this was so. As chapter three shows, at least part of the Tragedy's appeal lay in the way it could be made to portray difficult and unresolved issues of social identity in antebellum America, especially issues of gender. The chapter also suggests that such a focus, as embodied in the story's various elaborations, helps to reveal far-reaching concerns that both drove and were driven by those issues.

Chapter four discusses still deeper dimensions to antebellum confrontations with change. These dimensions were revealed as the story, in its many incarnations, brought out the implications of a shifting moral psychology that encapsulated the period's increasingly materialistic ideas, and ideals, of human nature. The principles and, especially, the language of this psychology were apparent in accounts of the Tragedy from the beginning, even as people responded to Sharp's death and to the Beauchamps' tragic fate. Those who adapted the Tragedy drew heavily, and often quite explicitly, on the principles and language alike. They said that their attraction to the story lay in the opportunity it provided to explore the moral, psychological issues it raised, and in their sense that audiences found such explorations interesting and important. The chapter suggests that the Tragedy's literary career also indicates how pressing those issues could be, in all their ramifications, for antebellum audiences.

Chapter five, finally, describes how fully the Kentucky Tragedy was implicated in antebellum politics, especially in the growth of an increasingly democratic, partisan politics during that time. The events were assigned great political significance from the moment of Sharp's murder, revealing important facets of American thinking about democratic partisanship at what, the events themselves suggest, was a formative point in its development. The environment such a politics created remained a backdrop for later representations of those events, and often an explicit part of the story, as well. At the same time, as this chapter stresses, the Kentucky Tragedy, as various writers continued to shape and represent it, also reveals how thoroughly antebellum political developments—involving both practice and ideology—were implicated in more general questions of identity and human nature.

In many ways, the Kentucky Tragedy in all its versions puts the pervasiveness of connections—or, again, interconnections—among antebellum social, intellectual, and political forms in peculiarly sharp relief. The changes Americans had to confront during the first half of the nineteenth century were not only far-reaching but also complex. They took place within a web of intertwined concerns, each building on the other, that made the emerging American world seem unusually threatening, defining possibilities and potentialities that appeared likely to move in uncertain, even contradictory directions. The Kentucky Tragedy, as it was interpreted and reinterpreted during the antebellum period, helps to illuminate why the era's tensions and anxieties were almost inevitable, given the course of events and the assumptions and ideals antebellum Americans used to define their lives.

To see this more clearly, however, we must first go back to Kentucky, to the murder of Solomon Sharp and to the tragic events that ensued.

*Chapter 1*

# GREAT GOD!! IT'S HIM!!!

In Frankfort, Kentucky, shortly after noon on Friday, July 7, 1826, twenty-three-year-old lawyer Jereboam Beauchamp was taken from a cell to a hill overlooking the city, just deserts, many felt, for his having murdered the influential and popular Solomon Sharp some eight months before. There, in front of over five thousand people, Beauchamp was hanged. By all accounts, he approached his death with dignity and composure, bowing to the people as he rode in a wagon to the gallows, speaking to those he knew. At the gallows, he asked for a drink of water and also asked a band in attendance to play "Bonaparte's Retreat from Moscow," a rousing fiddle tune. Then, the rope around his neck, he announced himself ready. The cart in which he was standing drove off; and Beauchamp struggled for a few minutes, then died.[1]

The composure with which Beauchamp approached his death was impressive, not least because of the horrible condition he was in. His wife, Ann, had been with him in his cell since his sentencing in late May, where they had determined to die together. On the Wednesday night preceding his scheduled execution, they had dosed themselves with what they believed to be a fatal amount of laudanum. The drug failed to have the desired effect, and the following morning the two were placed under a suicide watch and threatened with separation. Throughout the day, the Beauchamps listened as preparations for the execution began, and, toward evening, became visibly agitated when a military guard was assembled for the next day's events. As night came, Beauchamp wrote a little; Mrs. Beauchamp, who still had some concealed laudanum, took another dose, but she was unable to keep it down.

The following morning, the two appeared composed. As the crowd gathered, the Beauchamps asked their guard for a few minutes alone. He reluctantly agreed. Once he had left, Mrs. Beauchamp produced the knife she had smuggled into the cell and stabbed herself just below the breast. Beauchamp then took the knife and stabbed himself in the abdomen. As Mrs. Beauchamp approached death, her severely wounded husband was permitted to pay her a final farewell. He then began his journey to the gallows, weakened and in great pain. It was, most observers agreed, a moving scene.

The events that brought the Beauchamps to such a tragic end, though quickly surrounded by conflicts, controversy, and speculation, may nevertheless be sketched in a way that provides a reliable account of what had taken place. The story had begun in 1819, when Mrs. Beauchamp—then Ann Cooke[2]—and Solomon Sharp had engaged in a relationship that quickly became, perhaps, too close. Already one of Kentucky's leading politicians, Sharp was approaching the apogee of a career that had advanced steadily from relatively humble beginnings to near the top of Kentucky's political world.

Born in Virginia in 1787, Sharp had been taken by his family as a small child to Logan County, Kentucky, sometime before 1795. Logan County was located in what was known as the Green River country, on the western frontier of the state. At the time of the Sharps' arrival, it had a frontier rawness that was fabled. According to Sharp's Green River contemporary, the great Methodist preacher Peter Cartwright, Logan County was known as "Rogues' Harbor," a refuge for all sorts of criminals fleeing prosecution in more settled regions.[3] No less notably, it was to be the setting for one of American history's most exuberant frontier religious outbursts, occurring shortly after the Sharps arrived.

At the close of the eighteenth century, Logan was only just receiving permanent settlement from older parts of the United States; there remained a substantial number of squatters on the land. In subsequent years, the region remained largely populated by small landowners growing corn, wheat, hemp, and flax, along with a little tobacco. Among these middling sorts, the Sharps seem themselves to have been somewhere in the middle—not among the very poor, but not among the very rich, either.[4]

Like many young men in the backcountry South, Solomon Sharp found a path to greater prominence through the professions and then land speculation and politics.[5] He had begun to practice law in that part of the state by 1809, and by 1810 he had begun to acquire land in Logan and other western counties, some of it with his brother, physician Leander Sharp, who lived in Bowling Green, in neighboring Warren County. Solomon himself moved to Warren County early in his career and entered politics, representing the county in the state legislature from 1809 to 1811.[6]

With the coming of war in 1812, Solomon Sharp left the legislature to join the American cause. His participation was brief, only about six weeks, but he did attain the rank of colonel, a stepping-stone to still greater political prominence. By the end of 1812, Sharp had won election to Congress, where he served two terms before returning to Bowling Green. In 1817, he was returned to the Kentucky legislature, to serve another two terms. All the while, he continued to prosper, acquiring land and slaves while enhancing both his social and political visibility. His marriage to Eliza Scott, a member of a prominent Frankfort family, in December 1818 confirmed his growing stature in Kentucky's social and political order.[7]

It was at some point during these years that he also came to know Ann Cooke. She, too, had been born in Virginia, probably in 1786; her family had moved to Kentucky sometime after her father's death in 1805, and prior to 1810, settling in Warren County.[8] Cooke seems to have come from a well-to-do family. As her biographer J. W. Cooke has found, Ann's father had acquired substantial property in Kentucky prior to his death, leaving his family a prosperous estate in land and slaves. In the years after about 1817, however, she found herself in increasingly difficult circumstances, and increasingly alone. Three of her brothers died between 1818 and 1821, leaving only her, her mother, and her brother Peyton, who lived in Bowling Green.[9]

Despite their deteriorating situation, Cooke and her family seem to have known some of the region's leading figures. Among them was John J. Crittenden, the prominent Logan County attorney who was also emerging as one of antebellum Kentucky's most distinguished politicians. A contemporary as well as, apparently, a friend of both Sharp and Cooke, he was already on his way to becoming a major voice at both state and national levels from this point into the Civil War era. The Cookes were also close to John U. Waring, among the region's wealthier men, a political hothead—and one of Sharp's bitterest enemies. And they did know the Sharps. Solomon had done some legal business for them, and, when she happened to be in Bowling Green, Ann Cooke had occasionally called on Eliza Sharp.[10]

In May or June 1820, Cooke gave birth to her stillborn baby. She identified Sharp as the father, claiming he had seduced her in his office the preceding September. Sharp denied both the seduction and his paternity of the child. Cooke did little to pursue her claims at the time, but they were not to be quickly forgotten. They resurfaced in 1821 when Sharp, after a brief absence from politics, decided to seek a seat in the state Senate. That June, he was viciously attacked in a handbill issued by Waring. In it, Waring accused Sharp of land fraud, an accusation growing out of an earlier dispute between the two men, and of the seduction that had led to the birth of Cooke's stillborn child. Before the charge could affect Sharp's senatorial race, however, Governor John Adair nominated Sharp to be state attorney general, and Sharp accepted. In the subsequent confirmation hearings, the charges were again raised. A Senate committee investigated them, exonerated Sharp, and confirmed him to the post. He moved his family to Frankfort, the state capital, shortly thereafter.[11]

It was also at about this time that Cooke appears to have met Jereboam Beauchamp. The circumstances are far from clear, as is the character of their relationship. Beauchamp was born in September 1802 in what would become, in 1819, Simpson County, immediately south of Warren. His Green River origins were not unlike Sharp's, nor was the world in which he came of age. His father, Thomas Beauchamp, was a farmer and small slaveholder, and the family, like Cooke's, had connections to Kentucky's political leadership. One of Jereboam's uncles, also named Jereboam, was a longtime state senator from Washington County, near the center of the state, and was, like Sharp, able to claim the title "Colonel." The younger Jereboam Beauchamp went to school in nearby Glasgow, Kentucky, and did some teaching before moving to Bowling Green in 1820 to read law.

The following year, having completed his studies, Jereboam returned to his father's home in Simpson County for a respite and, apparently, met Cooke, who lived only a mile or so away. She had gone into seclusion on a farm she had purchased in Simpson County, a farm she had appropriately named "Retirement," where she lived with her mother and two or three of the family's slaves.[12] The relationship blossomed and Jereboam and Ann eventually became engaged. Within a short time Jereboam began his legal career. He was admitted to the bar in April 1823,[13] and in June 1824 he and Ann wed, settling together on her farm. She was thirty-eight years old; he was twenty-one.

Then, in 1825, within months of their marriage, the Beauchamps were put on their collision course with Sharp when the latter decided to resign his post as attorney general and run for the legislature as a representative from Frankfort. The election of 1825 was one of the nastiest in Kentucky history. Kentucky was in the throes of what one nineteenth-century historian, Lewis Collins, described as "the most embittered and violent conflict of parties" that had ever embroiled the state, the relief and court struggles extending from about 1818 to about 1826.[14] The struggles grew out of a conflict over debt and credit that had plagued the state since the onset of a severe economic depression in 1818. A product of tumbling agricultural and land prices, the depression encouraged a call for legislation to provide relief for indebted Kentucky farmers and landholders facing foreclosure and eviction from their properties. This agitation also led to the rapid emergence of two strongly divided relief and anti-relief factions in the state's political arena.[15]

The subsequent course of Kentucky's political history was not to run smooth, especially after the election of a relief governor, John Adair, and the seating of a relief majority in the state House in 1820 helped move relief efforts in rather far reaching directions. The assembly approved a variety of measures to allow debtors to delay payments, protecting landowners from speculators by forbidding sale of foreclosed properties at a fraction of their value, and limiting the authority of the banks. In addition, it also approved legislation protecting occupants of Kentucky land against the claims of absentee titleholders, many from Virginia.[16]

The legislation was controversial and, as people recognized then and have recognized since, of questionable constitutionality. It received an unfavorable reception in the courts. Upholding principles of contract guaranteed by both the Kentucky and federal constitutions, state and federal judges rejected the legislation, exacerbating divisions between the relief and anti-relief parties. The conflict became particularly bitter when, in October 1823, Kentucky's highest court, the Court of Appeals, affirmed the unconstitutionality of some of the key legislation. The court's decision produced widespread anger, and in the subsequent elections of 1824, the relief party gained strength in the legislature. A substantial majority elected a pro-relief governor, Joseph Desha. The new assembly was emboldened to abolish the existing Court of Appeals and to create a new one, with more limited powers. Early in 1825, Desha appointed the New Court's three new judges, with former lieutenant governor William T. Barry as chief justice. Francis Blair, another relief stalwart, was appointed clerk.[17]

The result was legal chaos, since the Old Court, as it was known, refused to step down and even continued to hear cases. Achilles Sneed, its clerk, refused a demand to surrender records to the New Court, leading Francis Blair to seize them forcibly. Neither side conceded the legality of the other, and state politics became still more sharply divided along factional lines, the older relief and anti-relief factions transforming themselves into Old and New Court parties.[18] This mixture of conflict and chaos almost ensured that the 1825 election would be one in which, as historian Collins said, "the passions of the people" were never more "violently excited."[19]

Solomon Sharp was a leading figure in the New Court cause. Although he had long been uncomfortable with at least some aspects of relief legislation, he had also been a strong supporter of what one admirer termed "popular power."[20] He had seen the decision of the Court of Appeals against relief legislation as unwarranted. As attorney general when the court controversy arose, he voiced some reservations about the act that had abolished the Old Court, but he used the powers of his office in favor of the New.[21] His decision to step down from the attorney general's post and to run for the legislature in 1825 was motivated largely by his belief, and that of his supporters, that he could more effectively support the New Court cause as a popular, and articulate, legislative leader.

Sharp's efforts as attorney general had already brought him a fair share of political abuse, something that continued through the 1825 campaign. Even before he announced his candidacy, rumors of the Cooke seduction appear to have emerged as an issue among both his supporters and his opponents. In addition, the Beauchamps appear to have learned that Sharp was not only denying having seduced Cooke, but also suggesting he could not possibly have been her baby's father. The stillborn child had been dark in complexion—had been, in fact, a mulatto—and he had a certificate from the midwife to prove it. Sharp's family later denied that Sharp had any role in spreading the rumor (while not denying the rumor's truth).

In the end, Sharp won the seat for which he had campaigned. Frankfort, where Sharp had sought election, was allowed two seats in the House. Although it was a New Court stronghold, the Old Court party had selected John J. Crittenden, among its most prominent and respected leaders, to enter the race. Despite the friendship between Crittenden and Sharp, the campaign, which also involved another New Court candidate, Lewis Sanders (who would replace Sharp after the murder), was full of acrimony, including the virulent personal attacks on Sharp for his actions as attorney general. The election itself was marked by allegations of fraud: Crittenden's biographer Albert Kirwan noted that there were more votes cast than there were qualified voters. Sharp was the top vote-getter, by only sixty-nine votes, with runner-up Crittenden taking the second seat.[22] Sharp was widely trumpeted as a candidate to be Speaker of the House when the legislature was scheduled to meet in November.

He never became Speaker, or anything else, because at about two in the morning on Monday, November 7, 1825—the day the legislature was to convene—he met his death. According to the accounts that began to appear shortly after the event, he and his wife were in bed in their Frankfort home when they were awakened by a knock on the door. When Sharp asked who it was, he was told, "John A. Covington." The visitor claimed to be looking for lodging; all the public houses were filled. Opening the door, Sharp was taken by the hand and asked, "Is this you, Col. Sharp?" Sharp then said, "I do not know that I am acquainted with you; I know John W. Covington, but I do not recollect of ever being acquainted with any person of the name of John A. Covington." The visitor replied, "Then damn you, you shall soon be acquainted with me," plunging a knife into Sharp's body. His wife ran to Sharp's side, as did his brother Leander, but, according to reports, Sharp could say nothing and died within minutes.[23]

People were shocked. The editor of one Frankfort newspaper, not at all friendly to Sharp politically, commented, "To invade the sanctuary of a man's private and family residence; to call him up from the bosom of his wife, and gain admittance by a successful claim on his hospitality, to stab him in the heart, is an act of atrocity and crime that strikes us with more horror than any thing we have ever felt."[24] The legislature, following the lead of Sharp's personal friend (and political foe) John J. Crittenden, used similar words to mark the "mournful and distressing occasion" of his death. At Crittenden's urging, legislators voted to offer a reward of $3,000 for the arrest and conviction of Sharp's killer. An additional $1,000 was posted by the trustees of Frankfort.[25]

Who had done it? Initially, some people suspected John Waring. Waring had been involved in many altercations in the past, was known to have circulated the 1821 handbill charging Sharp with seduction, and made a credible suspect in the case of Sharp's murder. Waring, however, could not have committed the crime. At the time of the murder, he was in Fayette County, about twenty miles away, recovering from wounds received in another altercation.[26]

Suspicion quickly turned to Beauchamp, for several reasons. First, there were the rumors about Sharp's relationship to Mrs. Beauchamp. Jereboam was said to have made threats against Sharp over the course of the campaign. Second, he was known to have been in Frankfort when the crime was committed, and during the night had been heard leaving his lodgings at the home of Joel Scott, recently appointed keeper of the Kentucky state penitentiary.[27] Finally, he left town the following morning, immediately after learning of the crime, and expressed no curiosity about it. Based on these suspicions, he was pursued by a guard made up of Frankfort citizens to his home in Simpson County, where he was taken into custody and returned to Frankfort for examination.[28]

He arrived on November 15, and the following day was formally placed under arrest. He was led before an examining court, where the county justices of the peace took preliminary testimony from members of the arresting party, the city patrol, and others confirming the suspicions that had initially led to his apprehension.[29] At this point, Charles Bibb, the Commonwealth's Attorney, asked for additional time to bring in more witnesses, a request to which the magistrates and Beauchamp himself agreed. The magistrates also determined, however, that Beauchamp should be held until the court was to reconvene, about a week and a half later. There was ultimately to be a second delay before the hearings were finally completed in mid-December.[30]

As the investigation continued, its results were not entirely conclusive. A knife had been taken from Beauchamp at the time of his arrest, and there were efforts, never successful, to link it to the murder, based mainly on the nature of the wound. There were similar efforts to match a footprint found outside the Sharps' home on the morning of the murder with his. In addition, a bloody handkerchief had been found near the scene of the crime, a handkerchief that prosecutors claimed belonged to Beauchamp. Unfortunately, the arresting party had taken it with them to confront Beauchamp, and during the return to Frankfort the handkerchief had disappeared. The prosecution's claim could not really be confirmed.

The most damning evidence appears to have developed shortly after Beauchamp's imprisonment. In the aftermath of the killing, Eliza Sharp had said that she had only glimpsed the murderer—although he appeared to be about Beauchamp's size—but that she had clearly heard the voice that lured her husband to his death. It was a distinctive, high-pitched voice that, not surprisingly, had made a strong impression on her. Accordingly, and with the encouragement of uncle Jereboam, by now his nephew's chief advisor, a test was conducted in which Mrs. Sharp was given an opportunity to hear Beauchamp's voice. She testified that it was the voice of the murderer.[31]

No less damaging was testimony from a Frankfort editor and lawyer, Patrick Henry Darby, who recounted an 1824 encounter on the road with a young man he now knew to be Beauchamp, though he had not known him at the time. Darby reported that the young man had proclaimed violent anger at Sharp and had even asked Darby to help bring suit against the politician for certain claims, claims not spelled out in the record. Saying that he was the husband of Ann Cooke and declaring Sharp had treated her badly, the young man had then threatened Sharp's life.[32] This, together with Mrs. Sharp's testimony and other evidence from the case, was ultimately enough to persuade the magistrates to hold Beauchamp for trial. He would go before the Grand Jury and the next scheduled term of the Circuit Court in March 1826.

From the beginning, Beauchamp proclaimed his innocence, as he continued to do until the end of his trial. Shortly after his arrest, at the urging of his wife, he wrote two letters to John J. Crittenden, protesting his innocence but also acknowledging the desperation of his situation. He had never threatened Sharp's life, he said, and was about to be punished for a crime he had not committed. His danger was all the greater, given Sharp's status and popularity as a politician. As to the possibility that he was responding to rumors of Sharp's seduction and defamation of Mrs. Beauchamp, he had long since decided to relegate the past to the past, and "never to make the wounds of that family bleed afresh, by reviving unpleasant feelings which time had measurably consoled."[33]

He was being framed, he told Crittenden; much of the evidence against him was manufactured, designed to implicate him in the crime.

At about the same time, he made the same point to George M. Bibb, like Crittenden, one of the state's leading politicians. A friend of Sharp, Bibb had been among the first on the scene after the murder. He had joined in the search for evidence at daybreak, helping to explore the surrounding area. In writing to George Bibb, Beauchamp focused heavily on evidentiary issues, arguing, for example, that his knife was not sufficiently broad to have made the wound, despite efforts to use it to link him to the crime. He stressed that Bibb himself had discovered that the footprint found outside Sharp's home did not match his, despite what was being widely asserted. He had never made the rumored threats, and was in danger of being denied a fair hearing due to Sharp's popularity.[34]

Nobody believed him, and from the moment of his arrest, discussion of the case always had to do less with whether than with why he had committed the crime. For many people, Beauchamp's had been a crime of vengeance, the result of his need to respond to the earlier seduction and more recent defamation of his wife. The explanation made sense, in large part because of the significance of a strict and bloody code of honor in 1820s Kentucky.

Honor is an idea with a long pedigree in European and American thought, and with many parallels in ethical systems around the world. It can have many meanings and contain many imperatives, but wherever it is found, it has a strong focus on integrity and reputation. This was true in 1820s Kentucky—and elsewhere in the United States—where, complicated by ideals of masculinity and status, it obliged the man of honor to be ever prepared to defend his reputation, and that of his family, against any aspersion.[35] Its demands included an obligation on the part of men to protect women in their families from depredation and to exact revenge in the event of disgrace. Given the rumors that had long surrounded Cooke and Sharp, it would not have been difficult to view the killing as the act of a young man who, having married Cooke, was honor-bound to avenge her disgrace. Hence, in denying his guilt, Beauchamp also had to deny that the revived rumors of seduction had profoundly affected him, saying, as he did to Crittenden, that he had put them out of his mind.

Even as Beauchamp became the prime suspect, however, there were many people who suggested that the murder was not entirely the result of a personal vendetta between Beauchamp and Sharp. Within a week of the crime, Amos Kendall, one of Frankfort's most influential editors, wrote in his powerful *Argus of Western America* that Sharp's talents and position, as well as the circumstances of the crime, "cause suspicions to flash across the mind that the assassin was not actuated wholly by personal considerations."[36] Sharp's murder, he suggested (and he would continue to suggest) was a carefully organized political assassination.

Such charges of assassination, leveled in a heated political setting, appear to have been given widespread credibility. Kentucky's political leaders had frequently come to blows in the heated battles over relief and the courts. Even as Beauchamp's own difficulties were moving toward their tragic conclusion, moreover, the governor's son, Isaac Desha, was facing a charge of murder that, appearing to be mainly a matter of robbery and mayhem, was nevertheless viewed by many as a political affair. The younger Desha, it was intimated, had been set up by his father's opponents.[37]

Under the circumstances, Sharp's allies in the New Court cause, especially Kendall, had little difficulty fanning the flames. Kendall had done much by 1825 to put himself in a position to fan those flames. New England born, he had settled in Kentucky in 1814, first in Lexington, where he served as a tutor in the family of the already prominent Henry Clay. Subsequently turning to law and then to journalism, he had made his way to Frankfort, settling into the editorship of the *Argus* in 1816. As Kentucky's relief wars had become hotter, Kendall, who had initially been something of a moderate on the issue, became an increasingly vocal partisan of the relief and, later, New Court sides. Initiating what would ultimately become a total break with his former mentor, he was destined, through his subsequent association with Clay's most bitter rival, Andrew Jackson, to become one of the most powerful men in America during the two Jackson administrations.[38]

Even in the mid-1820s, however, he was beginning to make a political mark through his role in the relief and court struggles, and it was in this role that he addressed the Beauchamp-Sharp affair. As a New Court partisan, Kendall essentially sought to link Sharp's murder to his Old Court rivals, albeit in a rather convoluted way. He, along with other New Court proponents, claimed that during the 1825 campaign Sharp's Old Court enemies had not only raised the earlier rumors about his seduction and defamation of Mrs. Beauchamp, but had done so in ways specifically intended not only to discredit Sharp but also to drive an honor-maddened young Beauchamp to seek revenge for his wife's disgrace.

Old Court partisans sought to distance themselves from Beauchamp and especially from the charge of having spread rumors about Sharp. The young man, they said, had acted alone, based on a hatred that went back well before the 1825 campaign. New Court partisans, however, added more fuel to their fire as they increasingly turned their focus less toward Beauchamp and Sharp and more toward the witness who had done so much to incriminate Beauchamp during the investigation, Patrick Henry Darby. Darby was one of the Old Court party's more outspoken figures. He was a relative newcomer to Kentucky, having, after an initial foray in 1823, settled there in 1824. But he was already an experienced controversialist. Darby had moved to Kentucky from Tennessee, where he had also been a political and financial associate of Andrew Jackson. As recently as the spring of 1823, Jackson had supported Darby as a "hard-money" candidate for the Tennessee legislature.[39]

It was shortly after this that Darby had resettled in Kentucky, moving to Frankfort, where he established a successful legal practice and where, as editor and publisher of a newspaper called the *Constitutional Advocate,* he entered the volatile world of Kentucky politics on the Old Court side.[40] Darby brought with him a reputation for hotheadedness. Reflecting on Beauchamp's execution, Andrew Jackson, who had known and liked Sharp, said of Darby, "his want of Judgt. & imprudence will injure any cause which he attempts to advocate."[41] Not everyone would have agreed; Darby seems to have been genuinely admired by Old Court colleagues. Still, he was rumored to have a strong hatred for Sharp—a rumor he denied—and even to have predicted during the 1825 campaign that Sharp, if elected, would never live to take office.[42]

Whatever Darby's true character, New Court partisans fixed on him as the man who had fed Beauchamp rumors of Sharp's perfidy, some even charging Darby with complicity in the crime itself. Kendall, for example, claimed at one point that two men had been seen in the vicinity of Sharp's house the night of the murder, and though he did not specifically name Darby, he certainly implied that Darby was one of those men. A short time later, in a lengthy public letter published in

Kendall's *Argus,* Solomon Sharp's widow, Eliza, made a similar suggestion. Denying that her husband had seduced Ann Cooke, Mrs. Sharp fixed on Darby as the "chief instigator of the foul murder which has deprived me of all my heart held most dear on earth."[43]

At the very least, Darby and his supporters denied the charge. Darby declared Sharp guilty of both seduction and defamation, and suggested that the New Court leadership, including Kendall, had composed Eliza Sharp's letter. It was, Darby charged, part of a plot to destroy him and his cause.[44] Beauchamp, Darby reiterated, had acted alone, for personal reasons, again claiming that he had heard Beauchamp threaten Sharp's life as early as 1824. And, he asserted, others had heard such threats, too.[45] This last was, of course, worrisome to the Beauchamps. As Ann told her old friend John Waring in January 1826, Darby's claim, which she said was false, did much to undermine her husband's defense.

In the meantime, the movement toward Beauchamp's trial proceeded. In the aftermath of his arrest and examination, his uncle Jereboam had arranged for John Pope, one of Kentucky's most prominent attorneys, to take Beauchamp's case. A former U.S. senator, Pope was a neighbor and friend of Colonel Beauchamp. He had been an early supporter of relief legislation, but had since become one of the leading figures on the anti-relief, Old Court side.[46] Pope and a young associate, Thomas Lacy, represented Beauchamp at the Grand Jury hearing in March.[47] The Grand Jury considered the evidence in the case for several days and even considered the possibility that Beauchamp had not acted alone. Finding insufficient evidence to implicate anyone else in the crime, the jury soon returned a true bill against Beauchamp, charging him—and him alone—with the willful and malicious murder of Solomon Sharp.[48]

Brought before the court, Beauchamp, through his counsel, asked for a delay in order to gather witnesses in his defense. The delay was granted and a special session of the court scheduled for the following May specifically to try his case. Controversy continued to rage as political charges flew back and forth, particularly between Kendall and Darby, over why Beauchamp had committed his crime and who, if anyone, had put him up to it.

In this politically charged atmosphere, Beauchamp's trial opened in a crowded Frankfort courtroom on Monday, May 8. The attorneys on both sides were among the most prestigious in the state. The chief prosecutor was Charles Bibb. He was joined by the state's attorney general, James W. Denny, and by Daniel Mayes, a prominent Frankfort lawyer who had been retained by the Sharp family. The lead attorney for the defense was John Pope, joined by Lacy and by Samuel Q. Richardson, one of Kentucky's best-known criminal attorneys. The judge was Henry Davidge. After several motions from the defense, including an unsuccessful motion against both Darby and Kendall for creating an atmosphere that would preclude Beauchamp's receiving a fair hearing, the trial moved on to Beauchamp's plea of innocence and to the selection of a jury. Testimony began on Wednesday, May 10—testimony that was to lead, less than two months later, to the sentence carried out on that Frankfort hill.[49]

Based on the trial record, it is not entirely clear what, over the ensuing days, went most strongly against Beauchamp. The evidence against him was pretty thin and almost entirely circumstantial; the handkerchief, a key piece, was still missing. No weapon had been found that could be clearly linked to either Beauchamp or the murder. Almost certainly, most observers agreed, he was hurt by the testimony of Sharp's widow, Eliza, who appeared early in the trial. Veiled and often overcome by emotion, she was led by the prosecution through a detailed account of the murder. Here, again, she reiterated that, having been exposed to Beauchamp's voice, she was absolutely convinced that it was the voice she had heard asking to be admitted to the Sharps' home on the night of the murder. "When I heard the voice in the house, he went over some of the words spoken by the murderer; and the impression made upon me by the voice was so strong, I thought I should have fainted" (181). Testifying that she had known of no hostility between Beauchamp and her husband, she remained steadfast in her identification of his voice as that of the killer.

Beauchamp was to be still further implicated by the testimony of a Simpson County neighbor, John Lowe (spelled "Low" in the transcript). Lowe, a nonslaveholding farmer, testified to having heard Jereboam make threats against Sharp sometime after his marriage to Ann. More important, however, was Lowe's testimony regarding Beauchamp's behavior when the young man returned home from Frankfort after Sharp's death. According to Lowe, Beauchamp had arrived waving a red flag and subsequently declaring that he had "gained the victory" (188), without saying precisely what the victory was. Lowe also testified that in the time since his neighbor's arrest he had received a letter from the Beauchamps concerning the case. The contents were not immediately disclosed, but, despite defense objections, he turned it over to the court.

Other witnesses also testified to having heard Beauchamp threaten Sharp at one time or another. One witness who had praised Sharp's skill as an attorney in an 1823 conversation reported that Beauchamp had been provoked to reply, "God damn Solomon P. Sharp. I don't want you to mention his name to me, nor that of any such damned rascal. If I ever get a chance, I will send him to hell, where he ought to have been many years ago" (193).

But the lengthiest testimony along these lines came from Darby, who recounted in detail his earlier conversation with the young man whom he had subsequently learned to be Beauchamp. The conversation had occurred, he said, in September 1824, as Darby was traveling from Nashville to Elizabethtown, Kentucky. Stopping for water at a well on the property of one Sanford Duncan, Darby had encountered a man who identified himself only as the husband of Ann Cooke. Mentioning the earlier relation between Sharp and Cooke, the young man had told Darby that Sharp had promised them $1,000, a slave girl, and two hundred acres of land if, following their marriage, they would leave him alone. Sharp, however, had subsequently refused to fulfill the promise. According to Darby, the man then asked Darby's help in making Sharp pay up. When Darby refused, the man became enraged, praising his wife's character and threatening to kill Sharp if the issue were not settled.

As Beauchamp's attorney John Pope sought to lessen the impact of Darby's testimony, much of his questioning focused on the possibility that Darby was seeking to ensure Beauchamp's conviction in order to keep suspicion away from himself and from the Old Court party. Darby denied this, adding that he had been especially concerned by a letter—introduced as evidence over Pope's objection—from Colonel Beauchamp to the younger Jereboam. The letter, written the preceding January, suggested that the colonel accepted Kendall's version of the crime. "I believe him to be a damned scoundrel," the colonel said of Darby, adding, "I do believe that he is the man that did do the murder, or was the cause of it," and pledging to see to it that Darby should get "what he deserves" (204). Emphasizing that Colonel Beauchamp was a New Court stalwart, whatever his nephew's views may have been, Darby claimed to have feared early on that New Court efforts might succeed in tagging him with the crime. Confronting such testimony, Pope questioned Darby hard, and, despite their political affinities—or perhaps because of them—as Darby stepped down, he appeared on the point of striking Pope. Order was restored only after Darby was physically removed from the courtroom.[50]

Not every witness, however, supported reports that Beauchamp had threatened Sharp. Several defense witnesses testified both to Beauchamp's knowledge of Sharp and to having no knowledge of any hostility between them. Others suggested that Darby could not possibly have met with Beauchamp at Sanford Duncan's well, questioning whether Darby had been there himself.

Evidentiary issues were important, but not entirely conclusive. A great deal of testimony focused on whether Beauchamp owned a knife that could have made a wound of the sort that had killed Sharp. There was strong disagreement. Still more focused on the handkerchief that had been found at the murder scene, and whether it could be used to link Beauchamp to the crime. Here, too, there was great disagreement, perhaps inevitable since the handkerchief had disappeared. Some witnesses who had seen it testified to having seen Beauchamp wearing it at around the time of the murder. Others, noting the cheapness of the fabric, described it as most likely having belonged to "a negro, or some poor slovenly man" and probably used to wipe a bloody nose (273, 307).

The loss of the handkerchief during the trip returning Beauchamp from Simpson County to Frankfort was also part of the story. During that trip, one of the guards had stuck it in his pocket and gone to sleep for the night. During that night, Beauchamp was heard to stir around, perhaps putting something into the fire. Had Beauchamp burned the incriminating evidence? No one could say.

More damaging and clearer testimony arose out of the circumstance of Sharp's having gone to the door to admit "John A. Covington" to his home. Sharp had not known a John A. Covington, but had been a friend and associate to John W. Covington, a prominent Green River landowner. Beauchamp had known and done business with Covington, as well, and several witnesses who knew both men testified to

Beauchamp's tendency, when talking about Covington, to refer to him as "John A." rather than "John W." as a matter of course. Even defense witnesses called to rebut such testimony admitted that Beauchamp had been known to miscall Covington's name, helping connect him to the crime.

So did testimony from Joel Scott, at whose place Beauchamp had stayed in Frankfort at the time of Sharp's murder. Not only did Scott place Beauchamp in the vicinity of the crime, but he also testified that he had heard Beauchamp go out and return to his room sometime during the night. Scott also testified, again, that Beauchamp had seemed incurious about the crime when, early on the morning of Sharp's death, he left the inn for home, citing other troubling, perhaps incriminating comments Beauchamp had made. Beauchamp had, for example, pointedly asked whether "there was any person suspected of the murder" or if there was "any way they can find out who had done it," arousing Scott's suspicions (213). Scott's testimony, along with that about Covington and especially Mrs. Sharp's conviction that his voice was that of the murderer, probably helped to turn the jury against Beauchamp.

But perhaps most important was evidence, and testimony, involving Beauchamp's neighbor, John Lowe. Again, Lowe testified that he had received letters from the Beauchamps during the time since Jereboam's arrest, and, despite defense efforts to exclude them, a powerfully incriminating letter and "document" were ultimately introduced into evidence. In the letter, Beauchamp wrote that he was innocent but that he had enemies who were busily trying to build a case against him, even to the point of bribing witnesses, if necessary, to bring about his conviction. He appealed to Lowe's honor and friendship for assistance, attaching a long document essentially offering Lowe directions for testifying in Beauchamp's defense.

In the document, Beauchamp tried to cover a lot of bases. Lowe was, for example, to testify that Beauchamp had been contemplating a move to Missouri, and that Beauchamp's presence in Frankfort at the time of the murder was coincidental. Beauchamp had been there mainly to straighten out some of his affairs in order to dispose of Kentucky lands. Lowe was also to note, accurately as it turned out, that Beauchamp had become the subject of a paternity suit and was hoping to avoid a warrant attached to that suit. (The suit, which Beauchamp later said was unfounded, had been filed only a few days prior to his departure for Frankfort to kill Sharp). Lowe was to testify that, on

Beauchamp's return, they had discussed the murder, that Beauchamp had been somewhat fuzzy about the details, and that he had suggested that it might have been political or, perhaps, that Sharp's slaves had conspired to do it.

The purported affair with Ann Cooke, Lowe was to report, could have had nothing to do with Sharp's death. The story, they all believed, had originated with John Waring. The Cookes had always denied it and, along with their friend Sharp, had hoped it would simply go away. Lowe was to say that Beauchamp had even expressed a willingness to work with Sharp on any land deals related to plans for moving to Missouri.

Lowe was present when the guard arrived to take Beauchamp into custody, and the document urged him to offer a well-outlined account of what had happened at the time. He was to describe how, at one point after the guard's arrival, Beauchamp had gone into the house, leaving Lowe to talk with one of the men, George P. Kelly, and to claim that Kelly had shown him the by now notorious handkerchief. He was to say that he had told Kelly that the handkerchief was not Beauchamp's. He was also to report an attempt by the guard to catch Beauchamp on the Covington business. Beauchamp, Lowe was instructed to testify, clearly knew that there was no John A. Covington, despite efforts by Kelly, in particular, to entrap him.

Then he was to report still more sinister developments. Lowe was to say that, after some more discussion, as Beauchamp prepared to depart, Kelly had taken him aside, offering him $100 to testify that the handkerchief was Beauchamp's, a bribe Lowe steadfastly refused to accept. This was not to be the only such effort Lowe was instructed to relate. He was also told to testify that he had been visited by Patrick Henry Darby in late February or early March. Darby, Lowe should testify, had had a lot of questions. Had Lowe heard Beauchamp threaten Sharp? Had Beauchamp habitually confused the Covington name? Lowe should say that he had told Darby no, and that Darby had then asked, patting his pocket, how much it would take to get him to testify to the opposite. Lowe was also to testify that Darby had told him that a handkerchief had been found and that he could have another hundred for identifying it as Beauchamp's. Lowe was directed to say that he had not approved of the transaction, and that he had told Darby "to *clare* yourself from here as soon as you please" (263).

But, Lowe was to say, Darby was not to be deterred. Beauchamp's directions instructed Lowe to claim that Darby said the Sharps were out to get him, that he genuinely believed Beauchamp guilty, and that he told Lowe that if he could not support him, then at least, perhaps, he could keep silent. Darby would pay him for that, as well. But, Lowe was instructed to say, he could not keep entirely silent. Instead, he was to say that he had gone immediately to Mrs. Beauchamp with the news, which she had urged him to remember. In an appended note, Beauchamp added that the parts about Darby and Covington were absolutely crucial. As the document was read, according to one observer, Darby, who was present, "rose from his chair and looked Beauchamp full in the face for the greater part of the time."[51]

Following the introduction of the letter and document, Lowe was called to the stand. He testified that he had never been offered a bribe by Kelly, and that he had never had any contact, either in person or by mail, with Darby. There had never been any conversation about possibly employing Sharp in any kind of land business. Beauchamp had never discussed with him the publication of rumors of Sharp's seduction of Ann Cooke. Beauchamp did not deny having authored the document, and it left little doubt that he had sought to induce a witness to commit perjury. If it did not seal his fate, it certainly undermined his credibility, and the defense could do little to counter its effects.

Testimony concluded on Monday, May 15, and summations, unfortunately not recorded, were to occupy most of the next four days. Finally, on Friday, May 19, at about five o'clock, the case went to the jury, which, after only an hour's deliberation, returned with a verdict of guilty. Matters were not, however, to end there. The next morning, before the sentence could be pronounced, Beauchamp's lead counsel, John Pope, noted that Ann Beauchamp had been arrested and brought to Frankfort to be examined as a possible accessory to the crime. He asked that the sentence not be passed until her role was clarified and, acting as her attorney, also asked that Beauchamp be allowed to attend the examination.[52]

The key witness in the examination was, again, John Lowe. He related how he had initially urged Cooke not to marry Beauchamp, in part because of the substantial difference in their ages and in part because Beauchamp had a reputation as a wild young man. Lowe testified that he had visited her after the marriage and that she had told him how happy she was, in part because Beauchamp had resolved to kill Sharp.

After Beauchamp's arrest, she had again expressed her happiness and, trying to induce Lowe to give favorable testimony for Beauchamp, had said that Sharp deserved to die. She added that Beauchamp had wanted to kill Sharp publicly, but that she had, on her knees, begged him to do it clandestinely so as to preserve his own life, and, again, she begged Lowe to work with her to save him, a request, Lowe reported, she would make repeatedly.

Lowe also testified that Ann Beauchamp told him that she had helped lay the plan. She told him how, in order to get a better knowledge of Sharp's house, her husband had "got in with a black man" to help acquaint him with the layout of the house, on the pretext of wanting to "get" one of Sharp's female slaves (317). He claimed that she told him how Beauchamp had also got shoes and a knife, unlike his own, in an effort to deflect suspicion. Finally, Lowe testified that there had never been any mention of any promise on Sharp's part of the sort Darby had testified to in court. Lowe said that when Ann Beauchamp spoke of vengeance, she spoke only of the injury Sharp had done her through the seduction and subsequent defamation of her character. Other witnesses essentially corroborated Lowe's story. Despite some ambivalence on the part of the justices of the peace who heard the testimony, they finally decided that, since she had participated in the crime only by planning and asking her husband not to kill Sharp publicly, she should not be charged.

The court then reconvened to pronounce Beauchamp's fate. Before the court could speak, however, Pope, on Beauchamp's behalf, offered two motions to try to get the verdict set aside. One was based on a strained reading of the New Court Act of 1824—he said it had inadvertently repealed state murder statutes. The other was a motion for mistrial because, he said, the Lowe letter and document should never have been admitted as evidence. The court considered Pope's arguments but, meeting on the following Monday, denied them. Beauchamp was then given the sentence of death, to be carried out on June 16, 1826. Responding with composure, Beauchamp asked for an extension, "not for a *few days* of a life, which his country forfeited," but so that he might "*write something* for the benefit of those nearer and dearer to him than *life itself*" (319). The court agreed, setting a new date of July 7. He was led away to his cell, where, by her own request, his wife joined him to await his execution.

The period between May 22, when Beauchamp received his sentence, and July 7, when he died, was not a quiet one. For one thing, Pope continued his efforts on Beauchamp's behalf. He took the case, appropriately, to the Old Court of Appeals, arguing, as he had earlier, that the 1824 act establishing the New Court had inadvertently repealed Kentucky's murder statutes. Here, again, the case became embroiled in the larger controversy. Robert Wickliffe—among Kentucky's wealthiest men and an Old Court leader—asked to be heard as a friend of the court to answer Pope. Agreeing with Pope's contention that the 1824 act had repealed the murder statutes, Wickliffe nevertheless argued that the common law against murder remained in force. More critically, and capturing the main thrust of the court dispute, he also argued that to accept the legitimacy of Pope's appeal was to accept the legitimacy of the 1824 act. This, he argued, should not be done. The act was, he asserted, unconstitutional and could, therefore, have no bearing on Beauchamp's or any other case. The earlier statutes remained in force and the Court of Appeals should deny Pope's motion, which it did.[53]

There were also some displays of public sentiment on behalf of the Beauchamps. According to reports, they were visited in their cell in a show of support from some of Frankfort's leading citizens. In addition, petitions asking that Beauchamp be pardoned or that his sentence be commuted began to circulate in Kentucky shortly after his conviction, and continued to reach the governor only days prior to the Beauchamps' deaths. Petitioners argued, as in one document from Henry County, north of Frankfort, that "the consciousness of his guilt will be a sufficient warning to him to forsake the paths of Vice & pursue the path of Virtue." Another, from a group of Kentucky women, representing several areas, noted that "the crime was great for which mr Beauchamp is sentenced to die—but the provocation was also great," and urged the governor to grant a pardon.[54]

Beauchamp, in the meantime, began his efforts to "write something," efforts that did much to keep the controversy alive. Beauchamp had admitted his guilt shortly after his sentencing, speaking to his uncle Jereboam and to the jailer, John M'Intosh, who passed the details along to Amos Kendall. Although it is not certain exactly what Beauchamp said, according to one account, he essentially confirmed some of the key prosecution testimony against him but also implicated Darby as an accomplice in the crime.[55]

Shortly thereafter, however, he began writing his document, which he completed by mid-June and immediately sought to have published. In it, Beauchamp continued to implicate Darby in Sharp's death. The original, very lengthy title, which Colonel Beauchamp registered on his nephew's behalf with the copyright office on June 17, was "Beauchamp's Confession, being an account of the most important circumstances which led to and attended the murder of Col. Solomon P. Sharp, who was assassinated in Frankfort on the night preceding the commencement of the Legislature of 1825 by one Patrick H. Darby and Jereboam O. Beauchamp, written by said Beauchamp immediately on being condemned to die for the murder."[56] Through his uncle, Beauchamp initially offered the manuscript to Frankfort printer Jacob Holeman, who refused to publish it. Holeman was also editor of an Old Court newspaper, the *Spirit of '76,* and had been one of Darby's more ardent defenders.[57] Beauchamp, facing death, continued his efforts toward getting his version of the events before the public.

By all accounts, one of Beauchamp's main purposes in writing a confession grew out of a hope that he could persuade the governor to grant him a pardon. Working to get the document published before his scheduled execution, he seems to have believed that implicating the Old Court party—and especially Darby—in the crime would carry weight with the New Court governor, Joseph Desha.[58] Talk of a deal along those lines had been in the air almost from the moment of Beauchamp's sentencing, as even such prominent figures as Robert Wickliffe warned that Desha and others had promised Beauchamp a pardon in return for a strike on Darby.[59] Beauchamp probably also hoped to portray the crime in a way that would lead to continuing public efforts on his behalf.

It is clear that Beauchamp continued to work for a pardon—and, according to some accounts, even to expect one—almost from the moment of his conviction. As early as May 22, the day of his sentencing, he had written to Amos Kendall decrying his treatment in the press and in the courts. He asked the editor to let "vengeance now be melted away in magnanimity to me, or at least in mercy to my wife and to my family, who are, you know, so much your friends." He appealed to Kendall to use his influence to get the sentence commuted to exile.[60] Assisted by his father and especially his influential uncle, a New Court ally of Desha, Beauchamp continued to plead with the governor for a pardon or at least a commutation throughout the final weeks of his life.

As late as July 5, two days before his death, Beauchamp reportedly sent a letter to the governor, via his uncle, asking relief from the sentence and suggesting that the publication of his confession might work to the political advantage of the governor and the New Court party. The governor rejected his plea.[61]

As a result of all this maneuvering, the final document is a complicated one. It was not published until August 1826, over a month after Beauchamp's hanging. The surviving manuscript had gone to Beauchamp's father after the execution, and prior to publication it had undergone some fairly heavy editing. According to its closest student, Fred M. Johnson, the manuscript itself may not be in Beauchamp's hand.[62] Still, circumstances point to Beauchamp's original authorship, and Old Court leader Joseph Underwood, who seems to have been familiar with the process of its publication, asserted that Thomas Beauchamp had taken pains to give it "to the world without mutilation."[63] Thus, it can probably be taken with some confidence as the account Beauchamp wanted people to read. In essence, Beauchamp said that he had killed Sharp because of the seduction and defamation of Ann Cooke and tried to show that, though he had committed the crime, his conviction had been the result of trumped up evidence and false testimony.

Seduction, honor, and revenge dominate the tale. At the outset, it is offered to the public as a paean to Beauchamp's own respect for honor and as a warning to those who, taking advantage of their social and political position, would delude an innocent, young woman and lure her to her ruin—as, the *Confession* says, Sharp had done. Readers never learn exactly how Sharp had worked his wiles, but do learn that Beauchamp had heard about Sharp's seduction of Ann Cooke shortly after it occurred, and had developed both affection for her and a hatred for Sharp from that moment. Having contrived to meet her—he told her that he had heard she had an extensive library and that he wanted to borrow some books—he learned of her desire for revenge and quickly resolved to be the instrument of that vengeance. As early as 1821, he wrote, he had confronted Sharp on the streets of Frankfort, challenging him to fight. Sharp, he said, begged for his life, even offering his entire estate should Beauchamp leave him alone, a bribe Beauchamp claimed to have indignantly refused. Sharp was able to get away, and though Beauchamp wrote that he pursued Sharp through Frankfort in hopes of another confrontation, he ultimately had to return to Ann without satisfaction.[64]

Though Beauchamp reported he was unsuccessful in this early confrontation with Sharp, he also wrote that he and Ann Cooke not only continued their relationship but also continued to nurse their hatred for Sharp. Beauchamp was resolved to marry her, but she was equally resolved that she could never marry anyone so long as Sharp lived. She even proposed killing him herself, at which point Beauchamp knew, he said, that he had to act. It had become, he understood, a condition of their marriage that he complete the job, and, once they did marry, he was honor-bound to do so—an obligation he readily assumed.

At this point, however, politics intervened. The New Court party had won the 1824 election shortly after the Beauchamps' marriage, and this added a new wrinkle to the Beauchamps' plans. Honor can be a complicated matter, and in 1820s Kentucky it demanded not only attempting to avenge a tarnished reputation but also doing so in an open, even a public, confrontation. Epitomized by the duel—and many of Kentucky's leaders were veteran duelists—it entailed both a public act of vengeance and a public display of courage, a willingness to risk one's life to defend a sullied reputation. Beauchamp had sought to accomplish this in his confrontation with Sharp on the Frankfort streets, or so he said.

After the election, though, he realized that however defensible, even obligatory, killing Sharp would be in a world where honor mattered, Sharp's political allies, including the newly elected Governor Desha, would exact retribution. They were not men of honor themselves, he said, and they could only be expected to put politics above honor should Beauchamp openly kill Sharp. Hence, Jereboam increasingly believed the killing would have to be done in private, and, preferably, away from Frankfort. Self-preservation allowed for this, he was to say, when the obligations of honor were so little respected by those against whose political interests he would have to act. He recounted an elaborate plot, mounted in the summer of 1825, to lure Sharp to the Beauchamps' home by sending him a letter signed "Zebulon X. Yantis" asking for assistance with some land claims. Sharp failed to take the bait.

But the reemergence of rumors regarding Cooke's seduction and stillborn child during the 1825 election gave new urgency to the Beauchamps' plans. Not only did rumors of Cooke's seduction reappear, but it was also then, according to Beauchamp, that they received a letter from someone Beauchamp trusted, but refused to name, saying that Sharp had been spreading the story of Cooke's mulatto child. This defamation, he said, had forced him to act. His wife had not, by the way, begged him on her knees not to kill Sharp publicly. He had already recognized the foolhardiness of that, and, with his wife's assistance, had begun to devise the elaborate plan of subterfuge that was ultimately to lead to Sharp's death. Even the paternity suit, he said, was part of the plan, something he had created to help explain his behavior at the time of the crime (in the manuscript, Beauchamp says that the young woman had already exculpated him of the charge).[65] He had already laid plenty of groundwork for evasion before he departed for Frankfort on November 1. He arrived early in the evening on November 6. Disguising his purposes at every step, he bided his time for only a few hours before he finally went to Sharp's house, putting on a dark mask and hoping to be taken, if seen, for a black man. And then he knocked on Sharp's door "three times, loud and quick!" (29).

Beauchamp's account of the murder itself was consistent with those in the newspapers, and those offered at his trial, save in one key particular. Beauchamp's account was written in a way that further dramatized his motivation and, especially, Sharp's awareness of what the killing was about. The Covington business was all there, but Beauchamp's version also reported that when Sharp finally realized what was about to happen, he cried out, according to Beauchamp's account, "Great God!! It's him!!!" Stabbed, Sharp then said, "pray Mr. Beauchamp." Nor were the rest of the Sharps entirely surprised, according to the *Confession*. As soon as Dr. Leander Sharp rushed in to where his brother lay dying, his first words were, Beauchamp's account claimed, "Great God Beauchamp has done this! I always expected it" (29–30).

Despite the Sharps' outcries, Beauchamp described how he continued to cover his tracks, in Frankfort and on his journey home. Much of what he said was clearly intended to rebut prosecution testimony, including an account of the infamous handkerchief. He had left it, he said, not at the murder scene but in his room at the Scotts'. There had been blood on it, but the blood was his own, not Sharp's. He had used it sometime earlier to wipe his nose. He had thought to return for it but decided doing so might further arouse suspicion, much to his subsequent regret.

Having arrived at his home—he had, incidentally, raised a victory flag as he approached his exultant wife—Beauchamp was soon to be confronted by the guard, bringing with it the handkerchief he had left at the Scott home. He told of his horror upon being told that it had been found at the scene, knowing that he was being set up. He did, he admitted, manage to get it while the guards slept, burning it in the fire.

It was after his arrest, according to the *Confession,* that the situation became particularly knotty. Initially troubled by the prejudice against him, he began to have hope when, he said, Amos Kendall and the New Court party sought to treat the murder as a political assassination. This, he said, also appealed to the Sharps, because it suddenly redeemed Sharp's reputation. By making Sharp a martyr to the New Court cause, he was somehow absolved from the charge of seduction, and Beauchamp suddenly became a less likely suspect. He was, therefore, happy to see the Sharps begin to tailor their story to fit a political scenario, for, according to the *Confession,* they even began to deny that Leander had cried out Beauchamp's name upon seeing his brother's body.

Then, however, came an unexpected turn. Kendall cynically linked Beauchamp with Darby and the Old Court party. This, Beauchamp wrote, was to be his undoing. He had never known Darby, Beauchamp said, but on the very morning of his return to Frankfort he learned that Darby had been saying that he had once heard Beauchamp issuing threats against Sharp. Early in the ordeal, Darby had actually come to Beauchamp's cell and repeated the assertion. He would, according to Beauchamp, change his version of the story many times, ultimately settling on the tale of Duncan's well. But the whole story was an elaborate lie, told only to save Darby's skin—and to exonerate Darby's party—by helping to convict Beauchamp as a lone assassin.

As the investigation proceeded, Beauchamp wrote, his situation became increasingly untenable, his fate governed by men and women, including the Sharps, out to get him. Stories, he said, were altered, created, and reconciled. Even Mrs. Sharp's testimony about recognizing his voice was improbable. He had disguised it when calling out to Sharp on the night of the murder. She could not have recognized it when she was asked to identify it as part of the investigation—or so Beauchamp had believed when he, with his uncle, proposed their test.

Much of the rest of the *Confession* was devoted to Beauchamp's trial, of which he said, "the world never witnessed more misrepresentation flowing from prejudice or worse motives" (58). He discussed the confusion of Covington names. He had said "John A." on purpose, he wrote, because Sharp would respond to the Covington name but would know immediately that the man at the door—Beauchamp—was not his old Green River friend. Beauchamp also decried the fabrication that had to be involved in linking him to the infamous handkerchief. He accused Joel Scott and other prosecution witnesses of perjured testimony. And he took on the problem of John Lowe. Lowe, Beauchamp said, had lied. The man had met with Darby—who was seeking to remove suspicion from himself—and had been offered a bribe to swear that Beauchamp had threatened Sharp. And Lowe had told Mrs. Beauchamp of the offer, even volunteering, himself, to testify to it and to anything else the Beauchamps might find useful. Calculating politically that anything that might implicate Darby might work to Beauchamp's own advantage with the New Court faction, including Governor Desha, Beauchamp had drawn up the infamous document. It instructed Lowe to testify to the attempted bribery, and to a few other particulars that had not taken place. But Lowe was a traitor, already working with Darby—either because he believed them guilty or for some more sinister reason—for the conviction of Beauchamp and the implication of Mrs. Beauchamp as well. And here, of course, was the final turning point of the trial that had resulted in Beauchamp's conviction.

At this point, the *Confession* moves in a variety of directions. Much of its concluding portion was apparently written after the governor's July 5 rejection of what turned out to be Beauchamp's final plea for a pardon, his uncle having told him that there was nothing else to be done. It reflects anger, desperation, and, perhaps, even a final appeal to public sympathy after political calculations appeared to have failed. It places his opponents in a particularly harsh light as it describes how, according to Beauchamp, the governor and the New Court party had never stopped playing politics with his case. Even the initiative for his final plea had come from them. Beauchamp had been given reason to believe, he said, that the governor's pardon was assured if he would confess and accuse several others, including Achilles Sneed, clerk of the Old Court, and John U. Waring, of having been his accomplices.

He was to go even further and outline a larger conspiracy to assassinate the governor and other New Court leaders. He would not be given a written pardon, but if he played along, the governor would give him a last-minute reprieve on the way to the gallows. This, Beauchamp said, he had refused to do. He did not trust the governor to fulfill the promise and would not help to condemn innocent men, only to die anyway.

Perhaps hoping to place a still harsher light on the governor's circle, Beauchamp also, in some sense, made amends. Darby, he continued to describe as a perjurer, but he also acknowledged that Darby had not been involved in the murder. He wanted to make clear, too, that neither his uncle nor his father had been involved in the intrigue he had described related to his quest for a pardon, despite charges from both Darby and Amos Kendall that they had. Honor alone had impelled him to kill Sharp, Beauchamp said, and he hoped his father, at least, could take some consolation from that fact.

Beauchamp continued to write up to almost the end of his life. He described his reaction to what he now represented as almost certain death. He focused on his fear but also his love for Ann and his hope for salvation. He even left an account of their first attempt at suicide. The final document also included a body of literary work that, confined together in Beauchamp's cell, Jereboam and Ann Beauchamp began to create shortly after his imprisonment. This included a set of letters from Beauchamp to members of his family begging forgiveness and offering consolation. There was also a body of poetry invoking the imperatives of honor that had impelled Beauchamp to act while celebrating the Beauchamps' love for each other even in the face of death.

The inclusion of this material in the final, posthumous document was probably the result of its final editor's desire to both redeem the Beauchamps' reputations and condemn those of their enemies. Most of the letters and poems, however, were written well before July 5, the date of Beauchamp's final appeal to the governor, and likely were intended at the outset to contribute to Beauchamp's efforts to gain a pardon, his initial intention being that the *Confession* should appear several weeks prior to his scheduled execution. They would help further arouse public sympathy to reinforce the political calculations on which Beauchamp had counted. It is probably for this reason that Ann Beauchamp had even tried to persuade Amos Kendall, of all people, to publish one of her pieces in the *Argus*—a proposed epitaph celebrating their love and honor—prior to the execution.[66]

Jereboam's letters to family members, all written prior to July 5, offer a mixture of hope and courageous resignation. One to his mother was both a confession of sins and an assurance to her that he had prayed and that he sought salvation. They would, he said, meet in heaven. Certainly, he hoped his friends would be able to save him from execution, but, if not, he was willing to die, having put his trust in God. He repeated these sentiments in other letters addressed to his mother during his final days.

There was also a letter to his brothers and sisters. Here, Beauchamp warned his siblings that there was a God, and a heaven, and a hell, and he urged them not to follow in his footsteps. They should learn to control their passions, to obey their parents, and, above all, to read the Bible, to pray, and to "get religion" (103). Beauchamp had repented his wickedness and was willing to face the consequences of his sins, exemplifying an argument that at least some supporters had made on his behalf.

The poetry, written in jail, supported the image of the Beauchamps set forth in the *Confession*. One of the poems, Beauchamp said, was written prior to his conviction, "upon being aroused from sleep by a vision of his wife's spirit." "Daughter of grief," Beauchamp called his wife, writing that, however venomous the world, "Thy Anna's heart is kind." Whatever happened, they would "meet in Heaven above" (91–92). In verses addressed to her husband a few days before their deaths, Ann Beauchamp called him a "more than mortal man" and praised him for his deed:

> Thy spirit feels its worth; a vilians [*sic*] heart,
> Thy dagger pierced; he perished by thy hand!
> Accused of Heaven, he felt the bitter smart,
> Assigned to guilt by Heaven's high command.

Beauchamp had destroyed "the vilest heart" that had ever been animated by "human blood" (93).

This was the theme that also guided Ann Beauchamp's proposed epitaph—to be engraved on their tombstone—included in the *Confession*. "A child of evil fate she lived," Ann Beauchamp wrote. And when Beauchamp had heard of her suffering, he rose, "burning for revenge." Those who saw the stone should "drop a tear"; the Beauchamps had died for honor, and for love (97).

It is uncertain when, if ever, the Beauchamps gave up hope—Ann composed a will on the day Desha rejected her husband's final plea,[67] perhaps signaling her resignation—but Jereboam's account of their intended suicides continued in the vein defined by their literary oeuvre. The decision was undertaken coolly and calmly, Beauchamp recorded. His wife divided the laudanum between them "with as much composure, as she ever shared with me a glass of wine." He recounted how they kneeled in prayer to make their peace with God and ask his guidance, then lay down in each other's arms to await death (88).

And death did not come. Reflecting on Thursday night and again on Friday morning—the day of his execution—Beauchamp recorded how much he and his wife longed for death, and longed to die together. Then, with their decision to stab themselves, Beauchamp brought his *Confession* to its final close, save only its appended instructions that they should be buried together, in a single embrace.

With this, events began to move inexorably toward Beauchamp's final moments on the hill. Having used the smuggled dagger, the two were soon discovered by an astonished guard, Mrs. Beauchamp in horrible pain. She was about to be removed to the jailer's house for medical attention, when Beauchamp looked at her and scrawled a brief note: "Your husband is dying happy! For you I lived, for you I die! I hear you groan! I hope you may yet be recovered—if you are, live till it is God's will to take you, and prepare to meet me in a better world!" He signed it, "Your dying husband" (91). She was then taken away. Beauchamp was examined and judged fit to meet his prescribed fate. Hearing what proved to be her death screams, however, he begged to see her one more time and was allowed to go to her to offer a final farewell. Beauchamp held her hand until she died, and "'Farewell,' said he, 'Farewell, child of sorrow! Farewell, child of persecution and misfortune! For thee I have lived, for thee I die!'" Then he embraced her, and was led away.[68]

Beauchamp approached death with visible composure, though in visible pain. As he moved toward the gallows, he had one last encounter with Darby, reiterating the charge of perjury but absolving him of any involvement in Sharp's death. Once on the gallows, he was asked, one final time, to account for what he had done. Questioned by the jailer, Beauchamp reasserted that during the 1825 campaign he had received a letter detailing Sharp's defamation of Ann Beauchamp, but, even facing death, he refused to reveal its author. He again said that though the verdict in his trial had been true, the evidence on which he was convicted had been false. He now made clear, even more than in the *Confession,* how great an influence his wife had exerted on him in her insistence that he kill Sharp. Then, saying, "I want to go to my wife," he bid farewell to those he knew, asked for some water, then for his last song, and met his death. After hanging from the gallows for about a half hour, Beauchamp's body was released to his father's custody, and Jereboam and Ann Beauchamp were buried together, in a single coffin, according to their wishes. The epitaph she had written was engraved upon their stone:

Entomb'd below in others' arms,
The Husband and the Wife repose,
Safe from life's never ending storms,
And safe from all their cruel foes.

A child of evil fate she lived,
A villian's wiles her peace had cross'd;
The husband of her heart revived
The happiness she long had lost.

He heard her tale of matchless woe,
And burning for revenge he rose,
And laid her base seducer low,
And struck dismay to virtue's foes.

Reader! if honor's generous blood
E'er warmed thy breast, here drop a tear,
And let the sympathetic flood,
Deep in thy mind its traces bear.

A father or a mother thou,
Thy daughter view in grief's despair;
Then turn and see the villian low,
And here let fall the grateful tear.

A brother or a sister thou!
Dishonor'd see thy sister dear!
Then turn and see the villian low,
And here let fall the grateful tear.

Daughter of virtue! moist thy tear,
This tomb of love and honor claim;
For thy defence the husband here,
Laid down in youth his life and fame.

His wife disdained a life forlorn,
Without her heart's lov'd, honor'd Lord,
Then reader, here their fortunes mourn,
Who for their love, their life blood pour'd.[69]

*Chapter 2*

# NO MORE ROMANTIC TRAGEDY

The Beauchamp-Sharp affair attracted widespread interest from the outset. From Sharp's murder to the Beauchamps' deaths, the events were widely reported, not just in Kentucky, but elsewhere in the United States. Such essentially national publications as *Niles' Weekly Register,* published in Baltimore, and the *National Intelligencer,* from Washington, D.C., covered the events. So did such a distant, essentially local paper as the Providence, Rhode Island, *Patriot,* which was running stories about the affair within weeks of the events.[1] *Niles' Register* even helped to spread the rumor advanced in Darby's testimony that a major cause of the killing was Sharp's refusal to come through on an offer of land. It also suggested that Sharp had "charged her with having had a colored child" in order to get out of the deal.[2]

There was also extensive coverage in such an unlikely place as *The Album, and Ladies' Weekly Gazette,* a relatively new magazine from Philadelphia devoted to literary endeavors and moral improvement. *The Album* provided an extensive account of Beauchamp's execution, documenting his composure as he approached his death, and giving particular attention to his final farewell to his wife.[3] In addition, within a short time of the execution, the report of Beauchamp's trial was published in Kentucky, and an abridged version appeared in New York not long thereafter, reprinting some of Darby's writings on the events, as well.[4]

In the aftermath, people were not entirely sure what to think about what had happened. Henry Clay, a few days after the execution—and only months following his noted duel with John Randolph—wrote to John J. Crittenden, that, terrible as what the Beauchamps had done had been, "the manner of the death of the unfortunate Beauchamp and his still more unfortunate wife must awaken a public sympathy which even his crime and her vices cannot smother."[5] Thomas C. Clarke, editor of *The Album, and Ladies' Weekly Gazette,* after having published accounts of the Beauchamps' deaths, chided those who would represent the couple as martyrs. Writing that "the most touching and sympathising appeals have been marshalled up to justify, or at least apologize for their infamous deeds," he warned that to "immortalize murderers" was to encourage similar crimes.[6]

## I

In Kentucky, the controversy over Sharp's murder was not to die quickly. It dominated the 1826 elections—in process even as the Beauchamps met their deaths—for each side used the case to attack the character of the other.[7] It was to remain alive for a number of years. As late as 1835, the infamous John Waring killed Samuel Q. Richardson, one of Beauchamp's defense attorneys, on the streets of Frankfort. There was some feeling at the time that the killing stemmed from hostilities that the case had engendered, although it may have grown out of an earlier dispute over land, as well.[8] Threats had passed between the two men for years. Waring was, after four trials, acquitted of murder. Among his attorneys, incidentally, was John J. Crittenden.[9] Even later, at the end of 1837, Old Court veteran Joseph Underwood made the case a central part of a larger attack on Amos Kendall. By then, both men had become leading figures in national politics, and from the floor of Congress, Underwood, an inveterate rival, raised questions about Kendall's role in encouraging Beauchamp to implicate Old Court leaders in Sharp's death in return for a pardon. The result was an inconclusive war of words that, nonetheless, returned the case to the national spotlight.[10]

In the immediate aftermath of the affair, however, much of the continuing controversy was a result of Patrick Henry Darby's anger over efforts to implicate him in the crime. His anger was great. He was even reported to have replied to Beauchamp's final apology and exoneration by saying, "For a young man, you are the most abandoned I have ever seen. I hope you will die, because I know you are not fit to live."[11]

Even before Beauchamp's execution, Darby had translated his anger into action by filing suit against the Sharps, Kendall, and uncle Jereboam for libel. He had also charged Kendall, Colonel Beauchamp, and the New Court party with originating "the whole calumny" against him.[12] Eliza Sharp, he said, had allowed herself to be used as "an instrument in the hands of my enemies, and the political factionists of the state, to wage a war of destruction, both against my life and character."[13] And he apparently located witnesses who could back up the testimony he had given at Beauchamp's trial, placing him with Beauchamp, for example, at Duncan's well.[14]

The suit did not go to trial until the following year, in June 1827, the venue having been changed from Frankfort to neighboring Woodford County, reputedly a place friendlier to the Old Court side. The defendants, advancing a plea of "justification," had as their lawyer William T. Barry, a leading New Court figure, a former U.S. senator, lieutenant governor, and first chief justice of the New Court. Darby's attorneys included Crittenden and John Pope, who had been Beauchamp's chief counsel.[15] The trial ended in a hung jury, its members apparently leaning toward Darby, but unable to agree on the amount of damages he should receive.[16]

The case was to drag on for several years. By this time, Kendall had begun his rise to national political prominence as a key figure in Andrew Jackson's organization. Not surprisingly, Darby's suit became embroiled in the partisan rancor of Jacksonian politics, especially during the heated 1828 presidential campaign. Conflicts between Kentucky's Jacksonians and native Kentuckian Henry Clay—among Jackson's most vocal opponents—were strong, and broke down (with some notable exceptions) on Old Court-New Court lines. Kendall at one point accused Darby, a Clay ally, of trying to use the case to undermine Kentucky Jacksonians while aiding the cause of Clay and President John Quincy Adams.[17] As for the suit itself, it was never to be retried. When it came before the court again in September 1828, both sides asked for a continuance in order to find more witnesses. In June 1829, Colonel Beauchamp formally retracted his earlier charges against Darby and withdrew his plea of justification. Darby then agreed to drop his suit against the colonel.[18] The remaining parties were spared further action when Darby died of undisclosed causes in December 1829, in Brandenburg, Kentucky, on the Ohio River.[19]

No less important than Darby's suit for keeping the controversy alive was the August 1826 publication of Beauchamp's *Confession*. The *Confession* was widely circulated; there was a Philadelphia edition, as well as the original Kentucky imprint, by the end of 1826. Offering its account of the murder as a matter of honor, as well its story of the perjury and treachery of Darby, the Sharps, Kendall, and Governor Joseph

Desha, it also increased the bitter divisiveness created by the original crime. By early 1827, the Lexington *Kentucky Reporter,* a paper with long-standing Old Court ties, was advertising it as a book which "treats of curious and interesting matters" that had attracted much attention in the state, printing a brief excerpt designed mainly to put the New Court's adherents in a bad light.[20] However complex its provenance, the *Confession* presented a singular portrayal of the crime, and one that was widely noticed.[21]

And it raised new controversies of its own. In 1827, two witnesses in the case, including John F. Lowe, sued Beauchamp's father for libel, declaring that the *Confession* had "falsely wickedly and maliciously" accused them of perjury. Thomas Beauchamp denied "any wicked or malicious design" in the publication, but also admitted that he could not justify the *Confession*'s charges. Judgment was entered against him in both cases.[22]

The *Confession* also helped to provoke one of the lengthiest and most partisan accounts of the affair, a *Vindication of the Character of the Late Col. Solomon P. Sharp, from the Calumnies Published Against Him Since His Murder, by Patrick Darby and Jeroboam O. Beauchamp.* Published in 1827 by Amos Kendall, and purportedly written by Solomon Sharp's brother Leander, the 140-page book did precisely what its title suggests. It offered a flattering portrait of Colonel Sharp, denying that he could ever have been guilty of the seduction and defamation of Ann Cooke Beauchamp, as Beauchamp's *Confession* had charged. At the same time, it created a scenario linking Beauchamp and Darby as accomplices in the crime.

Leander Sharp was deeply interested in vindicating his brother's reputation. Kendall reported as early as March 1826 that Leander Sharp was preparing some kind of document in defense of Solomon's character.[23] Dr. Sharp had, moreover, responded to the insinuation—advanced by Darby but noted even in *Niles' Register*—that his brother had been murdered for reneging on a promise of land to Beauchamp and Cooke. There had been no need for such a promise, Leander said, because Solomon had never seduced Cooke in the first place.[24] Since the execution, Leander Sharp had made at least two trips through the Green River country, including both Warren and Simpson counties, trying to gain still more evidence about the crime and the events leading up to it.[25] He wrote the *Vindication* specifically to address points made in Beauchamp's *Confession* and in the face of Darby's lawsuit. He wrote it, he also said, despite a death threat from John U. Waring, should he mention Waring in connection with the affair.[26] Unlike both the trial report and Beauchamp's *Confession,* Sharp's *Vindication* was not widely circulated; fears of additional legal action on Darby's part apparently led to its suppression.[27]

It is a long, detailed document. Much of it repeats points made initially by Kendall in the *Argus* as part of the attempt to implicate Darby and the Old Court party; it is not difficult to believe that Kendall must have played a strong role in the *Vindication*'s preparation. But the work is also filled with extensive supporting evidence and testimony for the points Sharp wished to make. It begins as a testimonial to Solomon Sharp's virtues, describing his relatively humble origins and the efforts that had made him a leading figure in the state. It provides evidence of his good character, including his respect for women, and recounts testimony that had led to his earlier exoneration by the Kentucky Senate from the charge of having seduced Ann Cooke.

It also presents unflattering portraits of the Beauchamps. Some of the strongest language is reserved for Ann Cooke Beauchamp. She was, according to Leander Sharp, small, dark, and not particularly attractive. She had "lost her fore teeth, was stoop shouldered, and in no way a handsome or desirable woman" (12). Worse, she tended toward impiety, was given to novel reading, and, particularly revealing, "was an avowed disciple of Mary Woolstoncraft" [*sic*] (12). At the time of the alleged seduction she was, Leander wrote, "a frivolous, waning flirt of 35, who had nothing but forwardness and pertness to recommend her" (13). Sharp went on to produce evidence that she had a reputation for loose sexual behavior. The entire chain of events had begun when, having managed to get herself pregnant, she chose Solomon Sharp as a respectable man to blame for her sin. But she knew he had not been the culprit, as did everyone else. As Leander argued, in Kentucky's honor-based world, her male relatives would have had the same obligation to respond to her dishonor by exacting retribution on her seducer—something they had apparently felt no call to do. She was simply an opportunistic liar looking for an easy way out of the mess she had created for herself. She had even written a letter, Leander Sharp claimed, exonerating his brother and naming the guilty man (15).

If Sharp had harsh things to say about Cooke, his words for Beauchamp were no kinder. As a young man, Beauchamp was, Sharp wrote, "inattentive to his studies, wild, unprincipled, and profligate" (23). Sharp also suggested that those portions of the *Confession* in which Beauchamp claimed to have come to a near instant hatred for Solomon Sharp could not be true, presenting documentation that Beauchamp had even handled legal cases for Sharp in 1823 and 1824. Beauchamp had become attracted to Cooke, moreover, less out of sympathy for her injury than because of her bad reputation, influenced, Leander Sharp wrote, "by a feeling more natural to profligate young men" (27).

The marriage itself was hardly of a noble character, according to Sharp. Having had a "profligate" relationship, Ann told Jereboam that she was pregnant with his child, or so several witnesses said. It was a lie, but one that, Sharp said, showed her power over the young man. And Beauchamp's was not a wholly selfless act. He was after what property Cooke had. And though it was not as much as he had expected, with the marriage, it became his.[28]

But the real villain of the piece was Darby. Sharp presented extensive evidence from Tennessee as well as Kentucky to establish Darby's bad character. Only cynically calculating behavior, not merit, had allowed Darby to make contacts among the best men in Kentucky, contacts he had used to work his way into the upper reaches of the Old Court party. In his partisanship lay much of Darby's animus toward Solomon Sharp.

According to Leander Sharp, Darby was at the bottom of the business that had led an enraged Beauchamp to kill the colonel. Darby, Leander said, had authored the infamous letter accusing Solomon Sharp of having defamed Mrs. Beauchamp through the story of the mulatto child. Leander Sharp also adduced evidence that Darby had visited the Beauchamps during the 1825 campaign, suggesting that Darby's purposes, while unprovable, were nevertheless sinister and successful, inflaming the young man to anger toward Sharp. Even before Sharp had formally announced his candidacy, Beauchamp was heard making threats against his's life.

As to the rumor of the mulatto child, incidentally, Leander Sharp suggested that it was not without foundation. Although he denied that his brother had been involved in its circulation, Leander was not above looking further into the matter, and contacted several witnesses who had seen the child shortly after death. They testified that it was certainly "coloured," as dark as other mulatto children. They also testified that on at least one occasion Darby had talked to the midwife, suggesting that Darby himself may have been the source of the rumor that had so inflamed the Beauchamps. As for Solomon Sharp, he had known about such reports and could have used them, but did not, refusing to "add to the distress of Ann Cook's family and her own disgrace" (86).

With this, Leander Sharp was prepared to offer his explanation of the crime. Solomon Sharp had enraged the Old Court party through his actions as attorney general, and his decision to run for the legislature created a determination in his enemies to destroy him. Knowing Beauchamp's character, they opened a correspondence with the young man detailing rumors of seduction and defamation. Beauchamp was quick to anger; he was also desperate. He had married, Leander wrote, an "infamous woman" (87) who had failed to provide property he expected from her and who had lured him into the marriage by a false claim of pregnancy. Hearing that Sharp was spreading rumors, and believing those rumors would still further cast him into ignominy, he decided to avenge both private and public wrongs by killing Solomon Sharp.

Turning to Beauchamp's by now widely circulated *Confession*, as such, Dr. Sharp emphasized its apparent intent to excite public sympathy and put pressure on Desha for a pardon. The result was, he said, a document that, in its most important particulars, was almost entirely false, an appeal and, at the same time, an act of revenge on those who Beauchamp believed had brought about his downfall. Parts of it, the doctor said, had been taken straight from Darby's anti-Sharp newspaper writings, building on ideas and beliefs that were already current, and already tending to create an impression of the murder as a private matter. Reiterating the infamous character of both Beauchamps, Leander Sharp again denied that Beauchamp could have been motivated by the imperatives of honor outlined in the *Confession*. "It is impossible," Sharp wrote, "that a profligate young man could have been induced, for the bare privilege of marrying his own mistress, to kill a man who was not pretended to have committed any offence but enjoying her before him" (109). If anything, Beauchamp had taken a tale fabricated by Darby and sought to make it his own as he created what he hoped would be a useful version of the events.

Sharp concluded his *Vindication* with testimony from John and William M'Intosh, the Frankfort jailer and his brother, and Benjamin

Edrington, who, with William M'Intosh, had helped guard the Beauchamps. All three supported Leander Sharp's claims. The *Confession,* they said, was mostly false, and Beauchamp had told them as much. Even as he awaited execution—hoping for some kind of reprieve—Beauchamp had continued to implicate Darby in the crime. John M'Intosh went on to testify that, despite charges in the *Confession,* Beauchamp had never received any inducement from Desha or anyone else in the New Court party to lie in return for a pardon. The jailer also said that, despite the picture of repentance presented, for example, in Beauchamp's letters to his mother, such professions of religion described had no foundation in fact; he was, to the end, a profligate young man. From all this, Leander Sharp concluded, the *Confession* was a tissue of lies. Solomon Sharp's memory should be "vindicated before the world, and as to the causes of his murder, there can no longer be a mistake" (139).

Given the many accounts, it is impossible to know who was telling the truth about the murder of Solomon Sharp. All conflict, all are self-serving, and none appears particularly reliable. As historian Fred M. Johnson said after a careful review of the record, there is no "smoking gun" to explain the crime fully.[29] It does seem likely that Jereboam Beauchamp did the killing. Little else is clear. Nevertheless, the combination of responses to the case, including those of Darby and Leander Sharp, make it possible to suggest some likely explanations for the events.

Assuming Beauchamp killed Sharp, it is necessary to begin with the alleged seduction of Ann Cooke, and on this the evidence offers little certainty. At minimum, it seems likely that at the time the seduction supposedly occurred, Sharp and Cooke knew each other. He had done legal work for her family, and she had apparently visited his home. That the relationship became sexual—a matter of seduction or not—is less obvious, with evidence pointing in both directions.

In vindication of his brother, Leander Sharp was right to raise the issue of the failure of Cooke's male relatives to rise to her defense. Given the obligation of male relatives to avenge the dishonoring of female family members, Cooke's brothers might well have been expected to feel or act on such an obligation had Solomon Sharp seduced their sister.

There were, however, extenuating circumstances. For one, it is relevant that, by the time of the alleged seduction, Sharp had worked his way into Kentucky's elite, while the Cookes were on a downward course. Given the nature of American ideas of honor, they could not have counted on the code of honor to protect them from prosecution should they have taken action against Sharp. Honor violence was closely tied to status; it was acceptable only among people of rank, and equality. It may also have been the case, as Leander Sharp suggested, that Ann Cooke's reputation for "looseness" precluded treating any affair with Sharp as a matter of honor, however it had happened. Her relatives' failure to act does not disprove the charge itself.

Moreover, the Sharps' efforts to deny the seduction were peculiarly inconsistent. Leander's *Vindication,* for example, gave credence to the mulatto rumor. It also gave credence to reports that Ann Cooke had been made pregnant by a friend of her family, since deceased, named in the letter in which, he claimed, she had exonerated her brother. This possibility had also been suggested by Sharp's New Court ally Lewis Sanders shortly before Beauchamp's trial, although Sanders later retracted the suggestion,[30] but a defense witness deposed for Darby's libel suit said the same thing.[31] Obviously, one or the other story could be true, but not both, and the inconsistency does not lend credibility to Leander's version of the events.

As such testimony also makes clear, incidentally, it is unlikely that Ann Cooke's baby was a mulatto child. Historian J. W. Cooke's contention that it was a "blue baby" makes sense, and is consistent with what the midwife, cited by Leander Sharp, said. Describing the baby's color, she would not "undertake to say that the death of the child did not produce the dark appearance of the said child."[32] It is also worth noting that the witness in the deposition reported that he had first heard about the mulatto child from Eliza Sharp, again casting some doubt on Leander's version of the tale.

In any event, it is, finally, difficult to get away from Ann Cooke's persistence in making her charge against Sharp. Even Leander Sharp had trouble explaining it away, saying only that she calculated some advantage in accusing a prominent man of being her seducer. Whether Solomon Sharp was the father of Cooke's child, as she charged, or someone else was, she probably had grounds for making the accusation. As Leander conceded, Ann Cooke may have been profligate, but she was neither stupid nor a fool. That Sharp was cleared of the seduction charge by the legislature could easily have been a function of her reputation and his status.

If some kind of affair did occur between Sharp and Cooke, it is likely that in the intervening years a situation developed that simply got out of hand, resulting in the deaths of Sharp and the Beauchamps. It may well have begun, as Darby charged, with an offer of a bribe by Sharp to Cooke and Beauchamp in return for their silence. *Niles' Register* reported something similar, but in slightly different terms, saying that Sharp "had seduced the woman, then found her a husband, on the promise of a piece of land, which he afterwards refused to give."[33] The significant age difference between the Beauchamps points to such a possibility. There are also hints in the record to support Leander Sharp's assessment of Jereboam's character as being that of a less-than-scrupulous young man. In addition to the paternity suit filed against him, in July 1823 he had been charged in Simpson County with disturbing the peace, though the prosecution was ultimately dismissed. More seriously, perhaps, only a few months after he was admitted to the bar he was indicted by the state for champerty: improperly participating in a lawsuit in which he had no natural interest. Here, too, the charge was ultimately dropped but may reveal some concern on the part of his colleagues about his professional behavior. It would be nice to know more details, but the Simpson County courthouse was destroyed by fire in 1882, and the files on these and most other cases were destroyed with it.[34]

In any event, it does appear that Beauchamp's relationship with Sharp was more complex than that presented in the *Confession.* It does not appear that he developed an early hostility toward Sharp, based on the alleged seduction of Ann Cooke. His story of a challenge refused was not witnessed by anyone and probably never occurred. Moreover, Leander Sharp's evidence that Beauchamp had done legal work for Sharp, including affidavits from the Simpson County circuit court clerk and the county sheriff, is convincing. Again, this was in 1823 and 1824, prior to the murder, and well after the purported confrontation on the Frankfort streets—even as, according to the *Confession,* Beauchamp was plotting Sharp's demise.[35] It thus seems possible that the two men had a relationship that, at some point, went bad. If Sharp had bribed the Beauchamps, and either reneged or delayed on the payment, it would certainly explain why the relationship had existed and why it had taken a turn for the worse.

There is no doubt that a bond existed between Ann and Jereboam Beauchamp. It could have been love, it could have been common interest, it could have been—and probably became—a mixture of both. Her sense that Sharp had wronged her was strong; so was her gratitude to Jereboam for taking Sharp's life. It is worth noting J. W. Cooke's finding that in her will, written two days before Beauchamp's scheduled execution, she left her property to Beauchamp's father.[36] But it is also significant that both Darby and Leander Sharp put property at the heart of the Beauchamps' relationship, at least initially. Beauchamp's *Confession* did the same, at least obliquely. In the probably apocryphal account of Beauchamp's challenge to Sharp on the streets of Frankfort, Sharp was said to have offered Beauchamp his "whole estate" in return for his life.[37] Failure to fulfill such a promise would have created a strong bond of outrage between the two Beauchamps.

Any determination to get back at Sharp would have been intensified by the events of the 1825 campaign. It may never be known how the mulatto rumor got started or who specifically contacted the Beauchamps to tell them Sharp was circulating it. As Darby accurately pointed out, even as Sharp announced his candidacy, his leading supporters, including Amos Kendall, were raising the specter of attacks on Sharp's "public and private character" in the campaign, vowing to fight fire with fire.[38] It seems at least possible that Sharp's allies, with or without Sharp's connivance, threatened to spread such a rumor in the hope of forestalling any efforts to use the alleged seduction against him. In any event, someone, for either personal or political reasons, did tell the Beauchamps about the rumor. It also seems clear that, at this point, the Beauchamps began to plot Sharp's death, enraged by the defamation, perhaps even viewing it as an additional effort by Sharp to get out of the earlier bargain.

Why the murder did not occur until November can only be guessed. There may have been the mixture of personal and political motives, including a rage increased by Sharp's political success and a resolve to kill Sharp at the most spectacular moment. Another possible motive has to do with the paternity suit filed against Beauchamp. It was filed on October 29, 1825, only two days before he set out for Frankfort. The suit could well have turned Ann Beauchamp's desire into an ultimatum, forcing Beauchamp to demonstrate his commitment to her by carrying out their determination that Sharp should die.

But where was Darby in all this? His possible role was central to the debate, both before and after the Beauchamps' deaths. He remains an elusive character. He seems to have had an almost unmatched ability to arouse hostility, especially from his political and personal opponents. On the other hand, he did have the respect of some of Kentucky's most prominent conservatives, receiving praise for his ability as well as his virulence in taking their side.

The course of Darby's libel suits may be relevant to understanding his role in the Beauchamp case. There had been substantial circumstantial evidence brought to bear against him as an instigator, if not an accomplice, in Beauchamp's crime. Nevertheless, he felt sufficiently secure to risk initiating and pursuing his action against Kendall, Colonel Beauchamp, and the Sharps, a course that could easily have backfired on him had there been any evidence against him of complicity in the crime. (The success of Lowe's libel suit in response to Beauchamp's *Confession* is probably also relevant here, given the role the *Confession* assigned to Darby in what it represented as Lowe's "perjured" testimony.)

Moreover, Darby does seem to have located witnesses who could corroborate significant elements of his testimony against Beauchamp. The defendants in the suits relied mainly on testimony against Darby's character, and chiefly from his political opponents. Perhaps this is why, in 1827, the jury leaned his way and why Colonel Beauchamp, after a couple of years, decided to withdraw his earlier accusations. Darby probably was the unprincipled hothead Andrew Jackson and others described. However, there is no compelling reason to doubt the genuineness of Beauchamp's exoneration of him. There is even reason to suppose a kernel of truth in his testimony at Beauchamp's trial.

Taken as a whole, evidence from the case and its aftermath tend toward at least one possible explanation for the events that took place. In 1819, Solomon Sharp had sex with Ann Cooke. Pregnant, by Sharp or otherwise, she accused him of seduction and of being the father of her child. Two years later, John Waring tried to use her claim to attack his old enemy, Sharp. Sharp dodged the charge at the time, but later, to ensure Cooke's future silence, he created an arrangement with her and

Beauchamp, then failed to make good on it. At this point, the situation became embedded in the ugly, violent politics of Kentucky in 1825. Someone, with or without Sharp's connivance, floated the rumor of the mulatto child in order to protect Sharp's candidacy for office. Already angered, the Beauchamps not only resented the potential defamation but may even have assumed that this was a new wrinkle in an attempt by Sharp to get out of the bargain he had made with them. So they killed him.

## II

Even as Darby, Leander Sharp, Amos Kendall, and other interested parties were engaging in their bitter recriminations over the Beauchamp-Sharp affair, its literary possibilities had begun to intrigue American writers, and others. Less than a month after the Beauchamps' deaths, Henry Clay remarked to his close political associate from Louisiana, Josiah S. Johnston, "You will have seen the tragical end of Beauchamp and his unfortunate wife," adding, "We live in an age of romance. Ask Mrs. Johnston if the story might not be wrought up into a fine popular tragedy—one similar to Geo. Barnwell?"[39] He was referring to George Lillo's popular 1731 play, *The London Merchant; or, the History of George Barnwell,* an important piece in the early nineteenth-century theatrical repertory, and one that had been performed in Lexington as early as 1815.[40] The story of a young man manipulated by a woman he loves to murder his wealthy uncle, it does have a certain resonance with at least some aspects of the Beauchamps' case. And it ends with the protagonists' deaths—although, in the case of the play, they both die on the gallows.[41]

At least one noted American playwright, Joseph Hutton, had a reaction similar to Clay's. As early as August 21, 1826, he had begun to gather materials relevant to the case—by this time already labeled the "Kentucky Tragedy"—for a piece he planned to call "The Power of Passion." By November, however, he had put his plans on hold, mainly because of an appeal from Leander Sharp, who wanted to provide additional "documents" to help shape the plot.[42] The play never appeared.

A few other works soon did. Going against his own advice about making the Beauchamps into martyrs, the editor of the Philadelphia-based *Album, and Ladies' Weekly Gazette* published a poem, signed simply "B." and written for the magazine, which built upon Jereboam Beauchamp's last words to his wife. It was entitled "On the Grave of ———":

> Fare thee well! poor child of sorrow
> Calm repose thy troubled breast,
> The sun can wake to thee no morrow
> Nor calumny disturb thy rest;
> Softly may the moonbeams wave
> Their silv'ry beauties o'er thy grave.
> Child of misfortune, none will spurn
> Thy humble mansion with contempt,
> The good will oft thy folly mourn,
> And none from folly are exempt;
> Humanity demands a tear,
> And virtue's self would shed it here.[43]

It may also have been soon after the Beauchamps' deaths that an anonymous composer wrote a ballad recounting the events, a ballad that ultimately entered into oral tradition. Entitled "Colonel Sharp" by the time it was first collected in North Carolina in 1913, the ballad told how "Andy Bowens Beecher" and "Andy Cooker's dame" carried out their vengeance against the infamous Sharp and suffered tragic deaths. The ballad drew heavily on the version of the crime promulgated in Beauchamp's *Confession.*[44] Folklorist Leonard Roberts collected a variant, called "Jeremiah Beechum," in Kentucky as recently as 1956.[45]

But more elaborate literary efforts soon began to appear, as well. In one sense, Beauchamp's *Confession* may have represented the first literary version of the events, not simply in its self-serving and often fictional content, but in the ways in which Beauchamp, or his collaborators, drew heavily on literary conventions and devices for the final document. Most obvious was its reliance on those literary conventions that had been associated with the tradition of sentimental seduction novels dating back to the eighteenth century.

Herbert Ross Brown, in his classic survey of early American sentimental fiction, described seduction, sensibility, and suicide as the "tearful triune of sentimental beauties," the key conventions of the sentimental tradition.[46] All appeared in Beauchamp's *Confession,* in its characterizations, in elements of its plot, and in its portrayal of the Beauchamps' deaths as self-sacrificing martyrdom. The document drew heavily on the sentimental tradition by representing Sharp as a seducer willing to defame a "worthy" young woman to satisfy his own lust and ambition. It evoked a common plot device and traditional imagery by reporting that after the seduction, Ann Cooke had "retired to a romantic little farm" where, with only books for company, she refused all society.[47] One of the earliest and most influential sentimental novels, Susanna Rowson's *Charlotte* (1794), provided a model for Cooke's retirement when, after the title character's seduction, she too "retired," saying she wanted only to hide her "shame and sorrow," to spend what was left of her life "in obscurity, unknown and unpitied."[48]

The *Confession* also presented a stereotypically heroic Jereboam who, like sentimental prototypes, had always harbored an "utter contempt and abhorrence" for any seducer and who had a feeling for love as the "sweetest of all passions, which reciprocated, hapily [*sic*] turns Earth into a Heaven."[49] Even Sharp's refusal of young Beauchamp's challenge, one of the key—and least likely—episodes in the *Confession,* was a frequent turn in sentimental novels. Richmond, Virginia, novelist Samuel Relf in 1797, for example, hinged his *Infidelity; or, the Victims of Sentiment* around a cowardly seducer's refusing the peremptory challenge of a young man "swelling with passion."[50] A similar episode appeared in Rowson's *Charlotte.* Such a story was vividly told, too, in Jesse Holman's *The Prisoners of Niagara, or Errors of Education,* published in Frankfort, Kentucky, in 1810.

Beauchamp's final words had literary precedent. In a 1784 story, the headstrong Auretta rebels against her parents in order to join a Mr. Wendell, whom she loves. Far from being a cynical seducer, however, Wendell commits suicide rather than let her go through with her plan. And he leaves her a poem, concluding, "Farewell all friends, Auretta farewell too, / I die in honor, now I die for you."[51] William Hill Brown's pioneering novel *The Power of Sympathy* (1789) even anticipated the Beauchamps' final wishes, as its protagonist, facing the death of the woman he loves, commits suicide, hoping to be buried beside her. Their monument, too, is to have a poetic inscription: "Stranger! contemplate well before you part, / And take this serious counsel to thy heart: / Does some fair female of unspotted fame, / Salute thee, smiling, with a father's name, / Bid her detest the fell Seducer's wiles, / Who smiles to win—and murders as he smiles."[52]

None of this is, of course, to suggest that the Beauchamps had read Brown or the obscure "History of Auretta" and had simply used them as sources for creating their own final message to the world. It is to emphasize that the language of such literature was part of the environment in which they lived and part of the framework in which they hoped their words would have appeal. Much in Beauchamp's *Confession* would have seemed familiar to readers of sentimental novels or, for that matter, fans of popular melodrama. And it could be interpreted to teach the same lessons, as well. The *Confession,* for example, was presented by its publisher as "a volume against seduction—promise-breaking—murder and suicide," and he urged people to "Read it, ponder upon it, and so sure as you live, you will be benefited by your own reflections."[53] In doing so, he echoed countless writers in the sentimental tradition, from William Hill Brown and Susanna Rowson forward. Its literary allusiveness undoubtedly helps explain why the *Confession* seems to have attracted a wide audience when it appeared and why it went through at least four separate editions prior to the Civil War.[54]

Beauchamp's *Confession* was not the only early, purportedly factual account of Sharp's murder to draw heavily on conventions of sentimental literature. The strength of those conventions is particularly well illustrated by an anonymously written volume of letters, purportedly by Ann Beauchamp, published very shortly after the Beauchamps' deaths. Long taken as real—and cited by historians—these letters have been proven fictional by such scholars as Fred M. Johnson and Jack E. Surrency. Johnson, in particular, has called attention to their literary character and their heavy reliance on the conventions of the sentimental epistolary novel.[55]

Presented as letters from Ann Beauchamp to the wife of the volume's editor, one W—— R—— of Charles County, Maryland, they were published, like Beauchamp's *Confession,* with claims of overt moral intent. The editor hoped Cooke's "letters" would exhibit "the dreadful effects of seduction and treachery, and the consequences which flow from the first fatal aberration from the paths of virtue and innocence." Here, the lesson was aimed particularly toward young women "who suffer themselves to be too much under the influence of feeling and passion; or, who repose too confidently on their own strength, and the honour of man," as the letters were intended to show Cooke had done. Thus, much of the story has to do with the destruction of "the peace and happiness of a young, innocent, and helpless woman," and W. R. writes of the murder, "we cannot but sympathize with the fate of those who executed it, and feel inclined to cast over their guilt and their frailty the mantle of extenuation."[56]

In keeping with the author's purposes, perhaps, the letters also represent the first attempt to imagine the seduction itself. They begin by tracing Ann Cooke's (spelled "Cook" in the book) meeting between Sharp (or "Sharpe" as the volume spells it) at a ball and her instant, ardent attraction to him. When, on a walk together, Sharp "imprinted a burning kiss" on her lips, Cooke is hopelessly infatuated.[57] From there, it is only a short time before she falls victim to Sharp's wiles. Pledging his love, he betrays her, leaving her alone. From there, the letters move to an account of her meeting with Beauchamp, of his genuine love for her, and finally of the vengeance compelled when Sharp compounds the sin of seduction with that of defamation. The work concludes with an account of the Beauchamps' final hours. Appropriately, it does so by quoting, in the form of a last letter from Cooke to her friend, the poem Ann Beauchamp wrote to be their epitaph and, in an epilogue signed by W.R., the last words Jereboam spoke to her as he was led out to die.

Over the next three and a half decades, the trends established in these early documents were to serve as the basis for an array of works that drew on the Beauchamp-Sharp affair. The story was quickly incorporated into a "true crime" tradition that developed during the first half of the nineteenth century and which was an important part of American popular culture during the period. As a number of scholars have discussed, the early nineteenth century was marked by the emergence of a variety of forms of "sensational" literature. This literature ranged from gothic novels bordering on the pornographic, to the confessions, real and imagined, of brutal murderers, to relatively unvarnished trial reports that gave a powerful reality to what people sensed as the evil in their midst.[58] Creating a moralistic framework within which readers could savor a voyeuristic exploration of immorality, this literature was among the most popular of antebellum forms.[59]

The Beauchamp-Sharp affair was tailor-made for the tradition, and accounts of it were published with some regularity. Among the first was the 1826 New York publication of an abridged version of Beauchamp's trial report, entitled *The Trial of Jereboam O. Beauchamp, for the Murder of Colonel Solomon P. Sharp, Together with the Tragical Death in Prison, by Suicide, of the Wife of Beauchamp, the Once Beautiful and Accomplished Miss Ann Cook, of Bowlinggreen.* The editors took fierce aim at all three principals, describing Sharp as a heartless seducer and the Beauchamps as greedy, overreaching, and lacking in virtue. The editors accepted as true the rumor, brought up by Darby, that it was Sharp's refusal to pay what the editors termed "hush money" that had led to his death.[60] And they used the case to present important lessons "to the youth of this world,"[61] suggesting that one should have enough piety and concern for public opinion to avoid putting oneself in Beauchamp's position of placing greed above reputation.

At the same time, the editors could not escape that imagery which Thomas Clarke of the Philadelphia *Album* had been so worried about. They took for granted the Beauchamps' love for each other, which, though it stood as proof "that love may endure even in the absence of virtue," could not fail to excite the sympathy of others. At the same time, they condemned Sharp, who had "done that which robs his memory of every claim to respect."[62] Drawing, as best they could, on some of the same sentimental conventions that also informed the *Confession* and the purported letters of Ann Cooke, the editors of the New York version of the trial also helped to place the report itself within the larger tradition of sensationalist crime literature.

The same may be said of another account of the affair, which appeared in Henry St. Clair's *United States Criminal Calendar: or, An Awful Warning to the Youth of America; Being an Account of the Most Horrid Murders, Piraces* [*sic*], *Highway Robberies, &c. &c.*, published in Boston in 1833. St. Clair had a clear awareness of what he was about. He recognized the contemporary taste for sensationalism, noting that "No part of a newspaper excites so much attention as the record of crime and calamity." The need, therefore, was to "gratify this feeling in the manner the most advantageous to the public." He argued that "holding sin up to abhorrence" could do just that and offered a didactic compendium of crimes from the colonial era to his own time.[63]

Taking his account almost entirely from Beauchamp's *Confession*, St. Clair put Beauchamp in company with such illustrious rogues as the infamous pirates Captain Robert Kidd and William Fly, serial killers Micah and Wiley Harpe, and other notorious desperadoes. The case, he wrote, could simultaneously "show the danger of calumny and warn the young and violent not to take the laws into their own hands."[64] St. Clair described how both Beauchamp and Cooke had let their passions get out of hand, and he gave their thirst for revenge a regional twist when he suggested that "human life is little regarded in the western states."[65] Consistent with Beauchamp's *Confession,* St. Clair condemned Amos Kendall for trying to treat the murder as a political crime. Through his account of Beauchamp's trial and of the Beauchamps' deaths, St. Clair presented the affair as wholly a matter of private vengeance.

Prior to concluding with excerpts from the Beauchamps' poetry, St. Clair offered his own ambivalent assessment of the events. Beauchamp, he wrote, "had no right to avenge the wrongs of another, or even his own, with his own hand, and every well-constituted mind must revolt at the assassination so treacherous and cruel as that of Sharp." Still, he said, it had to be acknowledged that Beauchamp was "actuated by a sense of honor highly commendable, had it not been misdirected." At the same time, "there was never villainy more cruel, more cowardly, more atrocious, than that of Col. Sharp." Arousing the Beauchamps' passions, "he deserved all he got and more."[66] Whatever misgivings St. Clair had about the Beauchamps, it was ultimately their martyrdom that most impressed him.

St. Clair's view was the one generally taken in subsequent accounts of the affair. Thus, a popular 1843 account of another case of seduction and murder, one known as the "Heberton Tragedy," concluded with a twenty-page rendition of the Beauchamp-Sharp affair. The editors asserted that it could "serve as a monitor to those who take advantage of female innocence, teaching them that though the object over which they recklessly triumph may be bereft of relatives to espouse her cause, yet there is an All-seeing eye from whose omniscient surveillance nothing escapes, and who will sooner or later bring the seducer to an awful account." Relying more on convention than fact, the editors praised the Beauchamps as a pious couple, and even said that Jereboam had "early displayed remarkable indications of genius."[67] Cooke, they wrote, distinguished by her beauty, innocence, and talent, was unable to resist the "insidious wiles" of the seducer Sharp.[68] Avoiding the ambiguities raised by her male relatives' failure to become her avengers, the Heberton editors simply made her an orphan, taking away her family altogether. The Beauchamps' deaths made them martyrs to honor and to love.

As the events themselves became more distant, purportedly factual renditions of the Kentucky Tragedy came to comprise a tradition of their own, drawing on Beauchamp's *Confession* and on each other. An 1850 Frankfort publication, *The Life of Jeroboam* [*sic*] *O. Beauchamp,* was, for example, little more than a gloss on the *Confession* and on St. Clair. It did, however, go slightly beyond the latter in concluding that Sharp "deserved all he got, and *much* more."[69] Taken as a whole, this tradition shows not only the continuing appeal of the story but also the continuing vitality of the conventions that could give it shape. Such conventions, it may also be noted, were often reinforced by illustrations purporting to represent the Tragedy's principals and events but bearing only scant relation to either. Drawing on stock imagery, these illustrations reinforced the literary conventions defined by the sentimental "triune" of seduction, sensibility, and suicide.

So great was the power of those conventions that, as the popular tradition developed, all the ambiguities of the original affair disappeared. Sharp became a seducer, motivated by the basest desires. Beauchamp became a heroic avenger, however greatly some writers might appear to fret about his disregard for law. Ann Beauchamp, beautiful and accomplished, became the vulnerable victim of the seducer's lust.[70]

This lack of ambiguity was particularly apparent in an 1858 reprinting of the *Confession* entitled *The Beauchamp Tragedy in Kentucky.* Taking as its beginning the purported dying words of a debauchee that "God made them lambs: we men are wolves," the book took for granted that women were powerless to resist the evil purposes of a determined seducer. Women, the editors wrote, are by nature weak; it is man's responsibility to recognize and respect their purity.[71] From there, in a lengthy introduction, the editors went on to condemn Sharp as the unscrupulous seducer of Cooke, presenting the Beauchamps as martyrs and as victims of his sinister web of lust and deceit.

## III

In the realm of popular literature, then, the Beauchamp-Sharp tragedy attracted attention throughout the antebellum period, even as accounts of that tragedy tended to move steadily toward a celebration of the Beauchamps and a condemnation of Sharp. The inherent drama was hard to miss, and its career underscores the ongoing power of frameworks of sensationalism and sentimentality to shape antebellum popular culture. The same power was apparent as a number of antebellum authors made conscious efforts to adapt the events of the Beauchamp-Sharp case to more clearly literary ends. As Henry Clay had thought they should, playwrights, novelists, and others found in the Beauchamp story valuable grist for their literary mills.

Although Joseph Hutton's initial effort to turn the story into a play never came to fruition, by the early 1830s other writers did manage to exploit the Tragedy's dramatic possibilities. The first seems to have been an anonymous playwright who in 1833 published a five-act drama entitled *Beauchamp, or the Murder of Col. Sharp,* a play which received at least one performance, although it is not certain when or where.[72] Asserting that the play was "Founded Upon the real tragic events and facts," the playwright claimed to be "a Resident Near the scene of the action, and acquainted with all the parties."[73]

The creator of this pioneering effort, who remains unidentifiable, relied on Beauchamp's *Confession* for plot and characterization, but the play is essentially a *drame à clef* from an Old Court point of view. According to the playwright, Beauchamp's murder of Sharp was an honor killing, undertaken to avenge Sharp's seduction and defamation of Ann Cooke. The play also suggests, however, that much of the blame for setting the tragedy in motion belongs to a thinly disguised Amos Kendall and Francis P. Blair, former clerk of the New Court ("Amus" and "Francis" in the play). By the time the play was published in 1833, Kendall and Blair had both become leading figures in Andrew Jackson's presidential administration, Kendall as one of Jackson's closest confidantes, Blair as editor of the most influential Jacksonian newspaper, the *Washington Globe.* Thus, the play may well have been written as an attack on the Jackson administration in general and on Kendall and Blair in particular. In this, it would have anticipated Joseph Underwood's resurrection of the Beauchamp-Sharp affair in his own attack on Kendall at the end of 1837.

Like Beauchamp's *Confession,* on which it draws, the anonymous Kentuckian's play creates a synthesis of the sentimental and the political. The author presents both the seduction and defamation as facts and, though the play portrays "Anna" as a woman dominated by her desire for revenge, stresses that her vengefulness was provoked by the betrayal of her innocence by Sharp. Beauchamp, all nobility, wants to share her injuries and even asks her to make Sharp's murder a condition of her acceptance of his love. Appropriately, given the play's political thrust, Sharp is a thoroughgoing villain, as are his associates, Kendall and Blair, who are assigned primary blame for spreading the story of the mulatto child. Revealing his true character, Amus even speculates at one point on what might happen to Anna after Beauchamp's execution, cynically musing that "the widow of a man that's hanged, you know, makes the best wife in the world."[74] The play concludes with an account of the Beauchamps' deaths based heavily on the *Confession,* to which the playwright apparently added a ballet accompanied by the music of "Bonaparte's Retreat."[75]

This anonymous Kentucky play was to be the most politically oriented literary treatment of the Beauchamp-Sharp tragedy. A more fully sentimental treatment would appear within a year or so of this anonymous version, Thomas Holley Chivers's 1834 *Conrad and Eudora.* Chivers was a Georgia physician who had attended medical school at Transylvania University in Lexington, Kentucky. While there, he read Beauchamp's *Confession* and was attracted to it. He may also have found some resonance in it because, according to his biographer, S. Foster Damon, Chivers had himself been abandoned by his first wife as a result of some now unknown slander.[76] In any event, the *Confession* figures strongly in Chivers's work, although he appears also to have known of the purported letters of Ann Cooke and even Leander Sharp's *Vindication.*[77]

Writing in verse, Chivers set his play in Frankfort, where the murder had occurred, but unlike his anonymous predecessor minimized without entirely eliminating the story's political dimensions. He focused mainly on the personal drama involving Eudora (Chivers's Ann Cooke), Conrad (his Beauchamp), and the seducer Alonzo (his Sharp). Chivers opens his play by imagining the seduction itself, in which the smooth-talking Alonzo challenges himself to overcome the resistance of an innocent, young, and fatherless Eudora. Overcome it he does, and he succeeds in doing so on the night he is to wed another woman, leaving Eudora abandoned and thirsting for vengeance.

Chivers's Conrad is a lifelong friend of Eudora—the age difference has disappeared—and, learning of the seduction, he is enraged. He goes to her and, together, they vow revenge, determining to act stealthily. From here, the play follows the *Confession* fairly closely, although in Chivers's play Darby becomes the prosecutor and a friend of Alonzo, as well as a conspirator in a plot to create the equivalent of Lowe's testimony in Beauchamp's trial. When this happens, rather than letting the jury determine his guilt, Conrad himself addresses the court with an appeal to honor, justifying the crime. If executed, he says, he will die for love. He is sentenced to death and, as the time approaches, he and Eudora, like their prototypes, stab themselves. Conrad appeals to his jailers to let him die with Eudora. His plea is denied, however, and he is led away to the gallows as the play concludes.

Chivers was a man of great literary ambition. A friend, and sometimes antagonist, of Edgar Allan Poe, he engaged in a literary career that led him to publish fairly widely. He had strong ambitions for *Conrad and Eudora.* In 1838, he revised it, retitling the work "Leoni; or, the Orphan of Venice."[78] He sent this new version to E. S. Connor, one of America's leading actors, hoping to have it performed. A few years later he sent "Leoni" to Poe, although Poe apparently did nothing with it. Still later, he sent another version of "Leoni" to the great Edwin Forrest, apparently as an entry in a contest Forrest had sponsored for the best "original tragedy."[79] In May and June 1851, what may have been this version of the play was published in a newspaper, the Macon *Georgia Citizen.*

Chivers drastically edited *Conrad and Eudora* to create "Leoni." Although he cited the Kentucky Tragedy as his source, and its events remain recognizable, the new play is set in Venice rather than Kentucky, and includes additional characters along with an array of subplots to complicate the action. The story begins after the title character's seduction by the cynical Alvar. Leoni (the new "Eudora") has known her cousin Alvino since childhood, and Alvar urges her to marry the young man, whom she had been too vain to appreciate in their youth. From here, the story begins to move in many directions, chiefly because of the subplots, but the basic element of Leoni's thirst for vengeance and Alvino's willingness to act for her, out of love, remains the focus of the play. On a dark and stormy night, Alvino goes to Alvar's home and calls him out. The two fight, and Alvino kills Leoni's seducer. Alvino is arrested and is sentenced to die. In the presence of the court, Alvino and Leoni, who have vowed to die together, take poison but survive its effects. They are imprisoned together. As Alvino's execution approaches, they hear the gathering crowd. Leoni stabs herself and dies. He does the same, but in a twist on the original story, his death comes at the very moment he is granted a reprieve.

Chivers's resetting of the story to Italy was consistent with what Arthur Hobson Quinn described as the "literary fashion" of the day.[80] It may also have been inspired by two other plays published shortly after *Conrad and Eudora* but before "Leoni." One was Edgar Allan Poe's uncompleted verse play "Politian." Portions of the play appeared as "Scenes from an Unpublished Drama" in the *Southern Literary Messenger* in late 1835 and early 1836. Parts of it were also printed in 1845 in Poe's *The Raven and Other Poems,* while two scenes remained in manuscript until recovered by the scholar Thomas Olive Mabbott in the early twentieth century. Poe placed the action in sixteenth-century Rome, but, as Mabbott demonstrated, he drew heavily on the purported letters of Ann Cooke as well as Beauchamp's *Confession,* quoting directly from both here and there in the play.[81]

There is really nothing to indicate what attracted Poe to the story, and, despite his debts to earlier documents, the play departs fairly significantly from more familiar versions of the events. The play tells the story of the orphan Lalage, who has been seduced and abandoned by the dissolute Castiglione, her guardian. His name echoed that of the noted sixteenth-century authority on manners, Baldassare, Conte Castiglione, whose classic 1528 work, *The Courtier,* was well known to antebellum readers, especially in the South.[82] Poe seems, however, to have chosen the name more for its period and aristocratic connotations than for any clear connection to the real Castiglione's moral and social ideas. In any event, Poe's Castiglione knows how deeply he has betrayed Lalage but refuses to make things right by marrying her. She has become, Castiglione says, a wanton woman. What he does not know is that she has also become obsessed with vengeance to the point of near madness.

Politian, whose name also had period and literary—though not clearly historical—connotations (he was a fifteenth-century Italian poet) is Poe's Beauchamp. He is the Earl of Leicester, in Rome for a visit, and has overheard Lalage singing to herself. Enchanted, he, too, becomes obsessed, in his case by a desire to meet the singer. When they do meet, they immediately fall in love and soon make plans to leave Rome, to live where her shame is unknown. First, however, they resolve to kill Castiglione. Drawing heavily on Beauchamp's *Confession,* Poe creates a scene in which Castiglione refuses a challenge from Politian. He then has the lovers resolve to kill Castiglione on the seducer's wedding day. Politian rushes off to do the deed, at which point Poe seems to have abandoned his efforts to finish the play.

The young writer's first foray into drama was not, as he himself reported, well received. Critics found the play hackneyed and affected, and they had particular reservations about the quality of the verse in which it was written. Poe was urged to drop the project and must have been persuaded to do so.[83] But his effort, if it inspired Chivers's revisions, also seems to have inspired a more successful playwright to take on the story. This was the actress Charlotte Barnes, daughter of theatrical parents and a stage veteran herself by the age of sixteen. Her *Octavia Bragaldi* opened in New York in November 1837 with Barnes, then age nineteen, playing the title role. The play proved quite popular. It was performed widely, and Barnes herself played Octavia Bragaldi as late as 1854—by which point, incidentally, she was married to E. S. Connor.[84] Quinn has cited the possible debt to Poe, noting, for instance, that she named her villain "Castelli."[85] Barnes herself acknowledged her debt to events that "occurred in the city of Frankfort, (Kentucky,) in 1825," events she learned about during a visit to the city. She had, however, added "interpolations" of her own and taken a few other liberties with the plot. The story illustrated, she believed, "the futile and lamentable results of revenge, even under circumstances which in the world's opinion serve in some degree to palliate it."[86]

Choosing an Italian setting, Barnes takes the Tragedy's events to fifteenth-century Milan. The play's central characters are the untitled but wealthy Francesco Bragaldi and his wife, Octavia. They have known each other since childhood but have, nevertheless, had a complex past. At age sixteen, Francesco had been sent to war, and though he was soon to return, a terrible thing happened during his absence. Octavia had been wooed by the cynical Castelli and, over her father's objections, had eloped with him. Castelli, too, had soon been sent to battle. When Octavia had begged to accompany him, he had refused, abandoning her completely. According to reports, he was killed shortly thereafter. Francesco, returning, had asked for her hand, and they were married.

But an awful truth now comes out. Through a series of events, Octavia and Francesco learn that the wedding with Castelli had been staged and was phony. He had simply wanted to have his way with her. They also learn that Castelli is alive and has returned to Milan. They vow revenge. Barnes recreates the scene of a challenge refused, then, echoing Poe, has Castelli assert that Octavia had been a wanton woman. This defamation is too much, and finally Francesco stealthily, and in disguise, kills Castelli. Arrested, he proudly proclaims his guilt. At her request, Octavia joins him in custody. There will, however, be no criminal process. Before he can go to trial, Francesco kills himself, and Octavia takes poison. They are buried together in a single grave.

If early dramatists transplanted the plot to what were almost Shakespearean settings, the first writer to render the story into fiction—clearly presented as such—went back to its Kentucky origins. This was Mary E. MacMichael, whose short story "The Kentucky Tragedy" appeared in Philadelphia's prominent *Burton's Gentleman's Magazine* in 1838—prior, it should be noted, to Poe's assuming the magazine's editorship in 1839–1840.

As a writer, MacMichael remains obscure, although she published a number of pieces, poetry and prose, during the mid-1830s. These appeared mainly in the hugely popular magazine *Godey's Lady's Book*, also published in Philadelphia. Some of her work indicates that she was herself a Philadelphian, and despite the discrepancy in the spelling, she may have been Mary Estell, who in 1831 married Morton McMichael, a prominent Philadelphia civic leader (and post–Civil War mayor). Morton McMichael was closely associated with Louis Godey and with other prominent literary figures, including Poe and Robert Montgomery Bird. He was even an editor of *Godey's*, along with Godey, Sarah J. Hale, and, briefly, Lydia Sigourney, from 1842 to 1846, contributing some pieces of his own to the magazine. McMichael had a reputation as a reformer—he is credited with dispersing a mob and preventing the burning of an African-American orphanage during Philadelphia's infamous 1837 anti-abolition race riot—displaying some of the same political and social proclivities found in Mary MacMichael's own literary work.[87]

In any event, MacMichael, like Chivers, moved much of the story's focus back to the seduction, and relied still more heavily on sentimental conventions. The story departs fairly significantly from the known events, and there is no place for politics in MacMichael's rendering of the tale. But it is still clearly related to—and MacMichael intended it to be understood in terms of the framework provided by—the Beauchamp-Sharp affair.

In her version of the Kentucky Tragedy, MacMichael actually told two stories, the first focusing on two young lovers, Claude de Wilton and Geraldine Hearthwood. The love is real, but not lasting, and when de Wilton ventures forth into the world, he ultimately abandons Geraldine, sending her a cold rejection letter, concluding with his "best wishes for health, happiness, and future prosperity."[88] Not only is she heartbroken, but she is also ill, of consumption, and soon dies.

The plot then returns to de Wilton, who has turned his attention to Ianthe Willoughby. Ianthe already has a lover, Frank Beauchamp, whom she has known since childhood, but under de Wilton's influence she rudely abandons Frank, who soon leaves Kentucky. Unlike many Ann Cookes, however, Ianthe, aware of his designs, resists de Wilton. Filled with remorse for rejecting Frank, she offers de Wilton only friendship, an offer he angrily rejects. And then the tragedy unfolds. In the course of time, Frank returns to Kentucky, and he and Ianthe determine to marry. De Wilton, too, has married and begun a prosperous new life. Still angry, however, de Wilton has cruelly spread an awful rumor about Ianthe, implying that he had successfully seduced her, a rumor that she fears could jeopardize her marriage. She tells Frank, who vows both his love for her and his duty to avenge her defamation. They marry and soon Beauchamp goes in the dead of night to kill de Wilton. Beauchamp confronts the villain and, in a twist on the usual plot, de Wilton declares his readiness to fight. Instead, Beauchamp shoots him dead on the spot. The story then passes quickly over the arrest, trial, and conviction, to conclude with the Beauchamps' mutual suicide. In this case, their efforts succeed, as the jailer, coming to take him away, finds them lying together in death. It is a story not to be forgotten, MacMichael assures her readers, and few, she says, have not heard of the "Kentucky Tragedy."[89]

MacMichael's was a pioneering work of fiction based on the case, but it was soon to be joined by what remains the most significant antebellum treatment, William Gilmore Simms's two-volume 1842 novel *Beauchampe.* Simms was a prolific novelist from South Carolina, arguably the only Southern novelist of any renown before the Civil War, as well as a vigorous conservative and proslavery polemicist. Simms said he had based the novel on fact, claiming "we have good authority for all that is given here"; but the story he told—running close to eight hundred pages—went well beyond any of the documentation in the case.[90] The claim to historical accuracy probably captures Simms's awareness of an American audience receptive to historical fiction, a popular genre in antebellum America. It may also capture some of the same playful reflexivity that shows up frequently in the text itself. As Simms himself acknowledged, though the novel drew on the Beauchamp-Sharp affair, it was also written within the framework of his own popular border romances, evoking the world of frontier America. And it did well. In 1856, responding to what he saw as a ready market, Simms published a slightly expanded version of the novel, entitling its first volume *Charlemont,* and retaining the title *Beauchampe* for the second.[91]

In either version, the first volume of Simms's long novel is entirely fictional, bearing little resemblance to any of the events associated with the Kentucky Tragedy. It is, instead, an extended tale of the seduction of the vain village beauty Margaret Cooper by Warham Sharpe, masquerading as a preacher named Alfred Stevens. She is loved by the good, honest William Hinkley, but is far too vain to appreciate a local boy. The original version ends as, having seduced her, Sharpe abandons her to her fate. The second volume is closer to the documentation, and Simms even quotes from the *Confession* here and there. In it, Hinkley has risen from his obscure beginnings to statewide prominence, Sharpe has become a powerful politician, and Cooper—having changed her name to Anna Cooke—has met and married Orville Beauchampe.

In his rendition of the tale, Simms makes Beauchampe a political protégé of Sharpe. Though Orville has married Anna knowing of her past seduction, it is only after the marriage that he learns that Sharpe was her seducer, starting the fatal chain of events in motion. Simms's Sharpe is a particularly ugly character, taunting his former victim, even making an attempt at another seduction when he visits the Beauchampes' home, before his duplicity has been revealed to Orville. It is even Sharpe who, confronted by Beauchampe over the seduction, desperately responds with the false information that Anna had delivered a black baby. Beauchampe kills the seducer on the spot. Simms spends little time on the trial, although he does return to the documents to say that Beauchampe was convicted based on perjured evidence. In recounting the suicide, however, he allows Beauchampe to succeed. Dying as he is put on the cart that would have taken him to the gallows, Beauchampe proclaims, "Daughters of Kentucky! you, at least, will bless the name Beauchampe!"[92]

Simms's novel received a mixed but generally positive reception. Poe famously wrote that "no more romantic tragedy did ever the brain of poet conceive than was the tragedy of Sharpe and Beauchampe," though he did complain that in the novel "too little has been left for invention."[93] Poe would later write that "the facts of this remarkable tragedy, as arranged by actual circumstances, would put to shame the skill of the most consummate artist."[94] However, Sarah Hale, chief editor of the *Lady's Book,* reported that at about the time Simms's novel was published, she had received a letter suggesting that the "famous Kentucky tragedy" be worked up into a tale. Simms, she said, had done it, and had done so in a way that would give the story "a permanent place in the national literature."[95]

Simms's novel also inspired the last antebellum literary work based on the tragedy, *Sybil,* a play by John Savage. Savage, a famous actor and playwright, was himself no stranger to matters of honor. He was married to an actress and, according to historian David Grimsted, once dueled and wounded a critic who had belittled Mrs. Savage's acting ability. When the critic persisted, Savage gave him a public thrashing.[96] In *Sybil,* Savage achieved a less ambiguous success. The play was extensively performed, including runs in St. Louis, New Orleans, San Francisco, New York, Philadelphia, and Boston. According to Savage, it even had a performance in Australia sometime before 1863.[97]

*Sybil* was also performed in Kentucky, to some controversy. Scheduled to open on October 7, 1858, at the Louisville Theater, and featuring the popular actress Avonia Jones, the performance was suddenly cancelled after objections from the Sharp family.[98] The family was much criticized, and the play made its Louisville debut on October 9, continuing for several performances. It played to full houses and enthusiastic audiences.

A writer for the *Louisville Daily Courier* had mixed feelings about *Sybil,* enjoying it as a drama that "ranks with the immortal works of the best writers for the stage," but condemning it as history, "an infamous libel upon the dead."[99] Having allowed the performances to proceed, the Sharp family reacted with renewed displeasure to the play's success. In a lengthy letter to the *Courier,* the family described the play—and other literary works, for that matter—as "a slander upon the truth of history, and the character of a man who filled important trusts in the State of Kentucky." They then presented a series of excerpts from Leander Sharp's suppressed *Vindication* designed to prove that their ancestor had not been a seducer and that the Beauchamps' characters had been less pure than playwrights and novelists might suggest.[100]

Savage defended his play. Acknowledging that he had drawn on the Beauchamp-Sharp affair, he said, nevertheless, that the play was only loosely based on events. While he had employed the usual documents, he had relied "far more upon his own fancy and invention" to make an entertaining play. Despite Savage's celebration of his own "fancy and invention," however, *Sybil* is in many ways little more than a dramatization of Simms's novel. The play opens after the seduction, but weaves in earlier events, including a tale of changed names and cynical impersonation. The seducer, Rufus Wolfe, masquerading as Alfred Stevens, uses his urbane ways to take advantage of a vain village girl, Margaret Cooper. Her avenger, Eustace Clifden, is a political protégé of Wolfe's. Clifden has married Margaret, now known as Sybil Hardy, with the full knowledge that she had been seduced and, as in Simms's novel, becomes Wolfe's bitter enemy on learning his true identity. Savage even paraphrases Simms when, after Eustace has taken Wolfe's life, Sybil assures him that "The wives, / The mothers, daughters of the State, are all / The debtors for the deed."[101] But Savage did depart from both Beauchamp and Simms in the tragic climax to his drama. In Savage's play, the jury refuses to convict Clifden, given the circumstances of the crime. Sybil, however, having feared the worst, goes mad. The stress has been too much for her, and she dies uttering her final words, "Not—Guilty," as the curtain falls.[102]

*Chapter 3*

# THOU ART HALF TO BLAME

The many authors and playwrights who saw literary potential in the events of the Kentucky Tragedy were working in an antebellum literary hothouse, writing at a time when American literary and popular cultures were exploding at an unprecedented rate. Print culture was expanding rapidly, from newspapers to widely read magazines to sensational sheets to, especially, novels. Drama, as plays went from stage to publication, was part of this explosion.[1]

The audience—or, rather, audiences—for this outpouring of popular expression remain, however, elusive. Each of the myriad forms had, to some extent, its own audience. Novels—and, it appears, printed versions of plays—tended to be aimed at a predominantly middle-class audience of men and women who could afford, among other things, the books and the time to read them.[2] Sensational sheets attracted urban workers. Still, one should be careful not to draw any lines too sharply. There was a great deal of influence back and forth from genre to genre. In regard to the theater, as such, audiences represented such a mixture that any lines of genre or appeal become still more confused, and confusing.[3]

The great variety of treatments of the Kentucky Tragedy emphasizes such problems of definition. Some, especially the trial accounts and reprintings of Beauchamp's *Confession,* belong to the world of sensationalism. Others reached an audience that, though widely distributed across regional lines, was primarily urban, middle class, and Northern. Simms, despite his Southern connections, depended on much the same audience.[4] More importantly, however, the shared themes and images in all the treatments suggest a common cultural background—crossing an array of class, regional, and gender lines—upon which the story's appeal rested, and that help us to place it in the context of its time.[5]

And again, the Kentucky Tragedy did have broad appeal. Its attractions are indicated, in part, by its continuing vitality in a range of forms, and by the explicitness with which virtually all the writers who adapted it asserted their indebtedness to the facts of the case. Its attractions may also have been shown by the extent to which a number of others, apart from those writers who focused on the Tragedy as such, used its incidents, whether taken directly from the sources or from other literary renditions, as part of their work.

Among these was Charles Fenno Hoffman, whose 1840 novel *Greyslaer* is sometimes considered to be a fictionalization of the Beauchamp case.[6] Poe, for example, discussed it in conjunction with Simms's *Beauchampe* as "a romance based on the well-known murder of Sharp," while suggesting that it had the same faults displayed by Simms's book.[7] There are certainly connections, although the connections are less important to the novel than are the events of the American Revolution that serve as its main focus.[8]

Still, Hoffman knew the Kentucky Tragedy. In an earlier, nonfiction book, *A Winter in the West* (1835), he wrote about it when he recounted a visit he had made to Frankfort. The story, he said, remained in currency. He described it as the story of the Beauchamps' "strange loves, of her cruel wrong, and his dark revenge, of the savage retribution they exacted from the author of their misery and crime, and the touching heroism of the death they shared at last together."[9] He also included, as an endnote, a lengthy account of the events, drawing heavily on Beauchamp's *Confession* and the published record of the trial.

Eschewing both the usual Kentucky and Italian alternatives, Hoffman set *Greyslaer* in Revolutionary New York. The novel follows the career of young Max Greyslaer, an American patriot. Much of it also deals with the travails of Alida de Roos, a strong-minded young woman Max loves and who, having earlier rejected him, has come to love Max. It is a complex story in which Alida is abducted by Tories, rescued by patriots and, on the eve of her wedding to Max, defamed by her onetime abductors, who want to prevent the marriage. There is even a rumor, echoing the Kentucky original, that she once had a child that may have been half Indian. When the slanderer is reported dead, Max is accused of murder and prosecuted by a Tory attorney hoping to use the affair to political advantage. Here, however, the ending is very different from that of the Beauchamp case, as Max's alleged victim is proved not to have been murdered but, instead, killed in battle. The novel ends happily as Max and Alida wed.

In addition to Hoffman's work, the Tragedy also played an acknowledged role in one of the first Canadian novels, Major John Richardson's *The Canadian Brothers,* originally published in 1840 and subsequently revised for an 1851 U.S. edition, retitled *Matilda Montgomerie.*[10] Set during the War of 1812, the novel follows the exploits of two brothers, Gerald and Henry Grantham, fighting for the British side. *The Canadian Brothers* was a sequel to Richardson's 1832 *Wacousta,* in which the brothers' family had been put under a curse. The sequel's subtitle is, appropriately, *The Prophecy Fulfilled;* the fulfillment comes with the brothers' deaths at the book's close, their deaths ending the family line.

Warfare takes their lives, but the chief agent in the destruction is the cold and beautiful Matilda Montgomerie, adopted daughter of an American officer. Her most vicious act occurs in Frankfort, where Gerald has been taken as a prisoner of war. They had met earlier in Canada, and he had fallen for her; she had told him of a thirst for vengeance that obsessed her, without revealing any details. Upon their meeting again in Frankfort, she declares that she can love him only if he agrees to avenge her wrongs. And now she tells him the details.

Earlier, she had been in love with an American officer in Frankfort. He, however, chanced to see her being embraced by her father, who, working as an American spy, was disguised as a black man. Her lover accused her of being black herself, telling others he had discovered her "in the arms of a slave."[11] Thus accused, she swore revenge, and she persuades Gerald to kill the villain who deprived her of her honor. The two formulate a plot to kill the officer clandestinely. The officer, however, turns out to be a Colonel Forrester, whom Gerald knew before, and for whom Gerald has great respect. Gerald is unable to go through with the murder. Matilda denounces him, saying she never loved him. She had taken it on herself to be the means of fulfilling the curse against his family, hoping through her plot to bring about two deaths—Forrester's in revenge for the wrong he had done her, and Gerald's as a member of the accursed family.

Richardson's novel departs from the events in important ways, and it is unclear what he used as sources for his version. But he did acknowledge his debt to the Tragedy, and used it to create a critical episode in his tale of war, death, and revenge.[12]

Less direct but no less evocative echoes of the Beauchamp-Sharp affair appeared in other works. Something of the Tragedy may have informed Henry Wadsworth Longfellow's 1842 verse play *The Spanish Student.*[13] Poe actually accused Longfellow of having plagiarized from "Politian" in the play, although the similarities do not seem nearly so great as Poe claimed.[14] At any rate, Longfellow's play was a tale of attempted seduction, set in Spain, in which the spurned would-be seducer successfully destroys a young dancer's reputation through slander and innuendo.

There also were echoes of the Tragedy in Julia Ward Howe's 1857 play *The World's Own,* performed in New York and Boston to a mixed—and often scandalized—reception.[15] Set in eighteenth-century Italy, the play focuses on Leonore, a haughty village beauty enamored of novels and reading, seduced and abandoned by a visitor, Lothair. The rest of the play follows her increasingly virulent quest for revenge and her relationship with Edward, a local artist who loves her. In the end, Edward, horrified by the vengeful woman she has become, encourages Leonore to end her life, which she does, understanding that her thirst for vengeance has made her a fiend. Though not wholly an adaptation of the Beauchamp-Sharp tragedy, the play showed enough similarity to the Kentucky story to bring about a New York republication of Beauchamp's *Confession* and a few related documents.[16]

## I

The Kentucky Tragedy thus inspired or at least informed a fair amount of literary work in antebellum America. There was, obviously, great variation, even in the most specific adaptations. Simms, Chivers (in *Conrad and Eudora*), and the anonymous 1833 playwright, as well as Savage, maintained at least some of the historical elements of the 1820s Kentucky setting, including its political intrigues. Poe, Barnes, and Chivers (in "Leoni") went for an exotic locale. MacMichael set her story in Kentucky, but it really could have been anywhere. Everything from seduction to false marriage to rumormongering marked Anne Cooke's dishonor. Sometimes Jereboam killed Sharp in stealth; sometimes in an open confrontation. Sometimes both Beauchamps died; sometimes only one. And if Hoffman's novel is included in the mix, then one time neither.

Still, even as the purportedly factual versions of the Tragedy tended to evolve in certain directions, so, too, did the more self-consciously literary ones. They all began with an acceptance of the story of seduction, despite any doubts raised in 1820s Kentucky. They portrayed a Sharp who was both unscrupulous and cowardly, drawing on both literary tradition and the influential *Confession* for the characterization: they invariably used the account of Sharp's refusal of Beauchamp's challenge, a story with literary roots of its own, to emphasize his venality.

The literary Beauchamps tended to have fewer rough edges than the documentary Beauchamps, even those whom the *Confession* tried to portray. Like the *Confession*'s Beauchamp, the literary version was a man of virtue and courage, motivated to act by an innate abhorrence of seduction and an abiding love for Ann. As for Ann Cooke Beauchamp, although literary efforts to render her character were ultimately to take very diverse forms,[17] as we shall see, there were some key transformations that brought most—if not all—together. Thus, the Ann who was victimized by seduction was also devastated by it, and in virtually all the treatments she went into seclusion, reluctant even to take up an acquaintance with the importuning Jereboam. More significantly, no one ever portrayed her as the "waning flirt of 35"—"stoop shouldered" and with her "foreteeth" missing—described by the bitter Leander Sharp.[18] She is always portrayed as beautiful and brilliant, her beauty and ability making her a worthy mate to the noble Beauchamp. Finally, all the authors dropped the difference in the original Beauchamps' ages: she had been forty when they died; he, twenty-three. Thus, in Barnes's play, they are husband and wife who had known each other since childhood. In MacMichael's short story, they are affianced prior to her becoming attracted to the seducer de Wilton. Chivers's Conrad and Eudora had been together in school. Whatever else authors might make of Ann Cooke Beauchamp, they followed tradition by making her, in age as well as beauty, an appropriate lover for her young champion.

Still, the very process of adapting the Tragedy was also influenced in some complicated, and not always consistent, literary practices taking shape in antebellum America. Print may have exploded in American life, shaping and creating audiences like never before, but not everyone was convinced that this was wholly to society's advantage. Such a concern actually carried forward fears going back for centuries, exacerbated, especially, as novel-reading became increasingly common beginning in the latter part of the eighteenth-century. Many observers worried about the effects novels might have on their readers, especially, though not exclusively, young women. In 1792, Mary Wollstonecraft—Ann Cooke's reputed "mentor"—had worried that "Novels, music, poetry, and gallantry, all tend to make women the creatures of sensation."[19] She was not the first to express such concerns.[20]

Nor would she be the last. People continued to worry about the effects of literature even as Chivers, Barnes, Simms, and others were adapting the story of Beauchamp and Sharp for popular audiences. The fears were not wholly specific to gender. Francis Wayland, in his influential 1835 textbook on *The Elements of Moral Science,* condemned "those who write, or publish, or sell, or lend vicious books," because of the power of such works to fill the reader's "imagination with conceptions of vice." It was, he wrote, "one of the most nefarious means of corrupting men."[21] One may recall, along these lines, the fear expressed by the editor of the Philadelphia *Album, and Ladies' Weekly Gazette* that "touching and sympathizing appeals" on behalf of the martyred Beauchamps might serve to "immortalize murderers" and encourage similar deeds, not to mention Henry St. Clair's apologia for his own digest of crime.

Still, there were also many people who saw much to be gained from reading, even fiction. "Mental culture" was an important element in antebellum social and cultural ideals, and many people saw reading as essential to the cultivation of the mind. Critic Francis Jenks, writing for the influential *Christian Examiner* in 1830, discussed the role literature could play in teaching readers to appreciate beauty and enabling them to go beyond "vulgar notions of utility" in their approach to life. It was essential, he said, to the cultivation of the "highest faculties" and to the realization of "the intellectual, moral, and religious man."[22] The writer of a note appearing in 1848 in Frederick Douglass's *North Star* described reading as one of the "noble employments of the soul" and the "groundwork" for all others.[23]

The problem was to read the right things, and to read them the right way. The basic arguments came together in an imagined dialogue on fiction published, significantly, in the *Lowell Offering.* This was a journal particularly devoted to teaching proper American values, its intended audience being young female millworkers, who were believed to have much to learn. Involving Annette, who sees little value in fiction, and Ella, who loves to read it and write it, the dialogue comes to terms with the possibility that "works of fiction have a most demoralizing and weakening effect upon the mind," as Annette puts it. Ella has to recognize the validity of Annette's concerns. Echoing Wollstonecraft, she, too, worries about "the poor, ruined females, who read of the imaginative until they entirely forgot the real." But Ella is herself able to handle such writing because she never allows herself to forget that it is, after all, only fiction. The issue is to read responsibly: "the power is wholly our own, to convert an active imagination into a curse or a blessing."[24]

Those who adapted the Kentucky Tragedy were highly conscious of such discussions. Professions of moral purpose—and guidelines to correct reading—appeared in several of the literary versions of the Kentucky Tragedy, as they had in the more "factual" accounts. The publisher of Beauchamp's *Confession* added a note describing it as "a volume against seduction—promise-breaking—murder and suicide"; St. Clair had claimed that the tale should "warn the young and violent not to take the laws into their own hands." So, too, had Charlotte Barnes asserted, in a prefatory note to *Octavia Bragaldi,* that the Tragedy's events "admirably illustrate the futile and lamentable results of revenge." Simms was especially self-conscious about creating a morality tale out of the Beauchamp story.[25] He began his novel *Beauchampe* by noting the ways in which he had drawn on the sources and the embellishments he had made. But he wrote that his real concern was with the "vital truths of the narrative." These were founded, Simms said, not so much in simple fidelity to the facts but in the extent to which, comparing his work with its sources, the "morals are the same." The vital truths were moral truths, and these were what readers should take away.[26]

In his approach, Simms also shared much with the *Lowell Offering*'s Ella, as he indicated in one of the many self-reflective passages dotting the novel. In a brief dialogue on reading, Simms had one of his main characters remark on the dangers of reading, fearing that the "intoxication would continue even after the draught has been swallowed, and would thus interfere with the hours devoted to other employments." Perhaps, says an older character, but anyone who could be so intoxicated "would most probably be intoxicated by more dangerous stimulants." He continues, "Everything, however, depends upon the habits of self-control which a man has acquired in his boyhood. The habit of self-control is the only habit which makes mental power truly effective."[27] Read properly, such a story as that of the Beauchamps and Sharp could have a salutary effect, as one reviewer of Simms's novel appreciated. It was a book in which readers could "see the seducer and slanderer of female innocence consigned to that immortality of infamy which he has so richly deserved."[28] Neither Simms nor Barnes could have hoped for more.

## II

Nevertheless, the ambivalence remained, as Simms's peppering of his novels with literary self-reflection and the defensive apologias of purportedly factual accounts underscore. It was an ambivalence addressed in many of the works themselves, as they openly confronted the concerns about reading raised more generally in antebellum America. One leitmotif running through the treatments of the Kentucky Tragedy—whether purportedly factual or clearly fictional—was the significance of reading to the Beauchamps' story. The influential *Confession* details how Jereboam Beauchamp used a common love of reading as his entrée for meeting and becoming more closely acquainted with Cooke. The story, as related there, emphasizes the kinds of relations Francis Jenks and others drew between reading and "mental culture," the ways in which literature can move one into a higher realm. At their first meeting, it was philosophy Ann and Jereboam read and discussed.

The thread of this idea was picked up in several of the texts, nowhere more directly than in the anonymous 1833 play *Beauchamp*. The play actually begins with a monologue from Beauchamp, trapped in the study of law, bemoaning the loss of a romantic spirit that had been his since childhood. When he first learns of Cooke, he also learns that it is a spirit they share, and this allows him to make clear that his attraction to her is more than physical. "One so near and so fond of learning and the wealth of Literature, must not be unknown to me," he declares. A short time later, anticipating Ella, he also makes clear to Ann that he knows how to separate fiction from life. Proclaiming his willingness to take her cause, he says, "Oh, 'tis not the pictured tales of romance that I seek, but the recollection of thy wrongs, and the rich treasure of thy mind and soul, hath brought me here."[29]

Not all of the representations of literature's role in the tale were so favorable, especially where Ann Cooke was concerned. In as early a document as the spurious letters, Cooke is presented as an object lesson on the evil effects of too much—or too careless—reading. Claiming to have been particularly moved by Alexander Pope's poem "Eloisa to Abelard," she draws all the wrong lessons from it, from an admiration for Héloise's all-consuming passion for Abélard to, even more, an appreciation for Héloise's powerful "independence of mind."[30] Farther on, she expresses a still more troubling appreciation for "the sceptical works of Hume, Voltaire, and Paine."[31] Her reading, as even she recognizes, has not been her strongest support in her efforts to resist the seduction that became her downfall.

On the question of reading, at least, the letters were not far from the portrayal of Cooke in the *Confession* and, even more, in Leander Sharp's *Vindication.* Her literacy and freethinking became a cornerstone in Sharp's attack on her character. He wrote that "She had read considerable, especially of Novels, and delighted to converse upon scenes of romance and fiction." He went on to suggest that "Of moral and religious principles, she was wholly destitute." When he described her as "an avowed disciple of Mary Woolstoncraft [*sic*]," he intended to make clear how her reading had left her infected with that "independence of mind" Wollstonecraft had championed for women. Christianity, Sharp wrote, "she denounced as a fraud on mankind, propagated and sustained by cunning and priestcraft."[32] Her too careless reading of the wrong things, if it did not lie at the bottom of her bad character, certainly contributed to the many traits that Sharp found so abominable, and so incriminating.

Cooke's problematic literary proclivities also entered into more clearly literary transformations of the Kentucky Tragedy. Poe's Lalage is portrayed as living in a dream world more fully defined by reading than experience. She anticipates her own presumed fate when, wholly lost in a book, her "fevered soul" becomes absorbed in a piece in which a beautiful woman died "full young": "She died!—the maiden died! / O still more happy maiden who couldst die."[33]

Simms, not surprisingly, was even more direct, and put Cooke's reading in the larger context created by his own reflections of the influence of literature. He set the stage through a conversation between his Sharp, Alfred Stevens, and one John Cross as, early in the novel, they discuss the ill-fated Margaret Cooper. She has, they have learned, a great dedication to reading, and Cross, a minister, is alert to the danger posed to Cooper by the possibility that she is reading the wrong things. After all, as he says, in places such as New York and Philadelphia there are thousands of people "Kept in constant employ sending forth those books of falsehood and folly which fill the hearts of the young with vain imaginings, and mislead the footsteps of the unwary."[34]

Margaret Cooper is just such a person, though given more to poetry than to fiction. She loves "the burning and thrilling strains of Byron, the tender and spiritual of Shelley, the graceful and soft of Campbell." For Cooper, as for Poe's Lalage, poetry has come to take the place of the world in which she lives: "The loveliness of nature itself, unrepresented by the glowing hues of poetry, grew tame, if not inoffensive." Cooper is what so many critics warned against, a "dreamer" who has lost her grounding under the influence of too much impassioned verse.[35]

Such treatments of Cooke emphasize still further the literary self-consciousness of those who wrote about her, and it was a literary self-consciousness that was widely diffused in antebellum America. Taken together, both the texts and the environment also suggest a setting in which fiction could be more than fiction, in which people could shape their identities, both individually and collectively, by what they read.[36]

## III

And, as historians have shown, there is evidence that they did. Catherine Kerrison, discussing the growth of novel reading in late eighteenth-century Virginia, has described the influence of novels on women's language and ideas during the period, citing, for example, the ways in which letters were written and understood within the framework novels helped create.[37] Others have noted similar processes extending through the antebellum period.[38]

Such processes were certainly apparent in the events and reactions surrounding the Beauchamp-Sharp affair. It is possible to note the extent to which the language of literature provided much of the Beauchamps' vocabulary as they composed both their final words and their final days. That language was apparent in at least some of the popular response to the Beauchamps' plight, in the petitions, for example, and in the immediate aftermath of their deaths. Defining villainy, heroism, and vulnerability, the language of popular fiction—whether elaborated or challenged by individual authors—moved beyond the literary realm to create a much larger context for representing and interpreting events. Its conventions had a resonance that went beyond the printed page.

Given such an environment, the characters of Ann Cooke Beauchamp become particularly revealing. She was subject to more varied literary transformations than any other figure, and these provide an important insight into the significance of the Kentucky Tragedy for understanding antebellum America. As a victim of seduction, Cooke was portrayed in two seemingly incompatible but actually complementary ways, each with strong conventional roots. Most simplistically, she was presented as just a woman. Acknowledged for her intelligence, it was nevertheless the case for some writers that, being a woman, her "strong mind," no matter how impressive, was no match to the seducer's appeals to her desires for love.[39] Such an explanation played readily into ideals of femininity that, as Sarah Hale wrote, celebrated women as being more given to the "true and fervent affections of the heart" than men.[40] Seeking and hoping for love, women were inevitably too eager to fall for its offer, whether real or pretended. The editor of the 1858 edition of Beauchamp's *Confession* wrote that woman "*must* love," and this made her especially vulnerable, as Ann Cooke was, to someone like Sharp.[41]

There was, however, another Ann Cooke who made her appearance in the literature, an Ann Cooke whose very haughtiness and vanity were the means of her undoing. In Samuel Richardson's *Clarissa,* the cruel seducer Lovelace once exclaimed of women, "How greedily do the whole sex swallow praise!" It was this trait, Lovelace assured a correspondent, that made them so susceptible to seduction.[42] In Chivers's *Conrad and Eudora,* the soon to be victimized Eudora expressed her own fear—soon to be realized—that "self-esteem may faun me into pride," leaving her vulnerable to Alonzo's blandishments.[43] The lesson that vanity could lead to disaster was commonly taught in the literary traditions upon which the Kentucky Tragedy stories drew most heavily. It was the core of Hannah Foster's classic American seduction novel *The Coquette* (1797), among others. And it figured in at least some treatments of the Tragedy.

Simms concentrated more on the pitfalls of vanity than did any other writer, although Mary MacMichael painted a vivid picture of her own. Both created Ann Cookes who were vain and haughty, and whose literary and intellectual proclivities made them feel superior to their neighbors. In both cases, the seducer was able to insinuate himself into their lives and achieve his purposes by appealing to such feelings. And if MacMichael's Ianthe was atypically able to resist the seduction, suffering later from de Wilton's false claims of success, Simms's Margaret Cooper could not. She "did not fall through vicious inclinations, but a wilful pride," Simms's evil Alfred Stevens reported to a companion, having achieved his purposes.[44] Preaching against the sin of pride, Simms's tale almost supported a comment by Eudora's mother, who tells Eudora that "thou art half to blame" for the seducer's success.[45]

Still, not everyone was as quick as Eudora's mother to blame the victim. As even Chivers developed his Ann Cooke characters, innocence was at least as important as vanity in understanding their fall.[46] Throughout the literary traditions on which the Kentucky Tragedy authors drew walked the figure of the young woman who, as one writer put it, "having herself no guile" became "much too confiding in others."[47] What another called a "fatal credulity," born of innocence and not vanity, had grave tendencies to put young women in jeopardy.[48]

Such a portrayal of Ann Cooke figures prominently in renditions of the Kentucky Tragedy. Both Charlotte Barnes's Octavia Bragaldi and Poe's Lalage epitomize such a character, tricked by their cynical seducers' false promises of marriage. A similar character appears in Mary MacMichael's story. Though her Ann Cooke character, Ianthe, is made vulnerable because of pride, the seducer de Wilton's earlier victim, Geraldine, had been fooled by a promise of marriage. Geraldine was distinguished by her innocence, and the "unreservedness, the unsuspecting trust" that led her to give her heart to another.[49] Here were innocent young women who, if they fell, could never be assigned the blame; their fall was, itself, a measure of their inner virtue.[50]

The innocent Ann Cookes comprised the version most closely connected to dominant antebellum ideas about gender, ideas that had achieved an increasing significance in the United States in the period since its founding. These ideas stimulated a growing conceptual separation of female from male and provided an underpinning for what may still be usefully described, despite some historical debate, as an ideology of "separate spheres," an ideology characterizing men and women as essentially different from each other, with each suited to a distinct "sphere" of activity. Specifically, women were seen as more fully suited for the duties of domesticity, motherhood, and the home, and men for what was viewed as the more volatile public realm.[51]

At the heart of this separation were those conceptions of masculine and feminine natures that also informed some of the concerns about reading during the antebellum period, as well as portrayals of an innocent Ann Cooke. One nineteenth-century commentator, writing in a way that also made clear the significance of separate spheres, summarized the differences. Gardiner Spring, a minister quoted in *Godey's Lady's Book* in 1854, wrote, "There is a feeling of heart, a consciousness of dependency, a natural and amiable timidity, a tenderness and kindness, which unfit a woman for the rude and tumultuous occupations, and which, while they assign to her a more retired sphere, as clearly disclose those qualifications which constitute her true dignity and glory."[52] The prominent Massachusetts politician Caleb Cushing wrote, similarly, "Hers be the domain of the moral affections, the empire of the heart, the co-equal sovereignty of intellect, taste, and social refinement." He continued, "Leave the rude commerce of camps and the soul-hardening struggles of political power to the harsher spirit of man, that he may still look up to her as a purer and brighter being, an emanation of some better world, irradiating like a rainbow of hope, the stormy elements of life."[53]

Portrayals of an innocent Ann Cooke both embodied such ideals and betrayed real anxieties about them. In developing a Lalage, an Octavia Bragaldi, a Geraldine Hearthwood whose timid virtues and "consciousness of dependency" leave them vulnerable to rude men in a tumultuous world, such writers as Poe, Barnes, and MacMichael created a scenario that puts ideals of virtue and dependency under great duress. Their literary transformations of the Tragedy, taking the most conventionalized versions of gender roles and showing how they might function under stress, highlighted both the content of those roles and the difficulties of maintaining them under challenging circumstances. And nowhere were the difficulties more apparent than in the case of an innocent Ann Cooke Beauchamp, led by her virtue into a horrible fate of seduction, betrayal, and death.

Even domesticity itself became an issue in the hands of the Tragedy's re-creators. Again, portrayals of a vulnerable, innocent Cooke embodied fairly precisely what were said to be feminine virtues, virtues that led to her fall. Most notable were her ability and desire to love, characteristics seen as both essential and ennobling, characteristics that, as historian Catherine Kelly has stressed, did much to reinforce separate spheres ideals.[54] Within that framework, and especially beginning in the 1830s, as writers began to exploit the power of the Kentucky Tragedy, an emphasis on such characteristics also led to a view of domesticity—maintaining the home—as both woman's highest calling and her most appropriate field. Here, she found her influence: "To welcome to the quiet hearth, the partner of her joys and sorrows, when worn and weary with the world's conflict; to rear her offsprings in the fear of God, and love of every thing good and holy," as one writer said. Here were both woman's duties and her glory.[55]

But, as the Tragedy indicates, such characteristics could also become the source of her endangerment. This possibility was emphasized especially strongly in such works as those of Poe and Barnes, in which the seducers accomplished their purposes by promising or even feigning marriage. One may note, as well, the tragic fate of the appropriately named Geraldine Hearthwood, whose hopes were raised and crushed by the perfidious de Wilton in Mary MacMichael's version of the tale. Deceptively offering what was seen as the most conducive path to feminine fulfillment, de Wilton, like Poe's Castiglione and Barnes's Castelli, played in a particularly venal way on those attributes that were supposed to be most ideally feminine—the desire for marriage and domestic tranquility. Innocence and domesticity might be virtues, but, if so, they were very dangerous virtues. As the Kentucky Tragedy could dramatize, these were virtues that left the virtuous extremely vulnerable. Through Ann Cooke's fall, the Kentucky Tragedy, at least in some of its renditions, raised some anxious questions about the viability of widely stated ideals.[56]

Portrayals of a vain and haughty Ann Cooke raise what initially appears to be a different set of concerns. From Leander Sharp forward, there was the Ann Cooke who was intellectual and proud, whose seduction owed less to innocence than to her own vanity. In some cases, consistent with Leander Sharp's portrayal, she was that disciple of Mary Wollstonecraft who rejected ideals of femininity and the constraints those ideals imposed.

In his treatment of the Tragedy, William Gilmore Simms described his haughty Margaret Cooper as just such a woman. Strong-willed and independent of mind, she had a deficit in true affection, a failing all too likely, Simms wrote, "in a woman whose mind leads her out from her sex!"[57] Margaret herself was given to reflections that, tacitly echoing Leander Sharp's portrayal, did show something of an influence from "Mary Woolstoncraft":

> Alas! no! am I not a woman, one of that frail, feeble sex, whose name is weakness?—of whom, having no strength, man yet expects the proofs of the most unyielding—of a firmness which he himself can not exercise—of a power of self-denial and endurance of which he exhibits no example. If I weep, he smiles at my weakness. If I stifle my tears, he denounces my unnatural hardihood. If I am cold and unyielding, I am masculine and neglected—if I am gentle and pliant, my confidence is abused and my person dishonored. What can society, which is thus exacting, accord to me, then, as a mere woman? What shame will it not thrust upon me—a woman—and as I am?[58]

Emphatically illustrating Cooper's "unfeminine" tendencies, Simms gave her words that went to the foundations of a dominant, separate spheres, gender ideology.

Simms's Ann Cooke was not the only woman who showed a lack of dedication to antebellum feminine ideals. Throughout the period, and especially after about 1830, many women were becoming more assertive in the public arena, to great controversy. From the activity of women encouraged by reform movements to the highly focused efforts toward woman suffrage and equality that had become widespread by the end of the era—not to mention the self-assertion embodied in literary work as such—many women had shown that a separate spheres ideology could not contain every woman's aspirations.

There were many seeds for such a development. As has often been noted, they were even contained in the separate spheres ideology itself. What were seen as women's unique virtues helped provide a justification for activism in an array of public arenas where "feeling" and "tenderness" were thought to be essential—in temperance, penal reform, education, and abolition—opening avenues to action in a broader world. No less crucial, however, was the influence of an American egalitarianism that could not be squared with the idea of separate spheres. In 1848, Frederick Douglass declared, "All that distinguishes man as an intelligent and accountable being, is equally true of woman; and if that government only is just which governs by the free consent of the governed, there can be no reason in the world for denying to woman the exercise of the elective franchise, or a hand in making and administering the laws of the land."[59] It was but a short step to denying the ideological foundations upon which separation was usually based. "You ask," in the words of the address from an 1850 women's rights convention, "would you have woman, by engaging in political party bickerings and noisy strife, sacrifice her integrity and purity? No, neither would we have men do it." The writers said, "We hold that whatever is essentially wrong for woman to do, can not be right for man."[60]

The tension such developments created actually appeared fairly early in chronicles of the Kentucky Tragedy as a result of the Kentucky women's petition to Governor Joseph Desha urging that Beauchamp be reprieved. The petitioners asserted their moral authority as women in order to stress their understanding of both the crime and the greatness of the provocation that had led to it. But they also asserted their right to speak, as one of Desha's male correspondents decried: "This is a publick affair, and why it is that females should undertake to direct or request the executive in this case is a matter of conjecture with me."[61]

In any event, and as people recognized, an egalitarian rhetoric implied not only a rejection of what had been described as a virtuous consciousness of dependency but also a rejection of the legitimacy of male authority, at least when it was based on gender alone. In 1837, the pioneering feminist Sarah Grimké angrily wrote, regarding the history of woman, that "from the days of Eve to the present time, the aim of man has been to crush her. He has accomplished his work in various ways; sometimes by brute force, sometimes by making her subservient to his worst passions, sometimes by treating her as a doll, and while he excluded from her mind the light of knowledge, decked her person with gewgaws and frippery which he scorned for himself, thus endeavoring to render her like unto a painted sepulchre."[62] The words Simms gave to Margaret Cooper virtually paraphrased Grimké's remarks, and, as his story makes plain, he was far from sanguine about what an independence of mind could do, either for her or for anyone else.

In the literature, Simms's was the most open protest against an egalitarian rhetoric, although whenever there was a strong-willed Cooke, her creators tended to suggest that her independence and ambition had contributed to her downfall by making her too open to flattery. But it would probably be a mistake to focus on either feminist or antifeminist tendencies in literary accounts of the Kentucky Tragedy. In this regard, MacMichael's version may be the most revealing, given its two-part structure and the two victimized women her story portrays. The first, Geraldine, is the epitome of innocence betrayed; Ianthe, of pride brought low. Neither is wholly up to the challenges she faces; both confront contradictions that are hard to resolve.

Bringing the two Ann Cookes together, however, was a very different figure, the Ann Cooke who sought to avenge herself against the seducer Sharp. For she is what every Ann Cooke became. Beauchamp's *Confession* had provided the model for such a portrayal. When Ann first broached the issue of revenge to Jereboam, she said that "her heart would never cease to ache, till Col. Sharp should die through her instrumentality; that he had blighted all her hapiness [*sic*]."[63] Writers who turned Cooke into a literary character echoed those words. Chivers's Eudora exclaimed, "I live to view the mirror of his blood."[64] For John Savage's Sybil, the last in the antebellum line, the anticipation of revenge was no less crucial to her life, for "Without this all-sustaining, grateful hope, / The solitude I breathe were death."[65]

The vengeful Ann Cooke was often characterized in the language of gender. As early as the fictional letters, Cooke recounts her seduction and the slander she has suffered, reporting, "I was roused, like the lioness from her lair, and swore by Heaven and earth to take such vengeance as only a woman's heart could feel."[66] Chivers, in his 1834 play, virtually paraphrased the letters as his Eudora declares, "Revenge in woman hath no limitations!" Chivers even linked the power of her anger to Cooke's more acceptably feminine attributes, to her great heart and her capacity for love. "Thou know'st a woman's love? how deep! how strong!" Her capacity for revenge, she says, is directly proportional to her capacity for love.[67]

Such a characterization had many dimensions, but one serves to highlight still further contradictions in the developing gender ideology of the time, particularly where feminine ideals were concerned.[68] As a figure like Eudora shows, the vengeful woman did not necessarily stand in opposition to a feminine ideal that privileged feeling. Instead, she could be an extension of that ideal, a character whose capacity for feeling could become dangerous under duress, turning quickly from love to hate as circumstances dictate.

Again, this was a characterization with many levels of significance, including psychological dimensions to be addressed more fully in the next chapter. But one implication with special salience grew out of a contemporary celebration, within the framework of a separate spheres ideology, of the special capacity of woman for feeling, for what Sarah Hale called the "true and fervent affections of the heart." This celebration was itself framed by a more general recognition of the importance of affection as a basis for social unity. It was a recognition displayed in many areas, personal, social, and political. There was, for example, an increasing tendency to define the family as an affective unit, its members held together not by structures of authority but, instead, by ties of feeling and love.[69] As a writer for a South Carolina magazine said in 1840, "The foundation of all domestic happiness between husband and wife is the consciousness that each entertains of enjoying the undivided affections of the other," and such feelings were to be extended throughout the family.[70] This view was easily expanded outward. By the middle of the eighteenth century, perhaps even earlier, the idea that affection produced the strongest social and moral bonds was widely held.

The ideal of affective unity was far from gender specific. Fathers were to share in the bonds of mutual affection holding families together, just as there was to be a mutual affection shared between husbands and wives. Men should seek a "concord of feeling" with others no less than women should.[71] Still, within this framework of affection, women had a critical role, one that cohered both with ideals of separate spheres and those of female domesticity. As wives and mothers, women were, as Daniel Webster proclaimed, "the affectionate and effective teachers of the human race."[72] They provided an emotional anchor and set the tone for family life, their influence reaching out through their men to the whole society. In a society celebrating affection, women, by their very natures, were assigned a pivotal role.

The Kentucky Tragedy—especially in its portrayals of Ann Cooke—dramatizes a sense of how fragile such a social framework must be, especially in the face of contradictions and ambiguities in feminine ideals. It was a framework demanding a certain kind of woman, but her existence, as the Kentucky Tragedy shows, was problematic. Turning affection on its head, those who adapted the story portrayed through Cooke a volatility of feeling that struck at the heart of the separate spheres—a capacity for feeling that, shifting from love to hate, could quickly destroy the world in which she lived. Here, that is, was a story that seems to have compelled those who confronted its events also to confront questions about either the validity or viability of dominant ideals of feminine character, about whether woman could, would, or should provide the kind of anchor society required.

## IV

Such ambiguities in gender ideology become still more fully disclosed when the literary constructions of Ann Cooke Beauchamp are connected to constructions of Sharp and Jereboam. As a seducer, Sharp was inevitably presented as cold and uncaring, most important for what he said about the possibility of counterfeit feelings and duplicitous pledges. He also provided a counterpart to Jereboam, whose feelings were real and whose promises were commitments.

In looking at the various portrayals, it is possible to understand his significance as a type from the perspective of the young antebellum literary theorist Ella, whose thoughts appeared in the *Lowell Offering.* Defending fiction, at least when properly read, Ella finds particular virtue in such stories of seduction and betrayal as the Kentucky Tragedy. It may well be, she argues, "that the novel-reader would be more upon her guard, as disappointed love is so often the theme of our fictions."[73] Similar thoughts informed even the earliest renditions of the Kentucky Tragedy, as in the claim of the editor of Cooke's spurious letters that his volume revealed "the dreadful effects of seduction and treachery, and the consequences which flow from the first fatal aberration from the paths of virtue and innocence." Sharp illustrated by example precisely the kind of man fiction could prepare its readers to resist.

But the Sharp figure also called into question a fundamental structure upon which gender ideals had to rest, a structure built on ideas of independence, dependence, and reciprocity. What one authority had described as a "consciousness of dependency" was, in itself, not simply a virtue that gave to a woman all that was "delightfully appropriate to her character and condition."[74] It was also the cornerstone, within the framework of separate spheres ideology, of what relations between women and men should be. Such thinking lay behind criticisms of Ann Cooke leveled by Leander Sharp and echoed by Simms condemning her for an independence of mind that betokened her failure to live up to feminine ideals. The editors of the 1858 edition of Beauchamp's *Confession* were still more forthright. Having quoted the "dying debauchee" to the effect that women are lambs and men wolves, they also advanced as a certainty that woman is "as God created her—subordinate to man." But female subordination was not the whole story where women and men were concerned, because, as the editors put it, "with her subordination comes his responsibility."[75] Men like Sharp—and the editors did not doubt his guilt as a seducer—comprised a danger going beyond the individual case. The editors revealed the one factor that contributed most to a lack of viability in a feminine ideal based on innocence. It was an ideal that also required a masculinity that respected innocence, something they said Sharp had refused to do.

Concerns about the seducer were widely held in antebellum America, even as the Kentucky Tragedy was unfolding. Such concerns are at least partially revealed by Patricia Cline Cohen's finding of a surge of seduction suits during that time, and beyond.[76] It is perhaps also relevant that such a novel as Hannah Foster's 1797 tale of seduction and betrayal, *The Coquette,* reached the height of its popularity between 1824 and 1828, when, as historian Elizabeth Barnes has found, it went through eight printings.[77] Both the literature and the concerns it embodied remained significant in the ensuing decades. Many people worried about the man who would toy with the affections of a woman, the man who "basely imposes upon the honest heart of an unsuspecting girl, and, after winning her affections by the prevailing rhetoric of courtship ungenerously leaves her to bitter sorrow," as one writer put it.[78] Such a character particularly intrigued Mary MacMichael. Her de Wilton, skilled at the "usual arts of seduction" and indifferent to the fate of his victims, was only one example of the many predatory men who figured in her fiction.[79] Given the gender ideology of the period, the seducer's significance is not difficult to understand. Female ideals depended on male reciprocity, something the seducer both brought into question and violated.

But the intricacy of interconnections among masculine and feminine ideals, dependence, independence, and reciprocity, finds its fullest expression when the character of Beauchamp, as he assumes the role of avenger, is added to the mix. To see this, it is useful to return to the notion of honor, the most obvious point of cultural resonance between Beauchamp's actions and antebellum American culture. Again, for many people, honor framed the events that ultimately brought Sharp and the Beauchamps to their deaths. It also served as a framework within which most of the writers portrayed and sought to account for what Beauchamp had done. Beauchamp's *Confession,* as the most influential account of the crime, was in large part an effort to frame Sharp's murder in terms of honor's demands. It cited Beauchamp's conviction that his death should serve to teach "a respect for those laws of honor, to revenge the violation and outrage of which, I so freely die."[80]

Still, Beauchamp's murder of Sharp, the *Confession,* and contemporary responses to the events emphasize how indeterminate the notion of honor could be, especially where issues of gender were concerned. Wherever they appear, ideas of honor, with their great focus on reputation, tend to be connected to social stratification. In a place like antebellum Kentucky—and elsewhere in the United States—such connections included not only class and status among whites but also racial inequality and slavery. All these distinctions were related to ideals of courage, reciprocity, and self-control, characteristics intimately tied to matters of reputation.[81] The obligation to defend one's family also linked honor to ideologies of gender and family roles. Honor, as many historians have said, was a concept that implied both white masculine privilege and white masculine responsibility. In conferring on white men the obligation to protect and defend their names and those of family members, it gave them rights of social control and leadership.[82] Again, Beauchamp's *Confession* said as much, asserting that upon his marriage to Ann Cooke his duty to act as her avenger became clear. Leander Sharp used the failure of Cooke's male relatives to challenge Solomon as evidence against her charge of seduction.

But such an understanding of honor was central to the Tragedy's events from the very beginning. Beauchamp himself certainly recognized this. This is why, when he wrote to John J. Crittenden declaring his innocence, he had to take such pains to claim that he had put the past behind him and had determined "never to make the wounds" of Cooke's family "bleed afresh." The debate over whether Sharp had been the victim of a political assassination likewise took for granted the likelihood that Beauchamp could have been impelled by honor to take Sharp's life. Both sides, that is, took for granted that rumors of Sharp's seduction and, especially, defamation of Ann Cooke Beauchamp could have been the immediate cause of the crime, however much they disagreed on the source of those rumors.

In literary treatments of the Tragedy, honor played such a significant role that, in many ways, variations in the Jereboam Beauchamp character were far more superficial than was the case for Ann Cooke Beauchamp. Writers inevitably portrayed Jereboam as a man driven by honor, and there was a consensus among them as to what this meant. It meant that, unlike Sharp, Beauchamp did take seriously his obligation as a man to defend the honor of women. Chivers even concocted a tale in which his Conrad, during a sojourn in Mexico, "cut the throat of a cut-throat, because / He insulted a lady in my sight!"[83]

Writers no less inevitably dramatized how, as an avenger, Jereboam took on what was clearly seen to be a male responsibility. In the *Confession,* the masculine duties of honor are emphasized when, shortly before their marriage, Ann Cooke proposes killing Sharp herself. Beauchamp recognizes he has to prevent this, giving him still greater resolve to play the masculine part. This episode was adopted by several of those who adapted the Tragedy, including Chivers and MacMichael. Savage's Sybil first appears in the drama while taking target practice. His Clifden, like other Beauchamps, recognizes that honor's imperative should be his, not hers, to fulfill.

But however presented, the masculine character of honor was asserted in all the treatments. Charlotte Barnes's Bragaldi, learning of his wife's dishonoring, immediately vows to challenge the evil Castelli, declaring his determination to "assert a husband's privilege t' avenge thy wrongs."[84] Simms and, thus, Savage made a similar point. When Ann tells him how Sharp has victimized her, Beauchamp declares that upon their marriage, as Savage put it, "You are mine, your wrongs are mine."[85]

The literature of the Kentucky Tragedy takes this masculine imperative a step further, however, especially as it evokes links among honor, manhood, and violence. Certainly, there is nothing new about such links, particularly between masculinity and violence. It is a connection of such long-standing pervasiveness that many people have seen a biological basis for it.[86] But the literature of the Kentucky Tragedy suggests its more particular significance in antebellum America: Equating the right—and presumed capacity—to act violently with masculine prerogative emphasized the putative differences between women and men, especially between ideals of male activism and female passivity, at the heart of antebellum gender ideals.[87]

As the Tragedy articulated this dimension of gender ideology, however, strong ambiguities began to emerge, embedded most fully in the relationship between the Beauchamps. The frequently used episode in which Jereboam must dissuade Ann from killing Sharp herself is one measure of those ambiguities. In the literature, there is no necessary connection between a murderous Ann and one who had previously chafed, as in Simms's version, against feminine norms. Chivers's Eudora, for instance, falls prey to her innocence but emerges with a powerful desire to be the agent of Alonzo's death. She pledges, at one point, to dress "in an Indian's garb, and paint me red, / The quiver'd angel of revengeful wrath, / And hunt him, like Diana, with a spear."[88] In all, the stress of circumstances brings out a Cooke drawn toward a masculine rather than a feminine response to dishonor.[89] Circumstances, not biology, appear to determine her course.

However, additional ambiguities are revealed by the ways in which every rendition of the Tragedy treats Jereboam's honor-driven determination to kill Sharp on Cooke's behalf. The determination is never his alone. In all the accounts, it originates with Ann Cooke. In most, she makes it her condition for marriage. When she does not, notably in Barnes's *Octavia Bragaldi,* where the two are already married, it remains a demand she continually places before her husband. Thus, though Beauchamp may be Sharp's killer, his wife is a driving force in the story's unfolding. As a result, all the literary renditions of the Tragedy raise questions of agency, of whether Jereboam is acting on his own or is directed by social imperatives and, more crucially, by his wife.

Within the rubric of honor, Ann's power becomes especially problematic. As many historians have noted, honor in antebellum America was in large part what Bertram Wyatt-Brown has described as an "external ethic."[90] It involved a large measure of display and visible self-assertion, even when it became intertwined with imperatives of violence and revenge; hence the demand for public violence and Beauchamp's need to justify the clandestine murder of Sharp. As everyone including the Beauchamps recognized, the strongest imperative of honor was that Sharp be killed publicly, following the forms and conventions of that ultimate expression of honorable violence, the duel. Chivers, in a brief dialogue between two minor characters, had one agree that, in Beauchamp's position, he too would have tried to kill the seducer. He adds, however, that Beauchamp "should have killed him in the open streets."[91]

In his own justification of the clandestine murder, Beauchamp had cited politics, along with Sharp's refusal of a challenge on the Frankfort streets to address the issue. This latter justification was, incidentally, hallowed by both literary tradition and the imperatives of honor itself. Refusal of a challenge was rarely thought to absolve anyone of a need to answer for an alleged act of dishonor; it could even serve as a valid excuse for murder.[92] The various subsequent accounts of the Tragedy show how widely this was understood.

In most renditions of the Kentucky Tragedy, however, any excuse Sharp's refusal provided for Jereboam's crime is less important than the power of Ann Beauchamp's insistence on Sharp's death, by any means necessary. The various Jereboams inevitably express reluctance to kill on the sly, even more than the Jereboam of the *Confession,* only to be pushed by their Anns to complete the job.

The boldest representation of Ann Cooke's power is in John Richardson's *Canadian Brothers,* as he draws on the Tragedy to fit the needs of his story of Gerald Grantham and Matilda Montgomerie. Gerald is far more torn than most over the prospect of clandestinely murdering the allegedly treacherous Forrester—Richardson's Sharp—rather than facing him openly. Matilda will have none of it, taunting him for his "child-like weakness," and mobilizes masculine ideals of honor to achieve her ends.[93] Although Gerald ultimately does not go through with the killing of Forrester, he comes very close, and remains a tortured figure in the face of Matilda's insistent demands.

There are a number of ways to interpret Cooke's use of Beauchamp, as portrayed in the literature. Richardson emphasized the sexual dimensions. Increasingly vehement in urging Gerald to act, Matilda's "eye sparkled and dilated, and the visible heaving of her bosom told how strongly her own feelings entered into the principles she had advocated. Never," Richardson continued, "did her personal beauty shine forth more triumphantly or seducingly than at the moment when her lips were giving utterance to sentiments from which the heart recoiled."[94]

Richardson used the Kentucky Tragedy to portray, in woman's sexuality and sexual attraction, a power to affect man's better judgment and, thus, to give her control over man's action. It was a point that a writer for that most influential of antebellum magazines, *The Lady's Book*, made in an 1832 article, tellingly entitled "Woman." This writer noted that "female beauty alone, has often produced among men fits of momentary distraction." Even the biblical King Solomon, this writer said, "felt all his glory, and his might, and his riches, and his wisdom, without their smiles, to be vanity and vexation of spirit."[95]

A similar scenario of female power was presented, at least implicitly, in other works. It was a scenario as old as the story of Adam and Eve, a story that itself served as a kind of template for virtually the entire tradition of seduction, betrayal, and revenge, dramatizing the complex intertwining of human sexual power and vulnerability. Simms, for example, described Margaret Cooper's fall as "the triumph of the serpent," making her the Eve who would ultimately lure an Adamic Beauchampe to his death.[96]

Even when there were no obvious undertones of sexuality, however, the effect of such dramatizations of Ann Cooke Beauchamp's power was to throw into question common assertions of feminine dependence and, conversely, masculine independence. In many ways, the Tragedy took to its logical conclusion the celebration of female influence, not by force but through feeling, however much that celebration was intended to rationalize a society embodying separate, and not really equal, male and female spheres. This was a complex issue, certain aspects of which will also be treated in more detail in the next chapter. For now, however, it is important to note how, dramatizing the ideologically ambiguous power of female agency and control, the Tragedy dramatized still further the extent to which existing gender roles and categories, placed under stress, rested on a very fragile base.

That fragility was pointedly brought out in the literary approaches to Beauchamp and in the problems they posed related to his determination to kill Sharp. As historians have discussed, the question of male agency and independence was almost obsessively addressed in antebellum American thought and culture.[97] Ideals of honor—heavily weighted in the South—and with them ideals of status and authority, were closely intertwined with a celebration of masculine independence, as scholars have shown.[98] "Masculine independence" was also important as a cultural underpinning to the market-based economy that was growing in dominance, North and South, as the Kentucky Tragedy was undergoing its more significant transformations from history to literature.[99]

Expressions of anxiety about living up to such an ideal abounded in antebellum America, enhanced by the need to demonstrate one's independence in a social and economic environment marked by both individualism and interdependence.[100] To a great extent, Beauchamp's character personified such anxieties, driven as he was by a combination of internal and external forces. In the *Confession,* Beauchamp, even as he sought to represent himself as a man in charge, could not avoid indicating the power of Ann's demands on him. And, of course, he ultimately became a pawn to legal and political forces that carried him to his death.

Writers who elaborated more imaginatively on the affair confronted this dilemma openly. Their Jereboams often showed a pained awareness of Ann's power and the obligations it imposed upon them, a pained awareness of the power of social imperatives. Honor itself became, frequently, an irresistible force rather than a measure of independence. Even Simms's Orville Beauchampe, on his way to kill Sharp, reflects on "the terrible responsibility to which his unhappy oath had subjected him."[101] As the literary Beauchamps dramatize, the ideal of masculine independence, like the feminine ideals accompanying it, might have an apparent validity in the abstract that could not be maintained in a difficult and complex world.

In its unsettling of gender ideals, the Kentucky Tragedy, through its many incarnations, indicates several things. One, obviously, is how powerfully explorations of gender, as such, appealed to antebellum writers and their audiences. The story of the Tragedy, in itself and in its transformations, was in many ways a story about gender ideals, their meanings and their instabilities. The story's popularity suggests that its concerns were concerns its audience found interesting to contemplate.

And the Tragedy's unsettling of what appeared to be well-defined social roles, based on gender, would have resonated especially strongly with the urban middle-class readers—and theater-goers—who comprised the main audience for literary adaptations of the Kentucky Tragedy. Certainly, its members did much to advance the persistent fascination with gender that occupied so much space in the burgeoning print culture of the age. But treatments of the Tragedy also suggest a larger concern for instability of roles and categories in American society. In the challenges all the characters had to face, there were large areas of uncertainty, affecting men and women alike.

During the antebellum period, many observers saw American society as being marked by social and cultural instability. The roots of this instability, as many people believed, lay in unprecedented levels of both social and economic mobility, entailing a lack of fixity that made it hard to get one's bearings. As the French traveler Michel Chevalier observed during a visit to the United States, "If movement and the quick succession of sensations and ideas constitute life, here one lives a hundredfold more than elsewhere; here, all is circulation, motion, and boiling agitation."[102] The overall effect was to seriously complicate how status—one's own and that of others—was to be understood. At one level, this meant, among other things, that one could never be too secure in one's achievements. There was always the sense that what one had—or was—today could easily be lost tomorrow. It was a world in which "manhood," for example, could never be wholly taken for granted but always had to be asserted and maintained.[103]

At another, in such a fluid social setting, even measures and definitions of status were not as clear as one might hope. John Mayfield and others have shown this was true even for the South, where plantation owning and planter status have often been supposed to provide a single standard for social measurement.[104] The whole thrust of such a setting was to create a world in which people could never be entirely certain what place any individual occupied in society, or what anyone's apparent status really meant.[105] It was a world in which appearances mattered, and fictions could—even should—be maintained in everyday life. People were well aware of the need to deal with such uncertainty, even in regard to somewhat trivial matters. The influential *Miss Leslie's Behaviour Book,* for example, warned young readers that "Women who have begun the world in humble life, and have been necessitated to give most of their attention to household affairs, are generally very shy in talking of housewifery, after their husbands have become rich." It advised that one should "converse with them as if they had been ladies always."[106]

No less serious, as Karen Halttunen has discussed, was the potential for imposture this environment created.[107] Sharp embodied this potential, at least in his literary personifications. In all, he was a man who operated under false pretenses, and in several, one who exploited false identities. Simms and Savage created an especially dramatic version when they made him a libertine in religious clothing. Theirs was a portrayal that vividly dramatized an unsettled environment in which social identities could be put on like a suit of clothes, apparent social attainment could not be entirely trusted, and social characteristics could be manipulated for personal gain. And such a Sharp was a peculiarly reprehensible as a seducer, an ostensible gentleman whose "false plumage" allows him to work on the weaknesses of innocent young women.[108] But he was a natural in a world where, as Chevalier wrote, "Men change their houses, their climate, their trade, their condition, their party, their sect," apparently at will.[109]

Writers who adapted the Kentucky Tragedy used Sharp in ways that emphasized their awareness of the sources of danger in such an uncertain world. Simms, Savage, and MacMichael actually transformed him into an outsider who, meeting a haughty but naive Cooke, assumes the false identity that contributes to his success and to her downfall. Others, however, went still farther below the surface to suggest that even apparent friends could don the "false plumage" of the seducer. Thus, Poe and Barnes drew on Kentucky events to portray a seducer who had long known his victim but who was able to trick her anyway. The danger of not knowing someone was a threat even when people were not literally strangers, a representation that in itself increased the power of a story based on the fragility of trust and the problem of appearances. As renditions of the Kentucky Tragedy dramatized, people living in a fluid society were forced to live in a world of appearances, and appearances could be deceiving.

The story of the Kentucky Tragedy, as a drama of seduction, betrayal, and revenge, epitomized the problems of this world. The seducer made particularly apparent the dangers in trusting appearances, just as the course of events from betrayal through revenge made clear the dangers inherent in gender ideals and in dreams of an affective community. The dramatic power of the story, its power to destabilize important and difficult categories and ideas, probably helps to account for the fascination it had for those who were drawn to it, as readers and writers, in antebellum America.

But that fascination, and even the fascination with gender itself, points to somewhat deeper concerns during the period. Social uncertainty was driven, in part, by social change. It was also driven by, and it drove, a series of concerns that were deeply humanistic and deeply psychological. People who confronted the Tragedy also confronted some profound and shifting issues of human nature and human motivation that reinforced a sense of fragility in regard to the larger social order. The result was to convey an image of men and women at sea, not only in regard to action but in regard to deeper questions of who they were, and what they could aspire to be.

Charlotte Barnes.
Courtesy of the Hampden-Booth Theatre Library at the Players, New York.

"The murder of Sharp." From Henry St. Clair, *The United States Criminal Calendar* . . . Boston, 1833. The Mandeville Special Collections Library, University of California, San Diego.

Solomon P. Sharp.
Kentucky Historical Society, Frankfort.

Amos Kendall.
Library of Congress, lc-usz62-16006.

William Gilmore Simms.
Courtesy of South Caroliniana Library,
University of South Carolina, Columbia.

Thomas Holley Chivers.
DeKalb History Center, Decatur, Georgia.

"The Beauchamps portrayed." From *The Life of Jereboam O. Beauchamp* . . . Frankfort, 1850.
William L. Clements Library, University of Michigan.

WOMAN:
"God's greatest trust, as well as Heaven's best gift to man."

THE
BEAUCHAMP TRAGEDY,
IN
KENTUCKY,
AS DETAILED IN THE
Confession of Jereboam O. Beauchamp;
TO WHICH IS ADDED
A Biographical Sketch of Col. Solomon P. Sharp,
AND
A HISTORICAL ACCOUNT OF THE OLD COURT AND NEW COURT PARTY CONTROVERSY, ETC.

The whole presenting a narrative of many exciting incidents in Kentucky life some thirty years ago.

*PRICE TWENTY-FIVE CENTS,*
(SENT FREE BY MAIL).

NEW YORK:
DINSMORE & CO.
1858.



From *The Beauchamp Tragedy in Kentucky* . . . New York, 1858.
Library of Congress.

*Chapter 4*

# THE MOST CERTAINLY HUMAN OF ALL LAWS

There were many avenues to that sense of fragility evoked by the tragic events of Sharp's murder and the Beauchamps' deaths. A Kentucky woman summarized what those events meant to her when she wrote, shortly after the Beauchamps had died, "Poor wretches, *better, far better,* would it have been could they have given up the ghost e'ere their eyes were opened upon this world of woe and wretchedness."[1] The possible sources for her response were various. If it were influenced by Protestant Christian evangelicalism, especially of the Kentucky variety, she would have been thoroughly indoctrinated in a view of the world that stressed the negative. "This world's a wilderness of woe / This world is not my home," as one of the period's classic folk hymns put it.[2] Southern evangelicalism, with its pervasive themes of world-rejection, provided a likely background for both the view this woman expressed and the language in which she expressed it.[3]

Informed by a residual Calvinism, similar views were widespread in antebellum America. They were probably strongest in the South, where cultural constructions tended toward a generalized pessimism about human nature and society.[4] As the regionally diverse literature of the Kentucky Tragedy emphasizes, however, misgivings about the world went beyond any pessimism rooted distinctively in the South.

The Kentucky Tragedy's presentation of a world in which basic categories of social identity, including those of gender and status, were unclear and contradictory raised a set of questions about possibilities for social stability, as we have seen. The Kentucky Tragedy also presented an agonistic world of competition that was almost Hobbesian in the assumptions that lay behind its chief characterizations. Dramatizing the necessity of mistrust, the Tragedy set its characters in a dog-eat-dog world from which conflict and violence could not be easily removed.

Such a view of the world would not have seemed eccentric in antebellum America, and it had many sources. It was closely related to ideas of honor that informed so much of the Kentucky Tragedy. There was a marked tendency for the man of honor "to imagine, that, like Cain, his hand was against every man and every man's hand was against him," as one such individual put it.[5] The honor violence epitomized in dueling, but also driving Sharp's murder, grew out of such a sense. People enraptured with honor saw the world as a hostile place in which threats were everywhere and in which one needed always to be prepared to respond.[6]

Such perceptions of the world were not, however, confined to those for whom honor was an ethos and an imperative. The same forces that destabilized social categories also helped create a perception that America, in the face of ideals of an affective community, was becoming increasingly competitive. Signs of competition were abundant in politics, in commerce, in labor, in religion, and in reform. The Tragedy built on the potential for an agonistic relationship between men and women, despite the compromise an ideology of separate spheres might seem to create. Sharp's determined assault on Cooke's virtue may certainly be seen in that light. So may Ann's manipulation of Jereboam, despite the usual motifs suggesting his own commitment to revenge. But, more generally, in its portrayal of a world of threats and mistrust, the Tragedy, in all its incarnations, presented an environment in which competition, and hostile competition at that, appeared to be the order of the day.[7]

The Tragedy also offered a fairly clear account of what motivated men and women in this dangerously competitive world. At its core, the story of the Tragedy dramatized the power of passion to push people to violent confrontations and death. Lust, ambition, anger, and obsession all played a role in the unfolding of the Tragedy, as so many of the accounts reiterated. Such passions created the interplay of antagonisms that led to its fatal climax. Here, ultimately, was why people fought. Few people would have found such a story lacking in either verisimilitude or in applicability to their nineteenth-century American world. As historians have shown, people often fretted about a world dominated by what they saw as tendencies toward selfishness, ambition, and greed. At a somewhat prosaic level, many people feared that communal ideals were being subverted by gossip, status-seeking, and imposture. More generally, people worried about an America being shaped by the rapid development of an individualistic, competitive economy in which self-aggrandizing men and women come to be dominated by a pursuit of gain, following a path marked by a willingness to exploit others.[8]

Such fears played a complex role in antebellum American thinking. They lay behind a key ethical tenet, North and South: that self-restraint was the crucial imperative in social life and moral behavior. Everyone has feelings, and feelings provide the basis for that affective community so many people prized. But feelings must be properly cultivated and controlled, prevented from getting out of hand.

This ethic of self-restraint appeared in many forms. It probably had its fullest expression in ideals of gentility that so dominated American thinking during the period. Easier to illustrate than to define, gentility proposed standards of behavior that both focused on feeling and celebrated restraint in its expression. In religion, this meant a quiet piety that centered on the pleasure and comfort faith could provide and on a relationship with God based on love and affection.[9] It contrasted with both the cold intellectualism of the Puritan and the ecstatic outpourings of the revivalist. In social life, gentility meant the cultivation of sympathy and a presentation of self that was modest, controlled, and amiable. In love, it meant that one should never be too bold and that love should come from the heart, filled with both sympathy and respect. Gentility entailed, as Karen Halttunen has said, the "exercise of perfect physical and emotional self-restraint," an exercise that was to govern every aspect of one's life.[10] The coherence of genteel with feminine virtues was strong, and at least some Ann Cookes—notably Charlotte Barnes's Octavia Bragaldi and Poe's Lalage—fit well within the framework of gentility, despite their inability to resist Sharp's advances. But self-restraint was to be a standard for everyone, male and female alike, and, as the Tragedy made clear, self-restraint was not an easy standard to maintain.

## I

The rubric of honor, so important to every rendition of the Kentucky Tragedy, gave special attention to ideals of self-restraint, despite its strong association with violence. This was particularly true of honor, which should be considered as much an ethic of display as of action. In many ways, honor focused heavily on projecting an image of self-control. At its most ceremonial, in the duel, the "code of honor," as it was called, was essentially a ritualized display of passion under control. However brought on, a proper duel was expected to involve a punctilious exchange of notes, written in the most careful language, observing the most formal courtesies. The meeting on the field was to provide an opportunity for principals to demonstrate a cool self-possession even in the face of death. It was not a denial of passion; it was a demonstration of emotional strength.[11]

Beauchamp and Sharp never dueled, but the story of the Tragedy cohered with this dimension of honor in more than one respect. Kenneth Greenberg has suggested that what really concerned those white Southerners enamored of honor was displaying control over death itself. As Greenberg says, facing death on the field of honor, or under any circumstances, was, for many people, the highest realization of honor's demands. Craven people were, by definition, devoid of honor.[12] The Beauchamps' suicides, calmly contemplated and attempted, as the *Confession* relates, may be seen in this light. So may Jereboam's oft-noted coolness in facing his own death on the gallows. According to most accounts, it was a coolness demonstrated especially well as he calmly gave the signal, himself, for the cart on which he was standing to drive away, leaving him to hang.

At the same time, in the Tragedy's events, and preceding the execution, there was much in Beauchamp's behavior that violated such honorable imperatives, including not only the clandestine killing but also Beauchamp's plea of innocence. Given standards of self-possession and courageous display, trying to escape the consequences of an honor killing was particularly inappropriate. One may recall the comment of one of Chivers's characters that the killing should have occurred "in the open streets." For this reason, there was also a tendency in the literary renditions to allow Beauchamp to restore his public honor through courageously offering his life, much as his execution behavior was probably intended to do. Chivers's *Conrad and Eudora,* though drawing closely on the documents, has Conrad preempt the jury's judgement, in some sense, by making a final statement to the court in which he acknowledges his guilt. He tells the court, paraphrasing the original Beauchamp but at a much more appropriate time, that "if I die,—my death shall be for love!"[13] Barnes's Bragaldi does more. Accused of murdering Castelli, he immediately confesses to the act. "I could stoop to murder," he declares, "Commit a crime to satisfy revenge, / But cannot stoop to lie. I slew Castelli."[14]

However, important as display was, there is also much in the record that emphasizes how much honor was about more than display, and this informed literary transformations of the Tragedy, too. Beauchamp's *Confession* asserted that, ultimately, Sharp's death had been necessary in and of itself, as the only way in which honor could be restored to the Beauchamps and even to society as a whole. Such a view is common in honor cultures. In societies that value honor, there is usually great concern not only for the loss of honor but also for its restoration. And in many such societies, people believe that honor can only be restored by killing. It is as if the offender were himself—or herself—a source of pollution that dirties the whole community; only complete removal can purify those who have been the victims. As anthropologist Christopher Boehm has described it, in the face of dishonor, killing becomes "morally necessary" for individuals and for society. As he has noted, whatever other codes may exist, at a certain point it really does not matter how the killing takes place.[15]

In antebellum America, such views were fairly widespread. Dick Steward, looking at Missouri duels from around this same period, has noted their "improvised" character—by which he means their departure from more formal models—suggesting that the chief concern in many "affairs of honor" had mainly to do with killing one's adversary.[16] Edward Baptist has found something similar in plantation Florida.[17]

None of this is to deny the significance of the more ritualized affairs that have led historians to stress display over murder in analyzing honor. Such more formal affairs were common and sometimes fraught with danger, but often involved mainly posturing and little risk. In 1845, a Georgia editor claimed to be so tired of what he called "bloodless fights" that he planned to stop noting local duels "if somebody don't get killed pretty shortly."[18]

Nevertheless, as Beauchamp's case and others make clear, one should not be too quick to divorce honor from killing. Beauchamp, beginning his *Confession* on the day of his sentencing—and writing while in hope of a pardon—must have felt his fellow Kentuckians would understand and appreciate what he was talking about when he set forth his duty to kill Sharp. That he had some reason for the belief is emphasized by the petition campaign for a reprieve that followed quickly on the heels of his being sentenced to die for the crime. It was also, perhaps, confirmed by the efforts of Leander Sharp and others to call into question the images of honor Beauchamp's *Confession* was intended to cultivate.

This notion of honor as blood was a major element in most subsequent treatments of the case, from the purportedly factual to the self-consciously literary. It was understood and celebrated even in those treatments where it was ostensibly condemned, as the preface to the 1858 reprinting of Beauchamp's *Confession* makes clear. The editors wrote that "the world detests the skulking assassin, but in its *secret* heart applauds whoever with sufficient motive rids it of a tyrant or social monster."[19] As Simms put it, echoing the Kentucky women who petitioned for Beauchamp's reprieve, murder might be a crime, "but there is a crime beyond it, in the shedding of that vital soul-blood, its heart of hearts, life of all life, the fair fame, the untainted reputation; and the one offense which provokes the other should be placed in the opposing balance, as an offset, in some degree, to the crime by which it is avenged."[20]

Thus, no matter how the murder itself is treated, Beauchamp becomes, in all the works, a man fulfilling honor's demands through violence, through killing a man who deserved to be killed. Ultimately, honor is equated with blood, with violence, vengeance, and death. Despite the disclaimers—Charlotte Barnes, for example, noting "the futile lamentable results of revenge" as a lesson to be taken from the story, or Henry St. Clair suggesting the story should "warn the young and violent not to take the laws into their own hands"—their Beauchamps remain heroic. And their Sharps, for all the moralizing, deserve to die.

This may be the most powerful common denominator of all the works on the Tragedy, and especially those with strong literary purposes. The ambiguities the principals expose in the social realm may be great, but the lines of villainy and heroism, sympathy and condemnation remain clear, as Simms's words suggest. The point is emphasized in virtually all the works by their portrayals of the Beauchamps' tragic deaths. In none of the works are they presented as people getting their own just deserts. Creating a dialogue between Patrick Darby and John Waring ("Upshaw"), the anonymous playwright of the 1833 *Beauchamp* has Upshaw lament the upcoming execution by saying how much he will regret seeing "this brave youth hanged for doing a virtuous act." Told that Ann has resolved not to survive her husband, he grimly commends her for preferring "a glorious death to living infamy."[21] This was a view every subsequent writer echoed. For all, the

Beauchamps' courageous deaths became an extension of a "virtuous act" that had brought them to a tragic end, not proof of the evil of their deeds. It may be to emphasize this point that two of the writers, Savage in *Sybil* and Chivers in "Leoni," allowed their protagonists reprieves, the claims of honor receiving here, at least, their due.

That honor sometimes required death is, therefore, something that virtually everyone who took on the Tragedy seems to have understood. If there was in honor some focus on passions restrained, there was also, in its more sanguine dimensions, an acknowledgment of the necessity under some circumstances to give passion its head, a recognition of a righteous anger that justified rashness and violence.[22] Such a perspective, in which an act like Beauchamp's was seen as both a symptom of passionate humanity and a corrective to it, underlay virtually all the accounts and adaptations of the Kentucky Tragedy.

## II

But honor is only part of the story, and if the authors who treated the Kentucky Tragedy altered and simplified the Beauchamps' story in order to give honor a clearer role in their characters' lives, one should be careful in analyzing their works not to oversimplify the process. Charlotte Barnes and Henry St. Clair, along with others, were not being disingenuous in both celebrating and lamenting the vengeance the two Beauchamps had enacted on Sharp. In introducing her play, Barnes quoted an injunction from the eighteenth-century Scottish critic Henry Home, Lord Kames, one of the most important influences on antebellum literary thought, that the best dramatic works dealt in "mixed characters"—characters whose virtues and shortcomings were far from clear cut, whose behavior displayed dimensions of both good and evil.[23] This injunction guided virtually all the dramatizations of the Kentucky Tragedy in a number of ways, none more forcefully than the representation of the drive for vengeance that dominated the actions of Ann and Jereboam Beauchamp.

To see this, it is helpful to retain a focus on the violence at the center of the Kentucky Tragedy. Violent tales had a powerful attraction in antebellum America, the Kentucky Tragedy representing simply one episode that fit well into the popular mold. Almost everyone who talked about it acknowledged this. Henry St. Clair, who had noted that

"No part of a newspaper excites so much attention as the record of crime and calamity," also suggested that "there is a propensity in man to take pleasure in the sight or relation of human sin and suffering." A writer for the Boston *Traveller,* having had the Beauchamp tragedy called to mind by Julia Ward Howe's *The World's Own,* went still farther. Citing the power of Beauchamp's *Confession,* in particular, this writer suggested that "not even Othello so much absorbs our interests or moves our emotions." This writer found the events in Kentucky "as sublime and terrible as any Aeschylus or Sophocles have immortalized in verse."[24]

The Boston critic's words are worth quoting, since at one level the drama of the Kentucky Tragedy fits into patterns that are neither distinctly American nor distinctly nineteenth century. There was much in the Kentucky story of betrayal and retribution, vengeance and death, that captured themes and images going back to the earliest history of Western drama, and one should not even limit one's purview to Western tradition in looking for analogues to the tragic story of the Beauchamps and Sharp. The Boston writer did see the fitness of classical analogies, asserting that the "action proceeds with the dreadful certainty of the Greek tragedy, where an invincible fate drives on the noble and generous to crime."[25] One should not be too insistent on using the term "tragedy" with great precision in discussing the Beauchamp-Sharp literature. It does not apply to every treatment of the story, nor were antebellum Americans precise in their own use of the term. It was applied to all sorts of terrible events, from human crimes to natural disasters. But the Boston writer does point toward elements in the story that had great resonance in antebellum America.

In her study of a celebrated seventeenth-century English murder case, historian Cynthia Herrup has written that "Crimes and trials fascinate us; they show us, at a safe distance, passions unrestrained."[26] Why people wish to see this remains a matter of conjecture. The appeal of the forbidden, a continuing need for catharsis in the face of violent emotions, even innate cognitive processes have been proposed at various times. Nevertheless, whether one adopts what is essentially a play metaphor, as Herrup does, or looks for some other basis for the apparently universal fascination with violence, Herrup's insight is useful. Such a story as that of the Kentucky Tragedy, inasmuch as it did place its characters under duress, not only tested roles of status and gender, as we have seen, but also examined the deeper drives and passions which were provoked and amplified by what everyone could understand to be an extreme situation, a powerful episode of betrayal and revenge. Doing so, it dramatized the dilemmas, and the suffering, such situations could create.[27]

In antebellum America, an interest in the extreme seems to have been especially great. It was reflected in the rise of the antebellum sensationalist tradition, with its various "true crime" genres and forms within which much of the purportedly factual literature of the Tragedy may be placed.[28] As Roger Lane has noted, this literature did not become popular because antebellum America was an unusually violent place. Murder, he finds, became a significant element in popular culture even as actual murder rates appear to have been going down.[29] It was precisely the extraordinary quality of murders that made them grist for the literary mill, and the more extraordinary the better. Much of this writing really was quite lurid, bringing together violence, a certain level of erotic voyeurism, and a fascination with evil.[30] Here was an emerging body of literature that, no less than the sentimental tradition, contributed to a context for adaptations of the Kentucky Tragedy.

Karen Halttunen and David Brion Davis have related this emerging literature to shifting ideas about the causes of crime. At one level, they have said, the shift resulted from the extent to which, in many areas, the United States was becoming an increasingly secular society during the first half of the nineteenth century. Many Americans thus sought secular explanations for the presence of criminal behavior. Sin was no longer enough, however strong the continuing influence of older Calvinist-derived notions of human depravity. Thus, for a variety of reasons—religious, cultural, and scientific—people were beginning to look more toward social and psychological sources for acts of crime and violence, the literature reflecting both their interest in and approaches to the problem. But, as in regard to other issues facing antebellum Americans, they seem to have been uncertain about what those sources were.[31]

At least some of the uncertainty about the sources of crime and violence was focused on the thorny issue of criminal responsibility. Everyone agreed that there were circumstances under which those who committed crimes, including violent crimes, should be held responsible for their actions, and circumstances under which they should not.

The framework of honor under which the Beauchamps' actions were understood is a measure of such a belief, honor's dictates justifying for some observers what the Beauchamps had done. This framework, however, was only a specific instance of a set of larger questions that had plagued criminal law for centuries, questions having to do with motive and intent and, more especially, with the difficulties in determining either. It mattered in law whether criminal acts, including murder, were intentional, so these were questions that could not be ignored.

Within the increasingly secular environment of the early nineteenth century, questions of criminal responsibility took on new urgency. Most starkly, as Davis and others have argued, this urgency was embodied in the growing use of the "insanity" defense in criminal and other proceedings, augmenting awareness of the role of mental competence in determining both criminal and civil responsibility. But the discussion this issue provoked, and the problems it entailed, went far beyond questions of insanity, as such, and entered directly into the more general issues of human drives and motivations that the Tragedy forced its audiences to confront.[32]

To see this, it is useful to consider, at least briefly, one of the most influential works on issues of mental processes and criminal responsibility from the antebellum period. This was the work of Isaac Ray, a Maine physician whose 1838 study *A Treatise on the Medical Jurisprudence of Insanity*—destined to go through multiple editions—was one of the richest treatments of the topic. Ray worked within the framework of faculty psychology, using a model that based human activity on the existence of certain "faculties" existing in the mind; in keeping with traditions of thought going back to the late eighteenth century, he located these faculties in the brain.[33] Thus, for him, insanity had to be understood to have organic causes, to be a disease of the brain. His was not an uncommon approach at a time when faculty psychology formed the mainstream of the discipline and in an era when phrenology and other investigations helped focus attention on the brain.[34]

Ray emphasized that symptoms of insanity are rarely easy to discover, and have many dimensions. Thus, for example, he distinguished symptoms visible in the intellectual realm from those in the moral realm—between an ability to grasp what was occurring in the external world and manias affecting "those sentiments, propensities, and passions necessary to man as a social and accountable being."[35] He also stressed the possibility that otherwise sane and reasonable people might suffer from a condition he described as a "partial moral mania."[36] In 1786, the Philadelphia physician Benjamin Rush—a pioneering American figure in the study of moral faculties—had described "a woman, who was exemplary in her obedience to every command of the moral law, except one. She could not refrain from stealing." Striking to Rush was the fact that, when detected, "she would both confess and lament her crime."[37] Ray cited the case, suggested the physical origin of the mania, and noted the complexity it posed for thinking about legal issues of insanity and criminal responsibility. How, he asked, should one adjudge manias affecting otherwise apparently sane men and women?[38]

It is in terms of such issues that the work of forensic psychologists took on great relevance to antebellum approaches to the Kentucky Tragedy, and especially to its literary treatments. Within the framework of violence and death surrounding Sharp's murder, what seems to have been especially significant for all of the writers was the extent to which the desire for vengeance on the part of both Beauchamps moved from hope to obsession. Both Beauchamps, as they were transformed from people to characters, developed a determination to visit vengeance on Sharp that, in the terms of such thinkers as Ray, bordered on mania.

Beauchamp's *Confession* had provided the background for such a representation. When Ann first broaches the issue to Jereboam, she says that "her heart would never cease to ache, till Col. Sharp should die through her instrumentality; that he had blighted all her hapiness [*sic*]."[39] Subsequent pages detail an almost complete focus on revenge by the two as they plot and plan Sharp's demise. In their literary versions, the Beauchamps were, if anything, even more thoroughly obsessed by a desire for revenge. Such writers as Thomas Holley Chivers and John Savage created versions of Ann Cooke who could think of nothing but Sharp's death. "I live to view the mirror of his blood," Chivers's Eudora had exclaimed; it was the "all-sustaining hope" of Savage's Sybil. They also portrayed a Beauchamp radically transformed by the knowledge of what Sharp has done. Chivers's Conrad, for instance, learning of Eudora's seduction, not only vows to be her avenger, but pledges to pursue Alonzo "like a bloodhound, day and night, / And finding him, make daylight through his heart."[40]

Significantly, as writers documented the power of obsession over their characters, they also created a situation in which those characters struggled with murderous desires. Much more than the Beauchamps of the *Confession,* the literary Beauchamps were both impelled and troubled by their passion for revenge. Thus, the novels and dramas are filled with expressions of doubt on the part of both Beauchamps. In Charlotte Barnes's play, after one particularly violent outburst from Bragaldi, eager to kill Castelli, Octavia cries, "What wild and threatening words are these, Bragaldi?" She urges, "Let not that spectre of departed woe / Rise up again to haunt our happy home!"[41] Chivers's Conrad, contemplating what he must do, declares his own reluctance by saying, "The cloud of conscience has eclips'd my soul!"[42] One may recall, too, Simms's Orville Beauchampe, troubled by "the terrible responsibility to which his unhappy oath had subjected him." Second thoughts abound in dramatizations of the Kentucky Tragedy, as characters confront an array of conflicting demands: domestic happiness, honor, and revenge. What David Brion Davis has noted of Simms's treatment applies more generally: the drama comes from such conflicts.[43] It comes from the battle with obsession. Obsession wins the battle, but not without a fight.

It was also a conflict that related directly to concerns about crime and criminal responsibility. The power of the irrational loomed large in literary treatments of the Kentucky Tragedy. As the Tragedy's principals struggled with their desires for vengeance, their authors, in keeping with concerns raised by Rush and Ray, gave an important place to what was often described as an "irresistible impulse" that could overcome inhibitions to violence. Hendrick Hartog has described how, during the antebellum period, defense attorneys sought to use a variation on the insanity defense in cases where a crime was the product of circumstances that had driven their defendants to a state like madness.[44] Literary treatments of the Kentucky Tragedy drew their dramatic tension from this same problem of impulse, from the idea that, as Barnes's Octavia Bragaldi says, "We never know the strength of our passions / Till time or circumstance doth draw them forth."[45] Those treatments did so in ways that both included and expanded specific issues of criminal responsibility to encompass some major and more general concerns in antebellum American culture.

Several of the writers who treated the Kentucky Tragedy were more generally interested in the power of impulse. Poe has long been noted for his explorations of the irrational, and the nonrational, whether through its dark side, as evoked in his tales, or through his poetry of sound and sense. There are actually parts of Beauchamp's *Confession* that anticipate some of Poe's darker stories with their interplay of rational planning and obsessive violence. Describing the efforts leading to Beauchamp's fatal trip to Frankfort, the *Confession* says, "Never was a murder planned with such studied precaution since the world began."[46] It is difficult not to think of the narrator of "The Tell-Tale Heart" (1843), who, denying his insanity, exclaims, "You should have seen how wisely I proceeded—with what caution—with what foresight—with what dissimulation I went to work!" as he prepared to commit an otherwise maniacal murder.[47]

But Poe was not alone in such an interest. Simms, for example, wrote a number of works devoted to exploring the nonrational in both psychological and spiritual dimensions, including, most famously, *Martin Faber* (1833) and *Confession* (1841).[48] In addition, he specifically described *Beauchampe* as one of his several novels with "a strong penchant to moral and mental analysis" related to questions of motivation and passion.[49] Mary MacMichael, in a story anticipating her treatment of the Tragedy, explored the transformation of a woman, "jilted" and slandered by a false lover, who declares that she has been converted "from a woman to a demon," like Ianthe, or Ann Cooke, obsessed with revenge.[50]

Some of the interest in the nonrational developed out of the same concerns that informed thinking about human faculties and criminal responsibility found in Isaac Ray's succinct identification of the moral realm with "those sentiments, propensities, and passions necessary to man as a social and accountable being." Ray's words, consistent with his understanding of faculties, are significant for their stress on the word "necessary." His was an anthropology, like that of most of his contemporaries, in which human faculties ranged from the deepest ground for thought to the most elemental drives, all of which were essential to human life. Francis Wayland, in his textbook on *The Elements of Moral Science,* identified three essential faculties—passion or appetite, which impels people toward immediate gratification; interest or self-love, leading to a focus on long-term happiness; and conscience, to restrain the appetites and govern the pursuit of interest.[51] Conscience, he said, should always direct moral choices, but no one could or would act without the impulse provided by efforts to satisfy the demands of appetite and interest.[52] John Savage, in *Sybil,* adapted this idea when, in a brief dialogue, one of his characters assured another that "Had your wild passions won a tame success / You'd soon have sunk into the dull routine / And healthy torpor."[53]

But the Kentucky Tragedy reveals how complex such thinking could be in antebellum America, especially as its events were transformed into literature. In keeping with the larger literary traditions on which it drew, the authors of the Kentucky Tragedy sought to take their readers through an exploration of the motivations driving the principals in the tale, not simply to document obsession but to investigate its sources and its power. Since the late eighteenth century, writers in the sentimental tradition had understood the complexities in issues of motivation and intent that also occupied the pioneering criminologists.[54] Virginia novelist Samuel Relf, in his 1797 *Victims of Sentiment,* had written that "To conceive of crime, we must previously admit an idea of guilt in the heart. Motives being the only true criterion by which to estimate the relative quality of action, it is not just to cull precipitant opinions from superficial outlines of conduct; but must probe and anatomize the heart and its propelling principles."[55] And, as was understood at the time, literature had special powers to allow such an examination. As antebellum essayist Anne C. Lynch wrote, fiction "enters the secret recesses of the heart, unveils the hidden springs of motive and action." It reveals, she said, "the secret workings of the human soul."[56] Taking readers inside the minds of the Beauchamps and Sharp, treatments of the Kentucky Tragedy were themselves expositions of such secret workings, expositions that both revealed and came to grips with the unresolved nature of thinking about the irrational in nineteenth-century thought.

As the Kentucky Tragedy's chroniclers presented the tale, their explorations of the irrational pointed toward a series of factors that led to the violence of the Sharp-Beauchamp affair. In at least some versions, the story of the Beauchamps was a story of personality, of personal characteristics that gave them an unusual propensity for extreme action. Both were sometimes represented as having an ardor of temperament that made them quick to anger, quick to resent. For Chivers, it was Eudora's having a "nobler, larger soul" than most people that made her desire for revenge so limitless.[57] Beauchamp, on the other hand, was often said, as in one purportedly factual account, to have been "naturally of a fiery disposition," leading him easily to conceive "a violent indignation against the conduct of Sharp."[58] Simms presented him this way. Charlotte Barnes described her Bragaldi as a man who was "all dignity and truth," whose sense of honor was so strong that any apparent calumny "Would send the angry blood into his cheeks, / Lend fire to every word, and prompt his arm / To silence the accuser."[59]

Such recourse to personality at least had the advantage of putting the Beauchamps at a safe distance from their audiences. So did approaches that offered something of an environmental explanation for the Tragedy, such as when St. Clair, in his account of Beauchamp's pledge to kill Sharp, wrote that it "may seem strange" that anyone would take such a vow, "but be it remembered that human life is little regarded in the western states."[60] Such an understanding of the crime was not unusual. Even at the time it occurred, Sharp's murder was sometimes described as symptomatic of frontier disorder. Hoffman, too, made this point, suggesting that, to his "Atlantic" audience, the Beauchamp-Sharp story may seem to have transpired "in another planet."[61] The Western dimension of the story especially intrigued Simms, who described the "rustic" Kentucky in which his story was set as a place of "fermenting morals" populated by people who were frank, open, and hospitable. It was also a place in which people were often wronged, but, as he said, when they were wronged they tended to respond quickly, fiercely, and without recourse to law.[62] Usually classifying *Beauchampe* among his several "border tales" with settings on the margins of civilization, Simms considered the frontier environment to be an important element in determining the nature of the novels' characters and events.

Those writers who used a frontier setting built on widely held ideas of frontier disorder and also drew on a familiar literary device for evoking the power of intuition and impulse—whether the power was seen as being for good or ill. It is worth noting the critic David Reynolds's comment that Emerson was among those who admired that most influential of literary forms evoking the frontier experience, Southwestern humor, for the way in which it played with the irrational.[63] Like the Southwestern humorists, those writers who adapted the Kentucky Tragedy articulated and reinforced a sense of the frontier as a place where impulse was unchecked, and as a distant environment in which one could see the passions at play freely.[64]

The same may be said about the tendency, embodied in works by

Barnes and Poe, along with Chivers's 1851 "Leoni," to remove the action of the Kentucky Tragedy in time and space, usually to Renaissance Italy. Such a setting was not only a matter of literary fashion in antebellum American plays but similarly called up an environment Americans had learned to associate with the free play of passion and impulse. It was an association Barnes evoked as her hero, having killed the seducer Castelli, declared, "A true Italian spirit warmed my heart, / Keen to perceive affront, and as the lightning / Swift to avenge a wrong."[65] It was a setting evoking an environment in which impulsive action seemed credible, but one that, like the frontier, remained geographically or temporally remote for many audiences.[66]

Still, what seems to have fascinated most writers was not the remoteness of the events but their foundation in more intimate human impulses, those that made the Beauchamps as similar to as they were different from the writers and their audiences. As Barnes quoted from Kames, dramatic characters "interest us the more deeply, as they display the emotions and passions of which we have all been conscious."[67] Here, again, issues of human nature and motivation were key.

Discussions of impulse, so central to understanding the Kentucky Tragedy, were heavily freighted in nineteenth-century America. As many writers described and attempted to schematize human passions and desires, they commonly referred to the most basic impulses as "primitive," even "animal." In an influential British work on popular education, the American edition of which appeared in 1834, the writer and educational reformer James Simpson paid particular attention to the need to train the heart as well as the head, the "primitive impulses" as well as the intellect.[68] He also created a table of faculties, emotional and intellectual, which together make up the human being. These included the "knowing" and "reflecting" faculties, such moral sentiments as those of benevolence, hope, "firmness," and even a love of "the ludicrous" embodied in the ability to laugh—a faculty which could be easily abused. But fundamental to every human constitution were what he called the "animal propensities," those propensities for food, sex, fighting, destruction, even acquisitiveness, that comprised the most basic drives.[69]

The language of animality was widely used in discussions of fundamental impulses. Isaac Ray joined Simpson in suggesting that criminal or deranged acts often revealed the triumph of the "merely animal" over what was more distinctly human, namely the conscience, as did

Francis Wayland.[70] Such language was also readily apparent in at least one document from the Tragedy, the spurious Ann Cooke letters, when the angered Cooke was made to exclaim that, after her betrayal, she was "roused like a lioness from her lair."

To see what gave such language peculiar resonance in antebellum America, however, it is necessary to examine more fully its role in the way people understood a more general problem that appeared particularly pressing to people during the era. This was the problem of relations between mind and body as it had occupied some of the most influential thinkers from the late seventeenth century through the antebellum period.[71] It was a foundation for the concerns about action versus intention that many people found so complicated during the antebellum period, especially as they sought to locate the faculties, somehow, in the brain. But the more specific connotations and resonances the language of "primitive" and "animal" impulses evoked during that time exacerbated the concerns that it raised.

Americans—and not just Americans, because the issues were important throughout the Atlantic world—were greatly interested in questions of human physicality during the nineteenth century. Such questions took shape at many different levels, and resulted from many different influences. One manifestation of this interest was the "physicalization" of crime—and other problems—found in such works as that of Isaac Ray. Phrenology, anthropology, and medicine all helped to create an increasingly physical view of human nature.[72]

One may see evidence of the concerns this anthropological materialism created in many arenas. One was an effort to find what was uniquely human, as opposed to "animal," in human nature. For Ray and Wayland, there was always conscience to set human beings apart from other creatures, but even conscience might be located in the brain, and hence as physical, as elemental, as any other element of "human" nature. For others, there remained a distinct dimension of human spirituality, and it is not difficult to see the vogue for everything from spiritualism to Transcendentalism as a reaction to tendencies toward an increasingly materialistic conception of humanity. Chivers was strongly interested in such issues. As his biographer, S. Foster Damon, noted, he was always drawn to a contemplation of the inner world, a focus that led him, by the time he wrote "Leoni," to an interest in Swedenborg and sympathy for Transcendentalism.[73]

Confrontations with materiality took many forms, from food faddism among intellectuals and reformers to, more profoundly, a widespread fascination with suffering and death.[74] The popularity of violent stories such as that of the Tragedy—placing lives at risk, bringing lives to an end—may be one reflection of this fascination. It is impossible, certainly, not to see evidence of this in the apparently widespread interest in the extensively detailed accounts of the Beauchamps' final hours, as, whether in purportedly factual versions or literary recreations, readers followed the principals through every moment of their inexorably approaching confrontation with death, receiving privileged insight into and a vicarious experience of the terrors that confrontation might hold.

But death was, in some sense, everywhere in antebellum America, and the larger framework of its cultural confrontations suggests the depth of concern materialism created as well as the strength of the Tragedy's hold on the American imagination. Deathbed accounts stressing eternal hopes, new forms of mourning, and a substantial body of "consolation" literature all took on great significance in antebellum literary and popular culture, and all sought to counter materialism by emphasizing the spiritual and emotional side of death to the exclusion of the physical.[75] By contrast, it is possible to note the emphasis on death's materiality in sensationalist murder stories that often described the goriest details of violent death.[76] Poe embraced such materialism in his peculiar 1845 story "Facts in the Case of M. Valdemar." In the story, M. Valdemar has been hypnotized at the moment of death and kept in a state of suspended animation for several months. Brought out of this trance, the narrator recounts, Valdemar's "whole frame at once—within the space of a single minute, or even less, shrunk—crumbled—absolutely *rotted* away beneath my hands. Upon the bed, before that whole company there lay a nearly liquid mass of loathsome—of detestable putridity."[77] It would be difficult to construct a more materialistic view of death and humanity or to find a more vivid exposure of the dilemmas Americans could confront in their increasingly materialistic world.

Questions of physicality, animality, and impulse were further complicated, and in ways that relate directly to the Tragedy, by their interrelationship with the two most divisive issues of the era, those of race and gender. The question of human differences related to both color and sex held a special place in discussions of human nature, as physical differences and scientific approaches to them were closely intertwined with ideas of impulsiveness and human development that went to the heart of issues of mind and body. The scientific tendency was, by the second third of the nineteenth century, to assert that people who were nonwhite or female were not only distinct from those who were white and male, based on physical differences, but that they were also more impulsive. People of African and Native American descent were, for example, often assigned a propensity for savagery on the basis of what were said to be more primitive, even bestial characteristics.[78] Sarah Grimké emphasized the implications of such thinking in regard to gender when, protesting the foundations of female exclusion from public life, she wrote that "Man has inflicted an unspeakable injury upon woman, by holding up to her view her animal nature, and placing in the back ground her moral and intellectual being."[79]

Language drawing on such thought played an important role in treatments of the Kentucky Tragedy. It was apparent in the spurious Ann Cooke letters not only when she declared herself "roused, like the lioness from her lair," but also "swore by Heaven and earth to take such vengeance as only a woman's heart could feel," interconnecting gender, animal impulse, and revenge. Chivers drew on interconnections among race, gender, and impulse when his Eudora pledged to dress "in an Indian's garb, and paint me red" in order to become the "quiver'd angel of revengeful death."

What really brought all these issues together, however, was the underlying power of sexuality.[80] Again, whatever happened in the events, those who transformed them into literature both took for granted Sharp's seduction of Cooke and used that seduction as the starting point for the story. They understood seduction to be a complex process that involved powerful drives raging out of control. In the case of Sharp, those who portrayed the seduction itself—chiefly Chivers, MacMichael, and Simms—presented him as a man whose pursuit of his sexual prey was itself obsessive. MacMichael's Sharp was especially predatory, having accomplished the seduction of the ill-fated Geraldine before turning his efforts to Ianthe, MacMichael's Ann Cooke. Simms's version was especially revealing. Having decided to conquer Margaret Cooper, but recognizing her ability to resist "all his usual arts of seduction," Simms's Sharpe simply "Knew not how to refrain" from continuing his pursuit.[81]

But the portrayals of Ann Cooke did most to capture the loaded combination of elements brought into play by the intertwining of biology and morality in the antebellum period. In many ways, they epitomize one of the era's more portentous ideas, the view that woman had a special vulnerability to mental instability "by way of her body's peculiar dominance," to use Isaac Ray's language.[82] As Ray's words help indicate, what was distinctive in woman was founded in her body, and what was distinctive about her body was, ultimately, her sex.

Constructions of female sexuality in antebellum America were complicated. On the one hand, just as some people sought to deny the physicality of death, so, too, did some seek to create an ideal of what is sometimes termed the "passionless female." This was an ideal that suggested, despite the ideas of Ray and others, that women were less driven by sex than men, that they were dominated by their spiritual natures.[83] That some people conflated the ideal with reality is certain. It is no less certain, however, that the ideal itself contributed to a fascination with female sexuality and sexual pleasure. This fascination drove the emergence, by the 1840s, of a substantial amount of popular literary erotica, much of it offering fantasies of female sexual pleasure quite different from the passionless ideal.[84]

Literature inspired by the Kentucky Tragedy was at least indirectly connected to that emerging tradition of erotica. John Richardson's excited Matilda Montgomerie, inflamed by her passion for revenge, virtually replicated some of its key conventions. Although Cooke's succumbing to Sharp's blandishments was always left to the audiences' imaginations, her sexual experience was strongly evoked by portrayals of her growing desire and increasing inability to resist. A brief episode from one of the more popular examples of antebellum erotica, George Thompson's 1849 *Venus in Boston,* may therefore be useful for providing a more explicit rendering of how seduction could be understood, a rendering highly consistent with what tends to be more obliquely presented in adaptations of the Kentucky Tragedy. In one episode from Thompson's novel, a female character who almost gives in to a seducer says, "when your arms just now encircled me, and your lips were pressed to mine, the dizzy delight which I experienced would, in a few moments, have made me your victim, had I not, by a powerful effort, overcome that intoxication of my senses which was fast subduing me."[85] This character acknowledges herself to have an "ardent nature," like many of the Kentucky Tragedy's Ann Cookes, and the language of sexual pleasure is clearly connected to the implicit language of surrender found in the Tragedy. Cooke's seduction, however manipulated by Sharp, cannot be separated from the power of her own desires, from her inability to resist the lure of momentary pleasure with Sharp, no matter how greatly and quickly she may subsequently regret it.

The concerns about sexuality underlying stories of Cooke's seduction had many sources, including changing ideas of gender and community in antebellum America. We have already seen something of the way in which sexuality could interfere with ideals of masculine independence and agency as the various Jereboams were, to some extent, driven by their Anns to murderous acts. In addition, given the emphasis on affection in community ideals and the idealized role of women in maintaining standards of affection, evocations of female sexuality would have had a special power to express social concerns. In the catalogue of the passions, and in popular understanding, even a virtuous love was inseparable from what theorist James Simpson called an "instinct of sex," love and sexual desire being manifestations of the same fundamental drive.[86] That Cooke could be, and usually was, the embodiment of both made this basic unity fairly clear, emphasizing the dangerous potentialities of affective ties. Stories of the Kentucky Tragedy thus captured a situation in which what should be "social passions" could become impulses for betrayal and death.[87]

At the same time, however, it is also important to note how much these concerns were based in problems raised by the increasing physicalization of human nature. In a few accounts, going back to the original, these concerns were synthesized through the story of the mulatto child. The story evoked a possible pursuit of pleasure on Cooke's part that, with more symbolic power than anything else in the antebellum environment, forced a confrontation with physical differences and their significance. Were those differences as absolute and meaningful as ideologists would like them to be? Could the drive for pleasure overwhelm the distinctions "nature" had created? It may be that, because this particular element in the story provided for such a dangerous exploration of female pleasure, it virtually dropped out of most of the literary works. Where it did appear—most notably in the novels of Richardson and Simms or the anonymous 1833 play—it was presented as definitely false, as a rumor that said more about Sharp's corruption than Cooke's passion.

The more pervasive synthesis of issues raised by materialistic conceptions of human motivation came from the link between sex and violence at the Kentucky Tragedy's core. Although there is no necessary connection between sex and violence, people have often seen one. The influential Lord Kames had, for example, declared that excessive sexual passion "tends violently toward its end."[88] In antebellum America, where sexuality had significant ramifications for thinking about social cohesion, such links would have had special salience. Violence, after all, epitomizes the absence of social harmony and stability—its character and results highlighting the human materiality people were confronting in so many ways. The Kentucky Tragedy, like much within popular traditions of sentimental, sensationalist, and erotic literature, built on such a linkage and helped to reveal its foundations. Through its story of seduction, betrayal, obsession, and revenge, it created a drama of inescapable animal appetites that made the body as central to experience as the soul.

The links between sex and violence, as such, were apparent in many aspects of the Kentucky Tragedy, including the seduction. As the Ann Cooke characters lamented their fate, they blurred any possible line between seduction and rape, describing what had happened in the language of violation and injury. Sharp's act thus became, for them, a violent one, a matter of power, aggression, and uncontrolled passions, even in its unleashing of female sexual desire.

The significance of links between sex and violence were still clearer, however, in that conundrum of female agency that so complicated issues of gender and identity in various renditions of the tale. Shortly after Jereboam's execution, the editor of the *Louisville Gazette,* who had been a friend of Sharp, engaged in an exchange with the *National Intelligencer* over how to interpret Beauchamp's act. He wondered whether "there was as much misfortune as crime in the melancholy and atrocious murder of Colonel Sharp." The point was not to defend what Beauchamp had done, according to the Louisville editor, but to inquire "whether it is not a misfortune to be the victim of infatuation and diabolical passions?" He asked, "Does it lessen the atrocity of the offense that it *is* united with other and indubitable sufferings and misery of mind?" One may hate the crime but still wonder whether circumstances "may *lessen* our detestation of the offender." If, moreover, Beauchamp truly believed that Sharp had slandered Mrs. Beauchamp, then there really was "some misfortune in the case" of one brought to grief by the combination of circumstances and his own understandably inflamed passions.[89]

Here, certainly, the editor takes us back to matters usually associated with honor—the masculine obligation to defend oneself and one's family from dishonor and defamation. But, in speaking of "infatuation and diabolical passions," he does so in ways that stress a psychological as well as a gendered dimension to what the concept entailed. What Richardson's erotically charged portrayal of the vengeful Matilda Montgomerie made explicit was at least implicit in other renditions. Love, as the pioneering psychological theorists pointed out, was inseparable from what James Simpson had called an "instinct of sex," its component faculty of desire.[90] Again, there were issues of agency, but now they were focused on problems of impulse and its significance. Showing an awareness of contemporary discussions of criminal responsibility and irresistible impulse, the Louisville editor also seemed to recognize that female power and a weakening of restraint flowed both from the inherent tendencies of men and women to be drawn to each other and from the elemental faculties that made men and women what they were.

Similarly connecting honor to the faculties and recognizing the faculties to be both natural and necessary, literary versions of the Kentucky Tragedy forced a still more complex, unresolved confrontation between ideas of human nature—the interplay of primal impulses, mind, and body—and questions of moral judgement. Simms, given his "penchant to moral and mental analysis"—not to mention his strong views on gender—was one of the authors to develop that confrontation most assertively. He could not, he wrote, "defend the taking of life, even by the laws," but, he said, "there are some honest impulses, in every manly bosom, which are the best of all moral laws, as they are the most certainly *human* of all laws."[91]

In the novel, Simms was talking mainly about conflicts between impulse and law, an issue to be examined more fully in the following chapter. But his words also display the pervasive power of the language of propensities and faculties for thinking about what Beauchamp had done, and not just those involving sex and sexuality. To the extent that honor involved a concern for reputation, as it did in every version of the Kentucky Tragedy, the concept was often described as a manifestation of the natural passions and faculties of self-love. Adam Smith, in the eighteenth century, wrote that "a desire of being approved of" was an endowment of nature and the root of honor.[92] By the nineteenth century, such a writer as James Simpson was prepared to base honor on the complementary faculties of "self-love" and a "desire for estimation," both of which he placed among the "animal propensities."[93]

But honor was no less closely associated with the angry violence embodied in fighting and duels, in vengeance and death. Here was the impulse behind the "affair of honor," the violent encounter that so often had insult—real or perceived—at its heart. Here, too, was a manifestation of what most people took to be an animal propensity: rage, a "propensity to contend and fight," as Simpson called it, an innate disposition to react violently to threat. Dangerous, it was also essential to the preservation of one's own life, and the lives of others, as both Simms and Simpson said.[94] It was in such terms that the great eighteenth-century criminologist Cesare Beccaria referred to honor as pre-social, writing that "whilst we act under its influence, we return, for that instant, to a state of nature."[95]

The Kentucky Tragedy was, in Beccaria's sense, an immersion into nature. Most obviously about passion, in the same sense that honor was also about passion, it was also about passion understood within the framework of complex, shifting ideas of human nature and even dilemmas in thinking about humanity, as such. To be most fully human, as Simms's comments make clear, was not to deny the "animal" propensities but to recognize their reality and to follow their promptings when circumstances required. At the same time, as a story of sex and violence, emphasizing the body as a locus of experience, the Tragedy also called attention to the increasingly materialistic understanding of those propensities and served to call into question distinctions between mind and body, as well as definitions of humanity, in ways that cohered profoundly with issues being raised in other, troubling arenas, including those of race, gender, and spirituality.

The result was, finally, to call into question, as well, that ethic of self-restraint so prized in nineteenth-century America. The Kentucky Tragedy brought attention to some of the most powerful, primal drives, those of sex, anger, and self-preservation, linking violence and desire in ways that took on special meaning in the context of antebellum life. As the Louisville editor noted, consistent with an emerging body of literature and anticipating subsequent literary approaches to the Tragedy, primal impulses, both inescapable and strong, placed every individual on top of a personal volcano, subject to potential situations and forces that were impossible to control. "We never know the strength of our passions / Till time or circumstance doth draw them forth," to return to the summary remark of Barnes's Octavia Bragaldi. In the competitive, fragile environment taking shape in mid-nineteenth-century America, as the Tragedy evolved from events to literature, such an unstable, essential view of human nature and its potentialities would have had a horrible fascination all its own.

*Chapter 5*

# ONE OBJECT—POWER!

The sense of fragility affecting the social and psychological thinking in antebellum America also affected the political realm. Even in the 1820s, when Beauchamp killed Sharp, America was a politically volatile place. Its politics were becoming more democratic, both in practice and ideology. At least where white men were concerned, political participation was being broadened and people were demanding their rights based on increasingly egalitarian political ideals. Much of this was epitomized in the emergence of Andrew Jackson as a political hero and Jacksonian democracy as a political movement after about 1824, even as the drama of the Beauchamps and Sharp unfolded.

Political life was also becoming increasingly partisan, and virulently so. Historians have debated, and continue to debate, when a truly partisan American political system emerged. There is no question, however, that by the time of the Beauchamp-Sharp affair the basis for such a system was being laid,[1] and, in Kentucky at least, the affair may even have contributed to that system's development, as we shall see. As the Tragedy was being transformed into literature, partisan developments proceeded apace throughout the United States. From the mid-1830s forward, America saw heated debates over powerful issues of class, gender, and slavery, as well as the formation of well-defined party organizations built, ostensibly, on clearly specified political ideals and interests—all of which affected political life in new, divisive, and unpredictable ways. The Kentucky Tragedy not only helps to emphasize the extent to which people perceived this developing political environment as a scene of conflict and confusion, but also helps indicate the ways in which political changes were linked to deeper concerns about the political and social order.

Politics had marked the Kentucky Tragedy from the outset. The killing of Sharp was quickly assigned to political causes, and most of the discussion from the time of Sharp's death to the deaths of the Beauchamps focused on political rivalries. As the Kentucky Tragedy moved from events to literature, political questions remained important. Dealing explicitly with the case's key political themes to varying degrees, all the various renditions contain important political motifs. This is because, in each, much of the drama unfolds around what had been a pressing issue since the era of the American Revolution, the issue of authority. Every work gives the issue a central place in the story, and the array of works does so in remarkably consistent ways. Taken together, the Tragedy's events and the literary transformations of those events indicate just how much difficulty there could be in coming to grips with issues involving the sources and legitimacy of authority. They indicate how much those issues were intertwined with more general sources of concern about a complex and unstable world.

## I

Problems of authority, as they could shape the drama of the Kentucky Tragedy, were anticipated in the political controversies that dominated discussions of Sharp's murder from the beginning. These were the controversies growing out of the relationships between Beauchamp's crime and the relief and court struggles that had led to the emergence of two strongly divided relief and anti-relief—and, by the time of the murder, "New" and "Old Court"—factions in Kentucky politics. The conflict, originating in problems of debtor relief and, more critically, legislative efforts to bypass court rulings declaring such relief unconstitutional by replacing the "Old" court with a new one, had reached a fever pitch in the months leading up to Sharp's murder. These months were dominated by hotly contested elections—including that of the pro-relief New Court governor Joseph Desha in 1824 and New Court proponent Sharp's in 1825—as well as ongoing conflict between the two courts and their proponents. Many people actually feared that Kentucky was fast approaching what elder statesman and anti-relief veteran Thomas Todd described as a condition of "insurection [*sic*] & anarchy."[2] Colonel Beauchamp, Jereboam's uncle, recognizing the mood, had worried that heated legislative debate over the courts might "blow us all sky high."[3] Sharp himself, during the 1824 gubernatorial election, had warned that the state was experiencing "a degree of excitement and division of parties that may disturb it for years to come."[4]

A sense of turmoil appeared to be widespread. There was some emigration from Kentucky during the time, and Baltimore-based *Niles' Weekly Register* reported at the end of 1825 that conditions were such that "the citizens of Kentucky are flying to other states in search of peaceful homes."[5] This may have been something of an exaggeration, and the kinds of economic conditions that had led to the relief struggle may have played as large a role as political turmoil in encouraging any emigration that did occur.[6] Nevertheless, one former Kentuckian, resident in Indianapolis, wrote that he "should feel a much greater inclination to live in Ky again if the political differences was subsided." And he did report that, in part due to those differences, Indiana "is populating fast with emigrants from Kentucky which I am glad to sea [*sic*]."[7] Sharp's murder was itself interpreted within the framework created by the more general sense of political turmoil in Kentucky. Whatever the actual cause of the crime, Kentucky's political partisans betrayed a sense that the state's political environment lent credibility to a claim that it was a political affair.

As New Court and Old Court sides exchanged their charges and countercharges regarding Sharp's murder, the one thing on which everyone agreed was that excessive partisan zeal engendered by the relief and court conflicts was the root cause of the crime. Patrick Henry Darby, the Old Court editor who bore the brunt of New Court attacks, was usually accused of being impelled by a mixture of "party rancour" and personal hatred to foment his plot against the New Court leader Sharp.[8] Those who sought to link Darby and Beauchamp politically also cited party rancor. One of Frankfort's New Court newspapers, the *Patriot*, described both men as "Old Court lawyers," subsequently characterizing Beauchamp as having been "a very active partizan of the old court in his country."[9]

Darby and his supporters expressed equal certainty about the motives of those who sought to implicate them and their party in the crime. At least some of the persecution of Darby, one Old Court writer suggested, was because the "rough handling he has ever bestowed upon the New Court sycophants, has inflamed the most direful hatred."[10] Darby himself ascribed his persecution to the partisan motives of such New Court stalwarts as Francis Blair and Amos Kendall. But scenarios implicating partisan motives in the case could go quite far. In early 1826, it was even suggested that Sharp's own party had instigated the murder for the purpose of "affixing a stigma on their adversaries."[11]

The transformation of Sharp's murder into a political event indicates several things about perceptions of partisanship in 1820s Kentucky. One is that those who described the killing of Sharp as the product of inflamed partisanship believed that people would not dismiss such an explanation out of hand. There is only indirect evidence for how these efforts were received at the time, although it may be relevant that Beauchamp's lawyers, in their motion at the beginning of his trial, argued that the pre-trial exchange of political charges and countercharges might prevent their client from receiving a fair hearing.[12] But the very violence and duration of the newspaper war indicates the power such charges must have had. Allegations of partisan murder had surfaced within days—if not hours—of the crime, and continued to be exchanged over a decade later, when, for example, Joseph Underwood attacked Amos Kendall on the floor of Congress. Those who created that war reveal a sense on their part of living in a political environment in which people were willing to believe—or, at least, were assumed to be willing to believe—that, prompted by partisan motives, those responsible for leading public affairs were capable of some very bad things.

There was much in the air to support such a perception. For one thing, Kentucky's political leaders were, many of them, no strangers to violence. It could have surprised no one that physical attacks and confrontations were part of the conflict over relief measures and court reorganization, as they had been over other issues in earlier times, and as they would be later. In the heat of the court conflict, even such figures as Governor Desha and Robert Wickliffe came near to blows on the streets of Frankfort, a confrontation prevented only when Wickliffe, making discretion the better part of valor, suggested that "We are old men and had better part."[13] The fiery Amos Kendall was, at one point, physically assaulted as a result of his pro-relief efforts.[14] Beauchamp's trial, it may also be noted, began exactly one month after Henry Clay's widely publicized duel with John Randolph.

The Beauchamp-Sharp affair also took place only shortly after what was, up to that time, one of the nation's most striking stories of partisan finagling, one with strong Kentucky overtones, as well. This was the infamous presidential election of 1824 in which John Quincy Adams was chosen president over Andrew Jackson, winner of the popular vote, with Clay again in the thick of things. Clay had given crucial support to Adams, and this had led to allegations of a "corrupt bargain" between the two men when Adams subsequently named Clay as secretary of state. The allegations were widely believed in Kentucky, where Jackson was far more popular than the New Englander Adams, and widely interpreted in ways that simultaneously captured and encouraged the most negative perceptions of political partisanship.[15]

Probably nothing, however, did more to reinforce fears of partisanship and the credibility of charges of partisanship in Beauchamp's case than the near simultaneous drama surrounding the case of the governor's son, Isaac Desha, who also stood accused of murder. Near the end of 1824, on a trip that took him through Kentucky, a Natchez, Mississippi, editor named Francis Baker had gone on a brief excursion up toward Maysville to see an old friend. He was accompanied by Isaac Desha. A short time later, Desha was seen bloody, disheveled, and out of sorts. Subsequently, Baker's body was discovered, his throat cut, his skull fractured, in a nearby gully. Based on several bits of incriminating evidence, Desha came quickly under suspicion. He declared his innocence, but was arrested, tried, convicted, and, at the end of January 1825, sentenced to die.[16]

Desha's case attracted no less national attention than Beauchamp's. Accounts appeared in newspapers around the country, including the *National Intelligencer* and even Benjamin Lundy's *Genius of Universal Emancipation,* at that point America's leading antislavery journal.[17] Shortly after Desha's sentencing, the *American Atheneum,* a New York literary magazine, exploited the case's notoriety by publishing "The Maidens of Mulberry Vale," a poem by "the late Francis Baker, Esq., whose recent murder has attracted so much public attention": "Then sweet as the Vale may their lives ever prove, / (Where fairest of the flowers their sweetness exhale,) / And truest of friendship, and purest of love, / Ever wait on the maidens of Mulberry Vale."[18]

People both in and outside Kentucky immediately saw Isaac Desha's case in partisan political terms. Like Beauchamp, Desha was convicted mainly on circumstantial evidence, and his supporters argued strenuously that the evidence had been created by the governor's political enemies to discredit the New Court side.[19] Claiming his client had been framed, one of Desha's lawyers, the former lieutenant governor and New Court justice William T. Barry, exclaimed, "Great God, has party spirit brought us to this!"[20] When, on the other hand, the conviction was overturned and a new trial ordered on what appear to have been valid grounds of tainted evidence and jury tampering, the governor's enemies claimed that the decision merely proved how corrupt the New Court party could be.

The case was to remain a volatile element in Kentucky politics for almost two years, including the period during which Sharp was murdered and the Beauchamps died. There continued to be vitriolic debate over whether Governor Desha would simply pardon his son, a debate that New Court partisans rightly feared would hurt their chances in the 1825 elections. At the time, Francis Blair, an ally of the governor, wrote to Henry Clay that the governor and "his wretched son have weighed upon our strength like the terrors of a guilty conscience, & have given confidence, enthusiasm & all the credit they have detracted from us to our opponents." He decried the fact that elections could turn on such a cause.[21]

The New Court side was left open to further condemnation when reports began to surface that Isaac Desha might not face a retrial. A recent law, passed under New Court auspices, had made it easier to exclude potential jurors who had formed a previous opinion on a case, and Isaac Desha's attorneys—the governor's political allies—had used this to forestall impaneling a jury in the case. The always-vociferous Old Court *Spirit of '76*, charging political interference, referred to Isaac Desha as a "royal murderer" screened from "the penalties of the violated laws of his country."[22]

Even as the Beauchamp-Sharp case took center stage in Kentucky's political affrays, Isaac Desha's was to have its own sensational moments. Most spectacular was the attempt Isaac Desha made on his own life in July 1826, only days after the Beauchamps' deaths. Despondent and, some said, drunk, he slit his own throat while out on bail and came very near to dying. He never breathed normally again. When in June 1827 he was deemed sufficiently recovered to face another trial, it was with a silver tube in his throat that had to be "frequently changed or cleaned."[23] In this trial, too, there was great difficulty in getting a jury, and when the judge decided that Desha should be held without bail, the governor finally came through with a pardon. Isaac Desha did not come to a happy end. In 1828, after his pardon, he left Kentucky for Texas, where he died in jail, charged with the murder of a man named Thomas Early. In his final days, he reportedly confessed to having killed Early, and Baker, as well.[24]

It was not difficult, following Sharp's murder, to see links between Desha's case and Beauchamp's. Even as Old Court partisans, for example, sought to respond to efforts to implicate them in Sharp's murder, they suggested that those efforts had to be considered in light of earlier attempts to treat the murder of Baker as a political crime. A correspondent to the *Spirit of '76*, decried the "effort made by the *Deshaite, Judge breaking, constitution breaking usurping faction*" to implicate his colleagues in Sharp's death. He noted that "when Desha, the Governor's son, was arrested for the murder of Baker, this same truth-loving, justice-doing party" had also claimed that "the murder was committed by Desha's political opponents, for the purpose of injuring the reputation of the family." He exclaimed, in print, "Great God! what species of creatures compose this gang?"[25] He was virtually quoting William Barry, as did a correspondent to a New Court newspaper, describing what the paper claimed was the role of Darby and other Old Court leaders in the Beauchamp case: "Great God!! To what may the ambition of an infuriated faction not drive unprincipled men?"[26] Talk of partisan murder was already part of the political environment during 1825 and 1826.

Much of this talk carried over into literary treatments of the Kentucky Tragedy. It probably did so, in part, because issues of partisanship played an important role in Beauchamp's *Confession*, the major document upon which most of the authors drew. The *Confession* described how Beauchamp's concern about New Court power, especially after Desha's election, had discouraged him from killing Sharp publicly; he claimed that partisan machinations would lessen his prospects for a fair hearing. At the same time, the *Confession* recounted Beauchamp's hope that if he could get "a jury of factions," composed of "violent new court men," they would likely acquit him in order to further implicate the Old Court party in the murder.[27] And the *Confession*, too, linked the Beauchamp and Desha cases, suggesting that if the governor was forced to pardon his son, he would have no choice but to pardon Beauchamp as well. More likely, of course, is that, unwilling to let Beauchamp off, Desha found it politically impossible to pardon Isaac until the situation had cooled—and, perhaps, had found it unnecessary until Isaac was threatened with possibly lengthy confinement. In any event, much of the thrust of Beauchamp's *Confession* was to place him as an honorable man in a corrupt world, and it cited the raw partisanship of Kentucky politics as the chief cause of that corruption.

Several of the authors who adapted the Tragedy offered a similar portrayal of partisanship, using it to signalize the corrupt environment in which Beauchamp had to act. The anonymous, essentially political 1833 play, with its thinly disguised characters, drew directly on the political conflict that created the actual murder's context. At one point, the play's Colonel Sharp laments that the court controversy was "likely to create greater disturbance in the country than we are aware of,"[28] paraphrasing the real Sharp's expression of concern during the 1824 gubernatorial contest, and suggesting, at least, the validity of the author's claim to have been present, on the scene. More importantly, in its clearly biased portrayal of Beauchamp's New Court antagonists, it virtually equated partisan politics with a willingness to do anything to support one's side.

In his 1834 play, *Conrad and Eudora,* Thomas Holley Chivers also demonstrated a familiarity with the more general outline of partisan conflict presented by Beauchamp's *Confession* and adopted it as his own. His seducer, Alonzo, is politically prominent. The action takes place as Alonzo is standing for election to the legislature in Frankfort. The killing, for Chivers, is wholly personal, but at one point his Eudora suggests to Conrad, as they plot murder, that it should be done during the election: "Then, no one will suspect by whom he's kill'd! / But all will say the rival party did it."[29] At the same time, Chivers also created a conspiracy among Alonzo's political friends to ensure that Conrad would pay for the crime.

William Gilmore Simms, in his novel *Beauchampe,* was particularly sensitive to the political context of the events, drawing heavily on the *Confession*'s picture of a corrupt, partisan Kentucky environment. His Sharpe is a thorough party man, and at least part of the plot revolves around Sharpe's attempts to enlist Beauchampe in his cause. Simms also drew on the *Confession* to add the strains of partisanship to the processes of justice. Though Beauchampe has committed an honorable act, he knows he cannot expect an honorable treatment. An honest jury would acquit him, but, he says, "You know the faction." Truth and honor will be severely tried, he says, when Sharpe's partisans "will strain every nerve—spare no money, and suborn testimony to effect their object"—which they do.[30]

Simms himself was no admirer of factionalism.[31] Nor were lots of other people. Beginning early in the development of the American republic and continuing through the antebellum era, as the nation's politics became, among other things, increasingly democratic and partisan, there was also increasing concern about whether partisanship was itself a good thing. The founders of the American republic had been vocal in their condemnation of parties, and the antiparty strain in American political thinking did not die quickly.[32] People were most troubled by what appeared to be a win-at-all-costs approach to politics that gave sanction to using any means available in the interest of victory. In Kentucky, anxiety over this approach was apparent in the relief and court controversies. An 1826 editorial in a New Court newspaper, the *Patriot,* described the differences between the two parties then contending for political support in Kentucky. Members of the Old Court party, it said, sought nothing less than "the entire prostration of their opponents."[33] The Old Court *Spirit of '76* was no less ready to charge the New Court faction with wishing to put its "vile purposes" above "the security of liberty" and "the happiness of the community."[34]

As it unfolded in 1825 and 1826, the Beauchamp-Sharp affair itself captured these concerns, as prominent figures sought to put partisanship at the center of an ugly crime. If anything, the affair helped define what partisanship entailed, both its dangers and its opportunities. In the hands of an Amos Kendall, one of the true pioneers of American partisanship, the episode was tailor-made for drawing the sharpest lines between oneself and one's opponents, for putting divisions in the most loaded possible terms. In an environment where antipartisan rhetoric was strong, the political transformation of the Beauchamp case undoubtedly supplemented other issues in helping to lay the groundwork for a true party system in Kentucky, defining partisans in wholly antithetical terms, ascribing motives to paint the opposition in the most sinister possible ways.

In the event, Kendall and his cohorts appear to have lost the battle joined over the Beauchamp-Sharp affair. Discomfort over hot partisan rhetoric, especially regarding the Beauchamp case, led to extensive New Court losses in 1826, as Kendall's efforts to implicate Darby and other Old Court figures in the crime appeared to have less and less foundation. But they appear to have won the war. The party they created and the partisanship they learned to manipulate had come to take a fairly clear shape by 1827. Energized by its ties to Jackson, what had been the relief and New Court faction was a fully established party within only two years of the Beauchamps' deaths.[35]

The literary renditions of the Tragedy were taking shape even as the party system was evolving into its more fully established form in the 1830s and 1840s. As those renditions indicate, the concerns of the 1820s did not disappear as the party system became more dominant. As they also suggest, conflicting views of party played an important part in antebellum political debate, not least because they became bound up in other conflicts within the political arena, kept alive by ongoing debates. In the developing party system itself, in the divisions between Whigs and Democrats that began to take shape in the 1830s, even as the earliest writers began to explore the literary possibilities in the Beauchamp-Sharp affair, debates over partisanship as such kept the issue in the public mind. Whigs tended to hold more to an anti-party rhetoric, while Democrats tended to be more openly accepting of a partisan system. There was, in some sense, a partisan debate over partisanship in antebellum America.[36]

Whatever the broader lines of debate, however, there were underlying ideas that both sides shared. And what both sides recognized was the emergence of an "agonistic ethos" not unlike that found in other areas of American society, in which competition had become the essence of political life.[37] Those who championed partisanship claimed that it brought an open play of interests and ideas to political life and saw this as something good. South Carolinian Frederick Grimké (brother of the feminist Sarah) assured Americans that "in spite of the eternal wrangling of parties, or rather in consequence of it, a keener sagacity, and juster views are created than would otherwise exist."[38] When times were most difficult, Grimké argued, was when "agitation, discussion, and the encounter of rival opinions will be productive of most advantage," and this was a condition created by the confrontation of contending parties.[39]

The appeal of literary adaptations of the Kentucky Tragedy suggests that not everyone shared Grimké's exuberance. Renditions of the Tragedy offered a far less healthy picture of partisan competition, representing it, much like many contemporaries of the Beauchamp-Sharp affair, as one where rewards tended to go to the most successful schemers, to those willing to win at any cost. Even as the partisan system took shape, that is, the literary tradition embodied in the Tragedy shows how strong antiparty fears, at least, remained through the antebellum period.

This strength was obvious in such politically oriented works as the anonymous *Beauchamp* or Simms's novels, where partisanship overlapped personal hatreds to drive the action. But all of the treatments created such an environment in ways that had political as well as social resonances. They did so by portraying strong connections between an agonistic world and problems of authority, evoking serious anxieties about both. At one level, related to larger social concerns embodied in the Tragedy, was the problem of trust, a problem epitomized in the character of Sharp, the seducer who used false promises and false appearances to entrap the vulnerable Ann Cooke. But, as stories of the Tragedy make clear, the problems Sharp represented involved dissimulation and something more than dissimulation. Readers had acknowledged the specifically political resonance of such a character as Sharp had become since early in the history of the seduction novel, the form of which treatments of the Tragedy so heavily drew. In 1804, John Adams had expressed his concerns about the fragility of the American republic when, confronting what he saw as its increasingly democratic tendencies, he commented that "Democracy is Lovelace, and the people are Clarissa," citing Samuel Richardson's popular eighteenth-century work.[40] People, to put it simply, may be easily seduced.

The growth of partisanship encouraged still greater anxieties about "political seduction" during the antebellum period. As Kimberly Smith has argued, by the middle of that period, as the Tragedy was being given shape, American politics had become a politics of public argument, a politics of words, and people worried about the power words could have, especially in a partisan environment.[41] Men of words were always prepared, as one Whig writer said, "to pervert the feelings and most sacred sympathies of the people to purposes of party aggrandizement," especially in a political realm where competition and scheming appeared to be so prevalent.[42] Chivers's Eudora was made to capture the concerns this raised when she fretted that "talking lovers are the falsest of their race. / They woo us with the sunshine of their thoughts, / As lecherous Sol doth woo the emerald spring."[43]

The problems of political seduction were, however, enhanced still further for many people by the no less significant impact of problems created by an increasingly democratic leadership, within the framework of an increasingly partisan politics. The process of democratization in early American politics was a symbiotic one in which popular leaders drew political legitimacy from numerical support, in which public opinion came to be seen as the key source for legitimacy in a democratic order. It was also a process in which older traditions of elite leadership—what Ronald Formisano has characterized as a "deferential-participant" politics—were replaced by a more egalitarian realm with political opportunities open to an array of individuals, not just an elite.[44]

The transition was not easy, and at least something of its meaning was made manifest in the relief and court struggles that formed the backdrop for the Beauchamp-Sharp affair. Traditions of "gentry" leadership and "deferential" politics had never been strongly entrenched in Kentucky, but the violent partisan controversies over relief and the courts encouraged some people to adopt a kind of "declension model" for political affairs. The Old Court *Spirit of '76* declared that there had been a "falling off in public morals and public virtue" since the early days of Kentucky politics, when the state had been led by men said to personify the gentry style.[45] New Court partisans, though quick to charge their opponents with aristocratic or, worse, "Federalist" tendencies, also looked nostalgically to what they said were better times.[46]

Reactions to Sharp himself tended to mobilize issues raised by the transition from a deferential to a democratic politics. He came from a part of Kentucky noted for its democratic proclivities, even at the time his career began.[47] His supporters and opponents alike frequently noted his nonelite background, despite what he later achieved. He also had a reputation for exploiting emerging forms of populist appeal. At the height of the court controversy he was often commended as a supporter of "popular power." But he was also vilified as, among other things, "a profligate in morals and a weather-cock in politics; a follower of majorities and a sycophant of power."[48]

This was the Sharp who appeared in the various renditions of the Tragedy. It was certainly the Sharp of the anonymous 1833 *Beauchamp,* who was accused by Darby, in a reflection of the playwright's own views, of being a devotee of "the shaking hand system."[49] It was also the Sharp of Simms and Savage, Savage's character holding up as an ideal the politician whose "crowd-controlling phrases" could find the "ready hotbed of the people's hearts."[50] A partisan, a manipulator of words, he was the demagogue whose spellbinding language could move a vulnerable population to do his will.

Since the early national period, such a figure had stood as a symbol of the dangers of democracy, exploiting narrow popular passions to achieve personal gains at the expense of the common good.[51] Through the antebellum era, he continued to embody the dangers felt by those fearful of democracy. William Branch Giles, opposing the extension of suffrage to nonpropertyholders in early nineteenth-century Virginia, wrote in 1817 that proponents of the extension rested their case on sheer deception, preaching what he described as the doctrine that "the people could do no wrong." Their arguments, he said, were merely efforts to gain popularity "by cajoling and flattering the people, under various ingenious disguises."[52] All of the Sharp characters, as men who "woo us with the sunshine of their thoughts," to use Eudora's phrase, fit neatly within the parameters of Giles's description. As such, they were characters who extended John Adams's analogy likening democracy to Lovelace well into the nineteenth century, into the age of Jackson and beyond.

It would be a mistake, however, simply to view treatments of the Tragedy as allegories of the dangers of democracy. Some of the writers, notably the anonymous author of *Beauchamp,* along with Chivers, Poe, and Simms, did betray conservative, even antidemocratic biases, but the dangers everyone portrayed went beyond simple questions of democracy and conservatism. Questions of leadership and legitimacy were far more powerful here, questions of the nature and clarity of authority.

The importance of such questions becomes clear in the representations of Sharp. Sharp was not only a wordsmith in every version of the Tragedy, but he was also a man of both prominence and corrupt character. A cynical political leader in all the renditions set in America, he became a debauched aristocrat when the tale was moved to Europe. One should not ignore the conventionality of such a characterization, given the great attraction aristocratic (usually Renaissance) Europe held for American writers, especially American playwrights. Hence, Barnes, Poe, and Chivers all presented Sharp in the person of a depraved nobleman, but one would hardly try to find antielitist purposes behind those portrayals—not, certainly, in works of such writers as Chivers and Poe. What one sees, instead, is another version of that questioning of appearances prominent in all the treatments of the story. It connects the dangers of deception not only to status but also to authority, leaving sources of legitimacy problematic and difficult to resolve.

This crisis in legitimacy was related to the more general changes that were making American society a society of strangers, one in which people had to depend on appearances while understanding appearances to be deceptive. The transition to a more democratic, partisan politics was, as many historians have noted, also a transition to a more impersonal politics. This may have been, as Bertram Wyatt-Brown and others have said, more characteristic of the North than of the South, but its signs were apparent everywhere.[53] As in social life, an impersonal politics was, of necessity, a politics of externals, of appearances and performances. And, again, appearances could be deceiving.

Within this framework, however, the character of Ann Cooke also takes on special significance. In virtually every rendering of the Kentucky Tragedy, there is a certain rootlessness about Cooke that increases her vulnerability to flattery and seduction. In Charlotte Barnes's version, Octavia Bragaldi—her Ann Cooke—had been the victim of a bogus marriage and a betrayal by the cruel Count Castelli prior to his departure for war. But Octavia's difficulties, one may recall, had resulted from her disobedience to her father's opposition to Castelli. Her fraudulent marriage and the tragedy that follows is the result of her disobedience to parental authority, as she recognizes in the end. Chivers built on a similar conflict, as Eudora is forced to choose between loyalty to her mother's love and succumbing to Alonzo's blandishments. She is moved when Alonzo tells her, "My love is not a mother's love, but more! / 'Tis love that groweth and keeps pace with joy"—a defiant notion in a matricentric age.[54]

Simms and MacMichael presented a message that was, at bottom, the same. Although their Ann Cooke was haughty and vain, unlike Octavia or Eudora, her ambitions for independence also led her to ignore any guidance that might protect her from harm. Simms offered the most self-conscious rendering of such a Cooke. The village belle Margaret Cooper, he wrote, had determined to reject the moralism of "those, the scorn of whom she anticipated," but in doing so, she had located no other principles to guide her choices. As Simms said, in figuratively fleeing her provincial home, she could "fly to no greater certainties than she now possessed." She could have learned nothing to guard her against "the principles of Alfred Stevens, and of these she knew nothing."[55] Adrift, she was vulnerable to his appeals. Such a characterization was of a piece with Simms's presentation of a Cooper whose ambition had taken her "out from her sex," leaving her with no tangible standards for identity and judgement. Rich in its gender implications, it was a portrayal that also had strong political implications, as well. Clear social categories can provide the customary authority that will protect the vulnerable from men like Stevens. A lack of clarity can make the vulnerability greater still.

Literary treatments of the Kentucky Tragedy dramatized significant political concerns in antebellum America. Questions of fluidity, competition, and trust loomed large in many areas of American life; problems of authority—even issues of parental authority raised by Chivers and Barnes—did too.[56] The Kentucky Tragedy, with its deceptive politicians and unscrupulous aristocrats and its rootless, vulnerable victims, helps to indicate how greatly the traditional sources of political legitimacy could no longer be relied on in American life, and how little had come to take their place.

Again, it would be entirely too simple to look upon literary renditions of the Kentucky Tragedy as anti-democratic tracts or, in their indictments of aristocrats, for that matter, as literary condemnations of established elites. It is difficult, however, to ignore their conservative tendencies in the face of a fluid, democratic environment.[57] In keeping with dominant modes of antebellum conservatism, these dramatizations conveyed both a sense of a need for authority and a sense of the dangers inherent in fluidity and change. Political categories were no more reliable than categories of gender, status, or even human nature. The Kentucky Tragedy dramatized that unreliability.

## II

As this discussion of problems of authority indicates, the political thrust of renditions of the Kentucky Tragedy rested on and highlighted links between the personal and the political in antebellum America. As the stories also show, ideas about the passions played an important part in defining such links, drawing political concerns in with key themes in social and moral thinking. Thus, the demagogue may have been a politician who played on the passions of the people, just as the seducer played on the passions of a vulnerable young woman. But like the seducer, he also pursued passions of his own. At one point, Barnes's Castelli, tiring of Octavia's complaints, exclaims, "no tongue / Shall ever triumph over Count Castelli. / One object—Power! One feeling—vast Ambition! / Alone shall urge or stir my passions now," suggesting an equation, even an intersubstitutability, between his overwhelming lust for sex and a lust for power.[58]

Such a linking of the personal and political through the passions was fairly common on the part of antebellum thinkers. There were, as Daniel Walker Howe has shown, deliberate efforts to use faculty psychology, with its identification of various faculties of feeling and reason—all essential, all dangerous—as a kind of palimpsest for the body politic. These efforts go back to the earliest days of the republic, and they remained influential through the antebellum period.[59] A Whig spokesman wrote an 1846 essay that summarized what they entailed. Evoking more general ideals of self-restraint, he praised what he called the "self-governing man." Such a man, this writer said, when confronted with a difficulty "does not call together all his powers, passions, appetites and desires, on a footing of perfect equality, and decide according to the major vote." All, he said, must be "present in the solemn council" and properly weighted. "So it must be," he argued, "with a self-governing people."[60]

Political passions raised problems and possibilities in the political realm similar to those affecting other arenas. Such passions could be disruptive or productive; they also provided a fragile but essential base for political community. In a sermon on American politics, the prominent religious thinker Horace Bushnell showed both what he assumed the passions' role should be as well as his sense of the problems they created when he condemned the "hollowness of political friendships and alliances" he believed to characterize American life. He termed them "mere coalitions of selfishness and ambition." Missing in politics, he said, were "True friendships, warmly returned and permanent as life." What was wanted in the political community was "a warm and a large heart" in the people, bring them together as a political community.[61] Here was a political version of that ideal of an affective community so prominent in other areas of American life.

Uncomfortable with partisanship, Bushnell also worried about the effects of what he saw as a "constant state of political warfare" in American society, "begetting a habit of universal mistrust."[62] Mary MacMichael, two years before she published her story of the Kentucky Tragedy, wrote an historical essay for the *Lady's Book* in which she raised similar concerns. MacMichael compared her present era with that of chivalry, finding much to praise in her own day, but much to admire in earlier times. What she appreciated about the age of chivalry was the existence of the kind of political community Bushnell admired, too. It was a community whose citizens were distinguished by "their ardent and devoted patriotism, their strong and unyielding faith, their generous sacrifice of selfish feelings and interest, their unwavering attachment." Tellingly, given her later treatment of the Tragedy, it was also a community in which "from the prince on his throne to the peasant in his shed, loyalty and faith were universally observed, when the courtesies of life were not mere external forms, when honesty was more than a byword, and fidelity and truth to woman was not considered a reproach."[63] Visualizing a world in which mutual affection was both real and constantly apparent, MacMichael's essay highlighted idealized links between the personal and the political that informed much of American thought.

As her treatment of the Tragedy makes no less clear, however, these links were not easy to control or to synthesize. Not only were "external forms" difficult to connect to internal states, as her Claude de Wilton proved, but an "unwavering attachment" could raise problems of its own. In her essay on chivalry, she acknowledged that "ardent and devoted patriotism," for all its virtues, also accounted for a bloody European history of nearly constant warfare. In her story of the Tragedy, an ardent attachment would lead to murder, suicide, and the deaths of both Ianthe Willoughby and her young Beauchamp. This problem of "unwavering attachment" had the moral and psychological implications that, as we have seen, did much to define antebellum cultural, psychological, and social concerns.

But, as MacMichael's work helps to illustrate, the problem also had distinctive political implications, particularly in regard to questions it raised about law and authority. At one level, such questions look back to issues of criminal responsibility and human agency that played such an important role in thinking about the Beauchamp-Sharp affair. This was the problem that Simms summarized in his comment that "there are some honest impulses, in every manly bosom, which are the best of all moral laws as they are the most certainly human of all laws." As Simms's language indicates, an act such as Beauchamp's not only raised questions of whether one could control one's passions, but also whether, in all instances, one should, a question that had political as well as moral implications. It was related to a thorny issue raised by virtually everyone who confronted the Kentucky Tragedy, that of the relationship between law and virtue, law and justice.

This issue was very much a part of the rubric of honor, which loomed so large in every treatment of the Kentucky Tragedy. As such, it was summarized in Beauchamp's *Confession* in the claim that "the laws of society" cannot inevitably provide "adequate redress for all injuries of one citizen toward another."[64] This view was echoed by many of those who accepted the ideals of honor, including those Kentucky women who, urging that Beauchamp be pardoned, asserted that the "crime was great for which mr Beauchamp is sentenced to die—but the provocation was also great." Traditions of honor and independence have, classically, been associated with tendencies toward impatience with and hostility toward the law, especially in the American South, and it is not difficult to relate such words to them.[65]

But the more general implications of such sentiments were rendered particularly well in John Savage's gloss on Simms's ideas. Savage's Beauchamp, facing trial, declares himself to be "hemmed in a dock, the bars of which / Have propp'd up every crime that law and gold, / Thirst, madness, tainted blood, foul head, black heart, / Or tortured nature e'er invented."[66] Moving from culture to politics, such words went beyond honor to convey more complex misgivings about the compatibility between law and morality, law and human agency, doing so in a way that dramatized still greater complications in antebellum political ideas and beliefs.

In a particularly telling remark growing out of the political crises that led to Sharp's murder, Kentucky's relief governor John Adair once lamented the emergence of a political world in which men appeared to have "become in feeling and conscience, *completely legalized*," guided more by the letter of the law than by ideals of political community.[67] Several factors would have conspired to encourage such a sentiment. One was the transition to a more impersonal politics. Holding the political community up to the same kinds of ideals conveyed by such later writers as Bushnell and MacMichael, the problem, as Adair stressed and the Beauchamp texts dramatized, was whether a "legalized" social and political order—one based on rules rather than feelings—could adequately address human needs and concerns.

The question of legalism was far from academic in antebellum America. It formed the core of some major political debates and distinctions. When, for example, Adair decried the "legalized" consciences of his political opponents, he was not attacking a straw man. The anti-relief, Old Court party, which he opposed, often did stress a rules-dominated approach to political choice, especially as its leaders focused much of their argument on the unconstitutional character of relief legislation and on the sanctity of contracts. In 1824, anti-relief leader Ben Hardin—Patrick Darby's law partner—argued from these grounds that relief's supporters, rejecting a strict constitutionalism, had essentially taught people to "contemn good order, and to be regardless of all subordination of law," leading the state to a condition of anarchy and violence. Making what was probably a reference to the Isaac Desha case—and anticipating the Beauchamps'—he said it was this that had led to "the most daring and atrocious murders and robberies. From the highest to the lowest in society," he said, "men are turned out cut-throats and assassins."[68]

Similar perspectives were to contend for years to come, and in many antebellum political arenas. Differences over legalism marked, at least roughly, the divide between the two major parties, whose roots lay in conflicts created by Jacksonian policies—policies themselves debated in legalistic and what might be labeled intuitionist terms.[69] Then and later, Whigs, dedicated to political stability, tended to see in proceduralistic constitutionalism a necessary force for the preservation of the political community. They saw virtue in the "external forms" that gave a proper shape to political loyalties and convictions.[70] Democrats tended to assert more scope for feeling and intuition, for, as Andrew Jackson himself once said, allowing personal "understanding" to settle issues of constitutional interpretation.[71]

But from the time of Beauchamp's crime to the end of the antebellum period, the question of legalism came up in a variety of contexts, and should not be understood as a question defined solely, or even primarily, in terms of party lines. Within the cultural framework of antebellum politics, where both feeling and restraint were acknowledged and valued, the motifs of legalism and intuitionism could be widely and variously deployed, and people of different political interests could use those motifs as their purposes required. This was particularly visible in the increasingly vociferous debate over slavery, the dominating issue in American politics as the Kentucky Tragedy took its various literary forms. The oppositional categories in that debate all gave a concern about proceduralism an important role, going well beyond simple party distinctions. At the core of abolitionism—a movement that had, after all, its share of Whigs—was a celebration of feeling, intuition, and empathy, and, above all, a sense that justice was more denied than served by laws that protected a brutal, evil system. Proslavery arguments—with their many Democratic adherents—tended more to legalism and the necessity for a rule-governed social and political order.[72] In their confrontation, champions of each side kept the conflict over legalism at the forefront of American political life.

The words of a Beauchamp who declared himself "hemmed in the dock, the bars of which / Have propp'd up every crime" had a powerful resonance within such a setting. Again, one should be careful not to read treatments of the Tragedy allegorically, or even as guides to individual author's positions on specific issues. Thus, for example, on the issue of slavery, South Carolinian William Gilmore Simms wrote extensively in defense of the institution, emphasizing the importance of constitutional order and stability, and Georgian Thomas Holley Chivers, too, was known to advocate a proslavery constitutionalism that he claimed was essential to preserve an orderly political society.[73] Nevertheless, even as they celebrated such a legalistic ethic in regard to slavery, they offered literary caveats to that ethic's moral foundations. Their quintessential hero was, after all, the man who could act independently, strongly, passionately when circumstances demanded, one who, as Simms said of Beauchamp, is guided by those impulses "which are the best of all moral laws."[74]

There may have been something self-serving in Simms's and Chivers's proslavery legalism, but the fact that their versions of the Kentucky Tragedy shared so much with others' emphasizes the extent to which all the debates over legalism looked deeper into the problems of antebellum political culture. The conflict between law and feeling was a major part of what the Beauchamp story was about. To what extent was an adherence to law necessary for stability and order? To what extent was a strict adherence to law a way of evading moral choices and even of preventing justice from being done? Did Americans really want a world in which, as John Savage's Sybil says, "law o'er justice vaunts"?[75]

## III

In his diagnosis of the sources of Margaret Cooper's vulnerability to the seducer Stevens, Simms cited, in addition to her vanity and haughtiness, one further factor, a factor he identified in language inescapably related to the increasingly democratic, partisan politics of antebellum America. Among Cooper's problems, Simms wrote, was, despite her scorn for village moralism, a desire to stand out in the estimation of others and a failure to understand "that public opinion, though a moral object against which woman dares not offend, is yet no standard for her government." He said, "principles are determined elsewhere," adding that "Whatever the world may think of them," such principles "are the only real moral securities on earth."[76]

The force of public opinion was deeply felt and strongly debated within America's changing political environment. The discussion was closely connected to majoritarian notions of democracy—increasingly troubling to many people even as Simms was creating his Margaret Cooper—and to possibilities for a "tyranny of the majority," to use the common phrase, but in ways involving far more than the power of "numbers" to oppress minority rights and interests.

As Simms's remarks indicate, there was a moral dimension to the problem of public opinion, a dimension that the French observer Alexis de Tocqueville captured, classically, when he characterized democratic tyranny as a force that had produced "less genuine freedom of discussion" in America than in any other country.[77] American writers worried about the problem of a democratic tyranny, and in language that draws attention to the links between the personal and political in Simms's portrayal of Margaret Cooper. Even such a democrat as the Boston essayist and radical Orestes Brownson feared that the power of public opinion was such as to make politicians speak "from truth and justice, wisdom and virtue, to the force of numbers"; the result was to destroy "manliness of character, independence of thought and action."[78] As a

Whig writer said, there was a "paralyzing despotism of 'Public Opinion' which threatens to banish all free and manly thought from among us."[79] Leaving aside for the moment the gender implications of such remarks, their assumption of a potential opposition between public opinion and principles, much as Simms portrayed it, could not have been clearer.

The problem could be exacerbated, as Brownson himself acknowledged, by partisanship. He himself refused to accept a party label "because we have a great dislike to party tyranny."[80] Whigs, who made anti-party rhetoric—if not anti-party practice—one of their chief tools, often contrasted the "liberty of freemen" with the "slavery of party."[81]

One of the many prescient observations made by the French traveler Michel Chevalier during his 1830s visit to the United States was that the country had "a society which moves by instinct, rather than according to any premeditated plan; it does not know itself." He continued, "It is divided between its instinctive perceptions of the future and its aversion to the past, between its thirst for freedom and its hunger for social order, between its religious veneration of experience and its horror of the violence of past ages."[82] The oppositions Chevalier saw were apparent to many people; they underlay, for example, Mary MacMichael's historical essay on chivalry and the problems of modern America. But none was more critical than that between order and freedom. As the Kentucky Tragedy texts indicate, it was possible to value both; it was not so easy to bring them together.

"Freedom" is a difficult concept to define, and such scholars as Edmund Morgan and Orlando Patterson have argued that, in critical ways, definitions of freedom depend less on a sense of what it is than of what it is not.[83] Freedom is understood mainly in opposition to some form of nonfreedom, such as slavery. Philosopher Susan Neiman has also pointed out the extent to which freedom depends upon uncertainty. To act freely, she has noted, is to act without enough knowledge or power to determine fully the consequences of one's actions: it is impossible to be simultaneously free, omniscient, and omnipotent.[84] One way to think about the moral dilemmas dramatized by the Kentucky Tragedy is to appreciate how symptomatic those dilemmas were of such larger concerns about freedom, coupled with a lack of clarity about what it meant.

Thinking about freedom in antebellum America had many dimensions. There was some tendency to equate freedom, generally, with unfettered economic activity, and to do so in ways that cohered with social and cultural tendencies in a world of competition and change.[85] The Jacksonian philosopher William Leggett, who had praised "the principle of unrestrained competition" in economic activity, essentially saw freedom as the right of individuals "to regulate their own pursuits of industry and improvement" free from government interference.[86] And, in general, there was a tendency to think about freedom in terms of the power of government in relation to individuals' lives and behavior.[87]

But underlying these tendencies were ideas about freedom that cohered closely with the more general issues of law and feeling portrayed in the various treatments of the Kentucky Tragedy. Whether in economic or political realms, freedom had come to take on a radical and highly individualistic cast, equated, essentially, with the exercise of an unrestrained will. The prominent democratic theorist George Sidney Camp wrote in 1841 that the essence of freedom lay in the right of individuals in a democracy "voluntarily to regulate their own conduct agreeably to the dictates of their own will," and his position was far from unusual.[88] Orestes Brownson defined freedom in similar terms. For him, freedom meant the "freedom to do whatever one has a natural right to do; and one has a natural right to do whatever is not forbidden by natural or absolute justice."[89] In 1846, a writer for the *Southern Quarterly Review*, evoking a similar view, praised John C. Calhoun for holding to a view of freedom that would "leave to each individual the most perfect liberty to seek his own highest good." It was the "freedom both to will and to do."[90]

There were caveats. Side by side with celebrations of the unrestrained will were more conservative warnings that true freedom could exist only where everyone appreciated how much its realization depended on fidelity to principles of "order, justice, reason, legitimacy," and not on the exercise of "mere personal will" alone.[91] Such caveats tended to be just that, however, caveats, and even they were framed by a recognition of inevitable dilemmas between following the dictates of one's will and obeying the law or observing any other "external forms," as MacMichael had called them. At the foundation of much of the antebellum discourse of freedom was a very Emersonian view that, as

Emerson himself said, placed "the laws of the world" on one side and "Will or Duty or Freedom on the other."[92]

The antebellum writers who dramatized the Kentucky Tragedy drew on and contributed to such a discourse of freedom. Although they rarely spoke of freedom as such, the contemporary discourse linking rule-breaking, right action, and a courageous moral independence suggests that it was very much on their minds. This was especially true in regard to their various Beauchamps, who invariably and deliberately reject the constraints of law and society to act solely according to a sense of right and justice, "agreeably," as Camp had said, "to the dictates of their own will." Although, certainly, such writers as Camp—not to mention Emerson—should hardly be thought of as exhorting their fellow Americans to murder, the various Beauchamps, through their moral independence, heroically personify a drive toward freedom with clear connections to the rhetoric of Camp, Brownson, and others.

These Beauchamps suggest several implications when framed by that conceptualization of freedom. One has to do with gender. As invariably portrayed, these figures synthesized ideals of honor with those of masculine independence and intuitionism. Within the framework of freedom, they also dramatized the masculine bias displayed when such commentators as Orestes Brownson made connections between "manliness of character" and "independence of thought and action" in the political realm. A number of historians have commented on antebellum tendencies to define citizenship in masculine terms.[93] To the extent that freedom was itself connected to political ideals, portrayals of a heroic Beauchamp help to indicate why this was so.

At the same time, renditions of the Kentucky Tragedy, as they work within the antebellum discourse of freedom, suggest, in their apparent popularity, both a longing for and an anxiety about freedom as it was coming to be conceptualized in antebellum America. At least one dimension of the story's appeal probably lay in its relationship to a concern raised by many observers about a loss of nobility in American life. Tocqueville noted the problem. In his words, Americans were a people whose "object is not to create heroic virtues but peaceful habits."[94] The prominent American Unitarian Henry W. Bellows made a similar observation when he suggested in 1845 that Americans "tend to very low and barren views of moral excellence." He meant by this that "There is nothing hearty, gushing, eloquent in the national virtue."[95]

To the extent that freedom entails both an unfettered will and an embracing of uncertainty, Tocqueville and Bellows were among many who believed that Americans had exchanged liberty for prudence, temporizing rather than acting courageously from a sense of right and duty.[96]

There was, and was intended to be, something poetic in the Beauchamps' challenge to law and order, connecting freedom, rule-breaking, and the deeper strivings of the soul. This was a message conveyed by virtually everyone who sought to give meaning to the tale, from the Beauchamps themselves to those who celebrated them in literary terms.

It may seem odd to connect murder with spiritual striving, but in the context of antebellum America the claim may not be too far-fetched. Just as an editor from Beauchamp's time could warn about a current tendency to "immortalize murderers," so have historians described what Karen Halttunen has termed a "popular cult of the murderer," including Beauchamp, during the first half of the nineteenth century.[97] Certainly there were many instances of individuals finding both freedom and even the ground for a sort of Emersonian self-reliance through violent action. Although, as an individual, he could not have been more different from Jereboam Beauchamp, Frederick Douglass is a powerful case in point, his violent resistance to the slave breaker Edward Covey providing a "turning point" in his life, a moment that "rekindled the few expiring embers of freedom, and revived within me a sense of my own manhood." Both the act and, as he said, a willingness to accept "even death itself" in consequence gave him a feeling of freedom he had never felt before.[98] Significantly, as David Leverenz has noted, Douglass even spoke of himself as being dominated by "a fighting madness" during that pivotal, violent moment in his life.[99] Beauchamp was no Frederick Douglass, not in life nor even in literature. But whether one wants to view his murderous act as a mode of self-realization, it partakes of the same order of aspiration that made such a goal so compelling. So, again, murder as spiritual striving? Perhaps not, but as we examine the interconnected sources of antebellum anxiety, tension, and discontent, we find a background of common concerns that helps explain why so many American writers—and their audiences—felt compelled to look at a sordid Kentucky tale and to see in it the makings of a celebration of duty, honor, love, and the heroic.

Nevertheless, there were ambiguities in the message, as well, ambiguities about how freely one could act, or should act, given the demands of human nature and society. The more radical versions of freedom rested on an intuitionist morality that essentially equated right with feeling: "The sense of right is felt to be the authoritative principle" in a democratic society, Frederick Grimké had said approvingly.[100] The feeling of justice or injustice was the surest guide to right action, the basis on which freedom had to rest.

But feelings could have moral shortcomings of their own, strong impulses producing problematic convictions of right and wrong, as many pioneering criminologists had said. The point was often raised in regard to the Beauchamps, in life and in literature. As treatments of the Kentucky Tragedy traced the motivations driving the Beauchamps' decisions, it exposed the power of irresistible impulses (rooted in such primal passions as sex and self-preservation) that drove their actions at least as much as dedication to principle and justice. Given the power and characteristics of impulse, a definition of freedom based on intuition and the unfettered exercise of the will could not avoid having dangerous implications. At the same time, the value placed on freedom could only have intensified concerns about agency raised by the understanding of impulse as rooted in primal, even animal characteristics.

So presented, freedom really did become a complex, problematic goal, and in ways that would have enhanced the tensions Chevalier, among others, observed. The longing for freedom embodied in the Tragedy involved a rejection of authority. But the Tragedy also captured the anxieties created when freedom had to be realized in a world where sources of authority, "order, justice, reason, legitimacy," were uncertain and unclear. As the Kentucky Tragedy taught, neither intuition nor institutions could provide a wholly satisfactory ground for freedom in a changing society.

In his remarks on American society, Chevalier made another point that was no less relevant to the Kentucky Tragedy's dramatization of the nature of freedom in antebellum thought. Discussing the power of public opinion in American politics, Chevalier wrote, "Democracy everywhere has no soft words, no suppleness of forms; it has little address, little of management; it confuses moderation with weakness, violence with heroism."[101] Treatments of the Kentucky Tragedy help to explain the confusions Chevalier observed. All evoked a paradoxical situation in which sympathy, affection, loyalty, and fidelity received their strongest confirmation in an act of violence, an act presented as essential proof that heroic virtue could exist in a democratic society. Whatever the authors' purposes, the result was to create a connection between freedom and disorder while highlighting the absence of a substantive concept of freedom independent from its links to the most volatile human drives.

# CONCLUSION

The Kentucky Tragedy shows how interconnected a variety of ideas and images became in antebellum America. It shows how those ideas and images were translated into popular forms during the second quarter of the nineteenth century, encouraged—or exacerbated—by changes in the social, political, and economic environments.

Like much in antebellum literary and intellectual life, stories of the Kentucky Tragedy tend to turn our attention toward the issue of individualism in its social, cultural, economic, and political forms, toward those questions of autonomy, agency, and isolation that often create a focal point for discussions of the impact of the developing market economy and of democratic partisanship on antebellum life. Presentations of the Tragedy—and the approaches various authors took to adapting the story—become more easily explicable when put in a historical context that stresses the extent to which many people saw individualism as a fact of American social, political, and economic life but had varying opinions about what to make of it. For some, it was a liberating fact, a basis for a society in which individuals could be empowered to escape the artificial constraints of older, more repressive ways of life. Egalitarian dreams along with possibilities for individual freedom appeared most capable of realization when every individual could seek his or her own goals unfettered by insidious forms or conventions. For others, the apparent triumph of individualism, and, especially, of the competitive individualism that flourished within the changing social and political environment, made the need for guidelines and a measure of restraint more pressing—whether restraint came from the self or from an appreciation for the social bonds and mutual, reciprocal obligations necessary to hold society together.

All of this was a part of the Kentucky Tragedy, and the story, in its various renditions and transformations, helps to emphasize how pervasive the problems of individualism were for antebellum Americans. It helps to illustrate how those problems appeared in a variety of arenas and, even more, how interconnected the problems were with each other. In all its myriad forms, the story indicates connections between the unfettered ego, its possibilities and dangers, and complex issues involving social identity and the stability of social categories, including dilemmas of gender and gender relations. The story sets demands for self and social restraint against the power of necessary but volatile human impulse, dramatizing dilemmas of ego and society raised by developing individualistic ideas and orientations. It shows how democracy and partisanship contain in themselves the possibilities for individual liberation as well as a dangerous autonomy, putting self above society.

Insofar as it confronted the dilemmas of the unfettered ego, the Kentucky Tragedy was also part of that web of interconnections between self and society created by the complexities of desire. As many observers noted, socially, politically, and economically, antebellum America was dependent on desire. The nation's growing market economy was, in essence, an economy of desire, depending on ever expanding, insatiable drives for acquisition and consumption for its health. Its democratic and ideological egalitarianism was built on similar drives for acquisition and consumption. The visiting French observer Alexis de Tocqueville was not the only commentator, then or later, to note the power of envy in American politics, and in social and cultural realms, as well.[1] Insatiable desire was the heart and soul of antebellum political economy and of the individualism, especially the competitive individualism, at its base.[2]

At the same time, as a story of sex and violence, among many such stories from the antebellum period, the Kentucky Tragedy alerts us not only to tensions and interconnections, but also to deeper concerns underlying antebellum America's political economy of desire. As a story of sex and violence, the Kentucky Tragedy confirms the work of those historians who have discussed how the body became an increasingly centralized site for political and social discourse in eighteenth- and, especially, nineteenth-century America.[3] In the motivating power it assigned to primal, even animal instincts, the story, in all its various permutations, located its most powerful messages in the use and abuse of bodies, in both the vulnerability and the heroism that could be expressed through the adventures of the physical self.

Such an approach built on that materialistic conception of humanity both reinforced and was reinforced by continuing developments in science, medicine, and social thought, all of which intersected to raise questions about what was mutable and what innate in human beings. As various writers laid out the Tragedy's story of seduction, betrayal, and violent revenge, they took their audiences to the core of such a materialistic view. They did so as they presented a tragedy set in motion by individuals, men and women, unable to control impulses of lust and self-preservation, creating a powerful moral drama out of the interplay of impulse and nobility, instinct and freedom. As translated by stories of the Kentucky Tragedy, the issues of materialism became entwined with those of social, political, and moral instability, such that frequently reiterated exhortations to moderation and self-restraint were themselves put on fragile and uncertain foundations. However elaborated, the story portrayed moral dilemmas made inevitable by a humanity that was itself inescapably physical, in which physicality expressed and defined both the highest and lowest forms of human aspiration.

The antebellum world was, as we have said, a world of tensions and anxieties, and the stories of the Kentucky Tragedy, with their gross, untamed physicality, help us to understand why this was so. The various changes characterizing antebellum American life took place within a context of a radical cultural and intellectual reorientation, a reorientation that made even the very natures of those affected by it appear unclear and uncertain. Contemplating issues of agency, motivation, and self-realization, the Tragedy, in its more developed versions, also contemplated a world in which visible anchors were few and, as the authors revealed, far from reliable.

We remain, in many ways, part of the Tragedy's world. Our admiration for the antisocial, violent hero remains undiminished. And many of the tendencies and tensions of antebellum life—its competitive individualism, its stress on appearances, even its seemingly archaic approaches to gender—remain with us as well. We continue to define courage, loyalty, and duty in essentially violent terms. Placing law on the side of rules and rules in opposition to heart-felt action, we remain wedded to scenarios in which law and justice, law and virtue, stand in a tense relationship that only violence can resolve. We retain that fascination with and fear of the physical self that underlay the Tragedy's appeal in its own time.

# NOTES

## INTRODUCTION

1. See Michael Sappol, *A Traffic of Dead Bodies: Anatomy and Embodied Social Identity in Nineteenth-Century America* (Princeton, 2002); see also, for a more general discussion, Roy Porter, *Flesh in the Age of Reason* (New York: 2004).

2. The most comprehensive collection of documents is Loren J. Kallsen, ed., *The Kentucky Tragedy: A Problem in Romantic Attitudes* (Indianapolis, 1963). Other valuable collections include Robert D. Bamberg, ed., *The Confession of Jereboam O. Beauchamp* (Philadelphia, 1966), and Jules Zanger, ed., *The Beauchamp Tragedy* (Philadelphia, 1963).

3. See L. F. Johnson, *Famous Kentucky Tragedies and Trials: A Collection of Important and Interesting Tragedies and Criminal Trials which Have Taken Place in Kentucky* (Louisville, 1916), 44–57; J. Winston Coleman Jr., *The Beauchamp-Sharp Tragedy: An Episode of Kentucky History During the Middle 1820's* (Frankfort, 1950); and, especially, the works of J. W. Cooke: "The Life and Death of Colonel Solomon P. Sharp, Part I: Uprightness and Inventions; Snares and Nets," *Filson Club Historical Quarterly* 72 (1998): 24–41; "Portrait of a Murderess: Anna Cook(e) Beauchamp," *Filson Club Historical Quarterly* 65 (1991): 209–30; and "Pride and Depravity: A Preliminary Reexamination of the Beauchamp-Sharp Affair," *Border States* 6 (1987): 1–12.

4. See Bertram Wyatt-Brown, *Southern Honor: Ethics and Behavior in the Old South* (New York, 1982), 306–7.

5. Willard Rouse Jillson, "The Beauchamp-Sharp Tragedy in American Literature," *Register of the Kentucky State Historical Society* 36 (1938): 54–60; Jack Edward Surrency, "The Kentucky Tragedy in American Literature: From Thomas Holley Chivers to Robert Penn Warren" (Ph.D. diss., University of Tennessee, Knoxville, 1977). There have been a few twentieth-century adaptations. The most notable is Robert Penn Warren's *World Enough and Time: A Romantic Novel* (1950; reprint, Baton Rouge, 1999).

6. David Brion Davis, *Homicide in American Fiction, 1798–1860: A Study in American Values* (Ithaca, 1957).

7. Important recent studies include Patricia Cline Cohen, *The Murder of Helen Jewett: The Life and Death of a Prostitute in Nineteenth-Century New York* (New York, 1998); Amy Gilman Srebnick, *The Mysterious Death of Mary Rogers: Sex and Culture in Nineteenth-Century New York* (New York, 1995); Andie Tucher, *Froth and Scum: Truth, Beauty, Goodness, and the Ax Murder in America's First Mass Medium* (Chapel Hill, 1994); Karen Halttunen, *Murder Most Foul: The Killer and the American Gothic Imagination* (Cambridge, Mass., 1998); John Brewer, *A Sentimental Murder: Love and Madness in the Eighteenth Century* (New York, 2004); David S. Reynolds, *Beneath the*

*American Renaissance: The Subversive Imagination in the Age of Emerson and Melville* (New York, 1988); and Stephen Kern, *A Cultural History of Causality: Science, Murder Novels, and Systems of Thought* (Princeton, 2004).

8. See Robert Darnton, "It Happened One Night," *New York Review of Books* 51, no. 11 (24 June 2004), 60–64.

9. See, e.g., Cohen, *Murder of Helen Jewett;* Srebnick, *Mysterious Death.*

10. George Miller, *The Epic Hero* (Baltimore, 2000), e.g., 379, 387.

## 1. GREAT GOD!! IT'S HIM!!!

1. This is a composite account based mainly on contemporary newspapers supplemented by secondary works, as noted.

2. Ann Cooke's name has been rendered in a number of ways. The leading expert on her life, J. W. Cooke, for example, renders it Anna Cook while noting the range of variations in his "Portrait of a Murderess: Anna Cook(e) Beauchamp," *Filson Club Historical Quarterly* 65 (1991), 218. I have chosen "Ann Cooke," following many of the major contemporary documents.

3. Peter Cartwright, *Autobiography of Peter Cartwright,* ed. Charles L. Wallis (New York, 1956), 30.

4. See J. W. Cooke, "The Life and Death of Colonel Solomon P. Sharp, Part I: Uprightness and Inventions; Snares and Nets," *Filson Club Historical Quarterly* 72 (1998): 24–41; James A. Ramage, "The Green River Pioneers: Squatters, Soldiers, and Speculators," *Register of the Kentucky Historical Society* 75 (1977): 179.

5. Joan E. Cashin, *A Family Venture: Men and Women on the Southern Frontier* (New York, 1991), 97.

6. Much of this discussion is based on Cooke, "Life and Death of Sharp."

7. Cooke, "Portrait of a Murderess," 210.

8. See Cooke, "Portrait of a Murderess."

9. See J. W. Cooke, "Pride and Depravity: A Preliminary Reexamination of the Beauchamp-Sharp Affair," *Border States* 6 (1987): 1; Jack Edward Surrency, "The Kentucky Tragedy in American Literature: From Thomas Holley Chivers to Robert Penn Warren" (Ph.D. diss., University of Tennessee, Knoxville, 1977), 16.

10. Surrency, "Kentucky Tragedy in American Literature," 16.

11. L. J. Sharp, *Vindication of the Character of the Late Col. Solomon P. Sharp, from the Calumnies Published Against Him Since His Murder, by Patrick Darby and Jefeboam O. Beauchamp* (Frankfort, 1827), 5.

12. Compilation of Beauchamp-Cooke family holdings from Simpson County tax lists, Simpson County Historical Society, Franklin, Ky.

13. Dorothy Donnell Steers, comp., *Simpson County, Kentucky, 1819–1825 Circuit Court Orders* (Franklin, Ky., 1985), 99; Mrs. James Beach Sr. and James Henry Snider, comps., *Franklin and Simpson County: A Picture of Progress, 1819–1975* (Franklin, Ky., 1976), 844.

14. Lewis Collins, *Historical Sketches of Kentucky* (1848; reprint, New York, 1971), 87.

15. Arndt M. Stickles, *The Critical Court Struggle in Kentucky, 1819–1929* (Bloom-

ington, 1929), 16–17; Matthew Gerard Schoenbechler, "The Origins of Jacksonian Politics: Central Kentucky, 1790–1840" (Ph.D. diss., University of Kentucky, 1996), 125.

16. Stickles, *Critical Court Struggle,* 25–26; Schoenbechler, "Origins of Jacksonian Politics," 151–52; Sandra Frances VanBurkleo, "'That Our Pure Republican Principles Might Not Wither': Kentucky's Relief Crisis and the Pursuit of 'Moral Justice,' 1818–1826" (Ph.D. diss., University of Minnesota, 1988), 4.

17. Schoenbechler, "Origins of Jacksonian Politics," 197–98.

18. Stickles, *Critical Court Struggle,* 68–69.

19. Collins, *Historical Sketches,* 92.

20. *Argus of Western America,* 30 November 1825 (hereafter cited as *Argus*).

21. Sharp, *Vindication,* 41–43; *Argus,* 30 November 1825.

22. Albert D. Kirwan, *John J. Crittenden: The Struggle for Union* (Lexington, 1962), 59.

23. Again, this is a composite account. But it draws heavily on the *Kentucky Reporter,* 14 November 1825; see also Jules Zanger, ed., *The Beauchamp Tragedy* (Philadelphia, 1963), 3–5.

24. *Kentucky Reporter,* 14 November 1825.

25. *Argus,* 16 November 1825.

26. J. Winston Coleman Jr., *The Beauchamp-Sharp Tragedy: An Episode of Kentucky History During the Middle 1820's* (Frankfort, 1950), 18.

27. F. Garvin Davenport, *Ante-Bellum Kentucky: A Social History, 1800–1860* (1943; reprint, Westport, Conn., 1983), 145.

28. Coleman, *Beauchamp-Sharp Tragedy,* 23; Lucius P. Little, *Ben Hardin: His Times and Contemporaries, with Selections from His Speeches* (Louisville, 1887), 140.

29. Coleman, *Beauchamp-Sharp Tragedy,* 22–23.

30. *Kentucky Reporter,* 21 November 1825; 5 December 1825; 19 December 1825; Orval W. Baylor, *John Pope, Kentuckian: His Life and Times, 1770–1845* (Cynthiana, Ky., 1943), 222; Loren J. Kallsen, ed., *The Kentucky Tragedy: A Problem in Romantic Attitudes* (Indianapolis, 1963), 167.

31. Baylor, *John Pope,* 223; *National Intelligencer,* 30 December 1825.

32. Franklin County Circuit Court Records, Case File #399 (*Commonwealth v. Jereboam O. Beauchamp,* 1826), Kentucky Department for Libraries and Archives, Frankfort; *Argus,* 22 February 1826; Willard Rouse Jillson, "Franklin County, 1820–1830," *Register of the Kentucky State Historical Society* 7 (1909): 52.

33. The letters are reprinted in Robert D. Bamberg, ed., *The Confession of Jereboam O. Beauchamp* (Philadelphia, 1966), 144.

34. Kallsen, ed., *Kentucky Tragedy,* 97–99.

35. Robert M. Ireland, "Homicide in Nineteenth Century Kentucky," *Register of the Kentucky Historical Society* 81 (1983): 134–53.

36. *Argus,* 9 November 1825.

37. Jeanette H. McCarthy, "The Strange Case of Isaac Desha," *Register of the Kentucky Historical Society* 60 (1962): 293–303.

38. This account is based on Donald B. Cole, *A Jackson Man: Amos Kendall and the Rise of American Democracy* (Baton Rouge, 2004), chapters 5–7 passim.

39. Surrency, "Kentucky Tragedy in American Literature," 25–26; Robert V.

Remini, *Andrew Jackson and the Course of American Freedom, 1822–1832* (New York, 1981), 47; Andrew Jackson, *Correspondence of Andrew Jackson,* ed. John Spencer Bassett, 7 vols. (1926–1933; reprint, New York, 1969), 3:198.

40. Surrency, "Kentucky Tragedy in American Literature," 26.

41. Andrew Jackson to Arthur Campbell, 12 July 1826, Arthur Lee Campbell papers, Filson Historical Society, Louisville, Ky.

42. Cooke, "Pride and Depravity," 4.

43. *Argus,* 24 August 1826.

44. *Spirit of '76,* 21 April 1826.

45. *Argus,* 22 February 1826.

46. Cole, *A Jackson Man,* 72, 98.

47. Baylor, *John Pope,* 222.

48. *Patriot,* 27 March 1826.

49. I have used the trial report reprinted in Kallsen, ed., *Kentucky Tragedy,* 166–320. Subsequent references are in parentheses in the text.

50. Baylor, *John Pope,* 230.

51. *Kentucky Reporter,* 22 May 1826.

52. Baylor, *John Pope,* 234–35.

53. Ibid., 243–45.

54. In Joseph Desha papers, Kentucky Department for Libraries and Archives, Public Records Division, Frankfort.

55. Sharp, *Vindication,* 106–7.

56. John Wilson Townsend, ed., *American Imprints Inventory,* No. 25, *Supplemental Check List of Kentucky Imprints, 1788–1820* (Louisville, 1942), 133; Coleman, *Beauchamp-Sharp Tragedy,* 40–41.

57. See Bamberg, ed., *Confession,* 15.

58. *Spirit of '76,* 14 July 1826.

59. *Patriot,* 19 June 1826.

60. *Argus,* 12 July 1826.

61. Ibid.

62. Fred M. Johnson, "New Light on Beauchamp's *Confession*?" *Border States* 9 (1987), 16.

63. Joseph R. Underwood, "To the Public" (n.p., [1838]), 8.

64. The document finally appeared as *The Confession of Jereboam O. Beauchamp. Who Was Executed at Frankfort, Ky on the 7th of July, 1826. For the Murder of Col. Solomon P. Sharp, a member of the Legislature, and late Attorney General of Ky. Written by Himself, and containing the only authentic account of the murder, and of the causes which induced it* (Bloomfield, Ky., 1826). For reasons of accessibility, I have used and cited the reprinting in Kallsen, ed., *Kentucky Tragedy,* 2–109. Subsequent references are in parentheses in the text.

65. The manuscript version is entitled "The Confession of Jereboam O. Beauchamp, written between May 22 and June 6, 1826, in jail while awaiting execution for the murder of Col. Solomon P. Sharp, a member of the Kentucky legislature and late attorney general of Kentucky," ms. in Jereboam O. Beauchamp papers, Filson Historical Society, Louisville, Ky., no page numbers.

66. See *The Trial of Jereboam O. Beauchamp, for the Murder of Colonel Solomon P. Sharp, Together with the Tragical Death in Prison, by Suicide, of the Wife of Beauchamp, the Once Beautiful and Accomplished Miss Ann Cook, of Bowlinggreen* (New York, 1826), 19.

67. Cooke, "Portrait of a Murderess," 228n.

68. *Kentucky Reporter,* 17 July 1826.

69. *Argus,* 12 July 1826; Kallsen, ed., *Kentucky Tragedy,* 96–97. The grave and badly eroded epitaph may be seen in Bloomfield, Nelson County, Kentucky. The state erected a marker, including a new stone with a clearer engraving of Ann Beauchamp's poem, in 1967.

## 2. NO MORE ROMANTIC TRAGEDY

1. Providence, R.I. *Patriot,* 30 November 1825, 7 June 1826, 22 July 1826.

2. *Niles' Weekly Register,* 29 July 1826.

3. *The Album, and Ladies' Weekly Gazette,* 26 July 1826, 2 August 1826.

4. *The Trial of Jereboam O. Beauchamp, for the Murder of Colonel Solomon P. Sharp, Together with the Tragical Death in Prison, by Suicide, of the Wife of Beauchamp, the Once Beautiful and Accomplished Miss Ann Cook, of Bowlinggreen* (New York, 1826).

5. Henry Clay, *The Papers of Henry Clay,* ed. James F. Hopkins et al., 10 vols. (Lexington, 1959–1992), 5:537.

6. *Album, and Ladies' Weekly Gazette,* 30 August 1826.

7. Donald B. Cole, *A Jackson Man: Amos Kendall and the Rise of American Democracy* (Baton Rouge, 2004), 93.

8. J. Winston Coleman Jr., *The Beauchamp-Sharp Tragedy: An Episode of Kentucky History During the Middle 1820's* (Frankfort, 1950), 68; L. F. Johnson, *Famous Kentucky Tragedies: A Collection of Important and Interesting Tragedies and Criminal Trials which Have Taken Place in Kentucky* (Louisville, 1916), 65.

9. L. F. Johnson, *Famous Kentucky Tragedies,* 60, 65.

10. *Washington Globe,* 13 January 1838; Joseph R. Underwood, "To the Public" (n.p., [1838]).

11. In *Trial of Jereboam O. Beauchamp,* 18.

12. *Spirit of '76,* 4 August 1826.

13. Ibid., 30 June 1826.

14. John Brown to Orlando Brown, 22 August 1826, Orlando Brown papers, Filson Historical Society, Louisville, Ky.

15. *Argus,* 20 June 1827.

16. Orval W. Baylor, *John Pope, Kentuckian: His Life and Times, 1770–1845* (Cynthiana, Ky., 1943), 249–50; L. J. Sharp, *Vindication of the Character of the Late Col. Solomon P. Sharp, from the Calumnies Published Against Him Since His Murder, by Patrick Darby and Jereboam O. Beauchamp* (Frankfort, 1827), 139.

17. *Argus,* 12 March 1828; see John Wilson Townsend, *Kentuckians in History and Literature* (New York, 1907), 77–78.

18. Woodford County Circuit Court Records, Civil Order Books, Order Book N,

pp. 273, 348, Kentucky Department for Libraries and Archives, Public Records Division, Frankfort.

19. *Kentucky Gazette,* 25 December 1829.

20. *Kentucky Reporter,* 12 January 1827.

21. Fred M. Johnson, "New Light on Beauchamp's *Confession*?" *Border States* 9 (1993): 17–20.

22. Simpson County Circuit Court Records, files 260-1827, 292-1827, Simpson County Archives, Franklin, Ky.; Dorothy Donnell Steers, comp., *Simpson County, Kentucky 1826–1831 Circuit Court Orders and 1826 Tax List* (Franklin, Ky., 1990), 74.

23. *Argus,* 29 March 1826.

24. *Niles' Weekly Register,* 26 August 1826.

25. Coleman, *Beauchamp-Sharp Tragedy,* 44.

26. Sharp, *Vindication,* 3; subsequent page references appear in parentheses in the text.

27. Loren J. Kallsen, ed., *The Kentucky Tragedy: A Problem in Romantic Attitudes* (Indianapolis, 1963), viii.

28. Compilation of Beauchamp-Cooke family holdings from Simpson County tax lists, Simpson County Historical Society, Franklin, Ky.

29. F. Johnson, "New Light," 21.

30. *Spirit of '76,* 21 April 1826; *Argus,* 17 May 1828.

31. Woodford County Circuit Court Records, case #569.

32. J. W. Cooke, "Portrait of a Murderess: Anna Cook(e) Beauchamp," *Filson Club Historical Quarterly* 65 (1991): 21; Sharp, *Vindication,* 82.

33. *Niles' Weekly Register,* 29 July 1826.

34. Dorothy Donnell Steers, comp., *Simpson County, Kentucky, 1819–1825 Circuit Court Orders* (Franklin, Ky., 1985), 116, 127.

35. Sharp, *Vindication,* 24–25; Coleman, *Beauchamp-Sharp Tragedy,* 3.

36. J. W. Cooke, "Portrait of a Murderess," 228n.

37. Kallsen, ed., *Kentucky Tragedy* 14.

38. *Spirit of '76,* 21 April 1826, quoting *Argus,* 29 June 1825.

39. Clay, *Papers,* 5:586.

40. West Hill Jr., *The Theater in Early Kentucky, 1790–1820* (Lexington, 1971), 102.

41. George Lillo, *The London Merchant; or, the History of George Barnwell* (London, U.K., 1948).

42. *Argus,* 21 August 1826; *Album, and Ladies' Weekly Gazette,* 1 November 1826.

43. *Album, and Ladies' Weekly Gazette,* 23 August 1826.

44. E. C. Perrow, "Songs and Rhymes from the South," *Journal of American Folklore* 28 (1915): 168; G. Malcolm Laws Jr., *Native American Balladry: A Descriptive Study and a Bibliographical Syllabus,* rev. ed. (Philadelphia, 1964), 257, 268.

45. Leonard Roberts, "Beauchamp and Sharp: A Kentucky Tragedy," *Kentucky Folklore Record* 14 (1968): 14–19.

46. Herbert Ross Brown, *The Sentimental Novel in America, 1789–1860* (1940; reprint, New York, 1959), 155.

47. Kallsen, ed., *Kentucky Tragedy,* 8.

48. Susanna Haswell Rowson, *Charlotte: A Tale of Truth,* 2 vols. (Philadelphia, 1794), 2:134.

49. Kallsen, ed., *Kentucky Tragedy,* 7, 11.

50. Samuel Relf, *Infidelity; or, the Victims of Sentiment. A Novel, in a Series of Letters* (Philadelphia, 1797), 189.

51. "History of Auretta; or, the Fatal Effects of Impatience," *Gentleman and Lady's Town and Country Magazine* 1 (1784): 57.

52. William Hill Brown, *The Power of Sympathy; or, the Triumph of Nature. Founded on Truth,* 2 vols. (Boston, 1789), 2:158.

53. Kallsen, ed., *Kentucky Tragedy,* 109.

54. Willard Rouse Jillson, "The Beauchamp-Sharp Tragedy in American Literature," *Register of the Kentucky State Historical Society* 36 (1938): 58.

55. Fred M. Johnson, "Letters of Ann Cook: Fact or Factoid?" *Border States* 6 (1987): 13–14, 20–21; Jack E. Surrency, "The Kentucky Tragedy and Its Primary Sources," in *No Fairer Land: Studies in Southern Literature Before 1900,* ed. J. Lasley Dameron and James W. Mathews (Troy, N.Y., 1986), 118; Mary L. Rion, "Civilization on the Frontier: Literary Activity in Kentucky before 1830" (Ph.D. diss., Johns Hopkins University, 1957), 431.

56. The volume is reprinted in Kallsen, ed., *Kentucky Tragedy,* 112–63; quotations from 113–14.

57. Kallsen, ed., *Kentucky Tragedy,* 141.

58. See David S. Reynolds, *Beneath the American Renaissance: The Subversive Imagination in the Age of Emerson and Melville* (New York, 1988); Karen Halttunen, *Murder Most Foul: The Killer and the American Gothic Imagination* (Cambridge, Mass., 1998); Daniel A. Cohen, *Pillars of Salt and Monuments of Grace: New England Crime Literature and the Origins of American Popular Culture, 1674–1860* (New York, 1993); and Patricia Cline Cohen, *The Murder of Helen Jewett: The Life and Death of a Prostitute in Nineteenth-Century New York* (New York, 1998), for major discussions of the genre and its popularity.

59. Reynolds, *Beneath the American Renaissance,* e.g. 91.

60. *Trial of Jereboam O. Beauchamp,* 4.

61. Ibid., 36.

62. Ibid., 37–38.

63. Henry St. Clair, *The United States Criminal Calendar: or, An Awful Warning to the Youth of America; Being an Account of the Most Horrid Murders, Piraces* [*sic*], *Highway Robberies, &c. &c.* (Boston, 1833), v.

64. Ibid., 285.

65. Ibid., 289.

66. Ibid., 308.

67. *A Full and Complete Account of the Heberton Tragedy: To Which Is Added Beauchamp, or the Kentucky Tragedy* (New York, 1843), 47.

68. Ibid., 48.

69. *The Life of Jereboam O. Beauchamp, Who Was Hung at Frankfort, Kentucky, for the Murder of Col. Solomon P. Sharp* (Frankfort, 1850), 28, emphasis added.

70. For a similar example, see John Brewer, *A Sentimental Murder: Love and Madness in the Eighteenth Century* (New York, 2004), esp. 205.

71. *The Beauchamp Tragedy in Kentucky, as Detailed in the Confession of Jereboam O. Beauchamp; to which is added a Biographical Sketch of Col. Solomon P. Sharp, and*

*a Historical Account of the Old Court and New Court Party Controversy, etc.* (New York, 1858), v.

72. Located in the Houghton Library at Harvard University, and catalogued under its title, it may be the play on the affair initially entitled *The Tragedy of Beauchamp, or the Noble Heroine* that was registered for copyright by Kentuckian William G. Dryden in 1830. Dryden's play has not otherwise been found. See John Wilson Townsend, ed., *American Imprints Inventory,* No. 25, *Supplemental Check List of Kentucky Imprints, 1788–1820* (Louisville, 1942), 139; Rion, "Civilization," 485n.

73. *Beauchamp, or the Murder of Col. Sharp. A Drama in Five Acts. Founded Upon the Real Tragic Events and Facts, which Transpired in Kentucky, Some Seven Years Since* (n.p., 1833), title page.

74. Ibid., 34.

75. Ibid., 36, handwritten marginal note.

76. S. Foster Damon, *Thomas Holley Chivers, Friend of Poe, With Selections from His Poems: A Strange Chapter in American Literary History* (New York, 1930), 35–36.

77. Charles M. Lombard, introduction to *Conrad and Eudora (1834) and Birth-Day Song of Liberty (1856), by Thomas Holley Chivers* (Delmar, N.Y., 1978), viii.

78. Thomas Holley Chivers, "Leoni," in *The Unpublished Plays of Thomas Holley Chivers,* ed. Charles M. Lombard (Delmar, N.Y., 1980).

79. Thomas Holley Chivers, *The Complete Works of Thomas Holley Chivers,* ed. Emma Lester Chase and Lois Ferry Parks (Providence, 1957), 1, 15, 75.

80. Arthur Hobson Quinn, *A History of the American Drama from the Beginning to the Civil War,* 2nd ed. (New York, 1951), 259.

81. Edgar Allan Poe, *Politian: An Unfinished Tragedy,* ed. Thomas Olive Mabbott (Menasha, Wisc., 1923), 41, 52.

82. Eugene D. Genovese, "The Chivalric Tradition in the Old South," *Sewanee Review* 108 (2000): 191.

83. Poe, *Politian,* ed. Mabbott, 80.

84. Jack Edward Surrency, "The Kentucky Tragedy in American Literature: From Thomas Holley Chivers to Robert Penn Warren" (Ph.D. diss., University of Tennessee, Knoxville, 1977), 122; Delmer Davis, "Barnes, Charlotte Mary Sanford," in *American National Biography,* ed. John A. Garraty and Mark C. Carnes, 24 vols. (New York, 1999), 2:187.

85. Quinn, *History of the American Drama,* 260.

86. Charlotte M. S. Barnes, "Octavia Bragaldi," in Barnes, *Plays, Prose and Poetry* (Philadelphia, 1848), iv.

87. *Dictionary of American Biography,* 10 vols. (New York, 1930–1936), vol. 6, pt. 2: pp. 142–43; Frank Luther Mott, *A History of American Magazines, 1741–1850* (Cambridge, Mass., 1930), 580n.

88. Mary E. MacMichael, "The Kentucky Tragedy," *Burton's Gentleman's Magazine* 2 (1838): 267.

89. Ibid., 271.

90. William Gilmore Simms, *Beauchampe, or the Kentucky Tragedy: A Tale of Passion,* 2 vols. (Philadelphia, 1842), 1:vii.

91. See W. B. Gates, "William Gilmore Simms and the Kentucky Tragedy," *American Literature* 32 (1960): 158.

92. William Gilmore Simms, *Beauchampe; or, The Kentucky Tragedy. A Sequel to Charlemont*, new and rev. ed. (1856; reprint, Chicago, 1890), 400.

93. [Edgar Allan Poe], Review of *Beauchampe, or the Kentucky Tragedy*, in *Graham's Magazine* 20 (1842), 157.

94. Edgar Allan Poe, "The Literati of New York, No. VI," *Godey's Lady's Book* 33 (1846), 157. The magazine's title varied over the years. I have silently standardized it, as cited here, for clarity.

95. *Godey's Lady's Book* 24 (1842), 288.

96. David Grimsted, *Melodrama Unveiled: American Theater and Culture, 1800–1850* (1968; reprint, Berkeley, 1987), 37.

97. John Savage, *Sybil: A Tragedy in Five Acts* (New York, 1865), 6–7, 98–100.

98. *Louisville Daily Courier*, 8 October 1858.

99. Ibid., 11 October 1858.

100. Ibid., 25 October 1858.

101. Savage, *Sybil*, 85.

102. Ibid., 98.

## 3. THOU ART HALF TO BLAME

1. For a good overview, see Isabelle Lehuu, *Carnival on the Page: Popular Print Media in Antebellum America* (Chapel Hill, 2000).

2. Ronald J. Zboray, *A Fictive People: Antebellum Economic Development and the American Reading Public* (New York, 1991), 133–34.

3. David S. Reynolds, *Beneath the American Renaissance: The Subversive Imagination in the Age of Emerson and Melville* (New York, 1988), 3–10; Lawrence W. Levine, *Highbrow/Lowbrow: The Emergence of Cultural Hierarchy in America* (Cambridge, Mass., 1988), 24–25, 30.

4. Michael T. Gilmore, "The Book Marketplace I," in *The Columbia History of the American Novel*, ed. Emory Elliott (New York, 1991), 55.

5. See Michael O'Brien, *Conjectures of Order: Intellectual Life and the American South, 1810–1860*, 2 vols. (Chapel Hill, 2004), 1:499–501; Jonathan Daniel Wells, *The Origins of the Southern Middle Class, 1800–1861* (Chapel Hill, 2004), 45–49.

6. Charles Fenno Hoffman, *Greyslaer: A Romance of the Mohawk*, 2 vols. (New York, 1840).

7. Edgar Allan Poe, "The Literati of New York, No. VI," *Godey's Lady's Book* 33 (1846), 157.

8. Homer F. Barnes, in *Charles Fenno Hoffman* (1930; reprint, New York, 1966), 124, minimizes the influence of the Kentucky Tragedy; but see Jack E. Surrency, "The Kentucky Tragedy in American Literature: From Thomas Holley Chivers to Robert Penn Warren" (Ph.D. diss., University of Tennessee, Knoxville, 1977), 131–32, for the opposite view.

9. Charles Fenno Hoffman, *A Winter in the West. By a New Yorker*, 2 vols. (New York, 1835), 2:161.

10. John Richardson, *Matilda Montgomerie; or, The Prophecy Fulfilled: A Tale of the Late American War* (New York, 1851).

11. John Richardson, *The Canadian Brothers; or, The Prophecy Fulfilled: A Tale of

*the Late American War,* 2 vols. (1840; reprint, Toronto, 1976), 2:175–76. I have chosen to cite and quote from the earlier Canadian version of Richardson's novel because it is both more accessible and more legible than the U.S. edition. However, the cited passages appear in both.

12. Klinck, introduction to Richardson, *Canadian Brothers,* xvi–xvii; Surrency, "Kentucky Tragedy in American Literature," 8n.

13. Henry Wadsworth Longfellow, *The Spanish Student,* in *The Poetical Works of Henry Wadsworth Longfellow,* 6 vols. (New York, 1966), 1:99–184.

14. Edgar Allan Poe, *Essays and Reviews,* ed. G. R. Thompson (New York, 1984), 751–55; see also Kenneth Silverman, *Edgar A. Poe: Mournful and Never-Ending Remembrance* (New York, 1991), 252.

15. Julia Ward Howe, *The World's Own* (Boston, 1857).

16. *The Beauchamp Tragedy in Kentucky, as Detailed in the Confession of Jereboam O. Beauchamp; to which is added a Biographical Sketch of Col. Solomon P. Sharp, and a Historical Account of the Old Court and New Court Party Controversy, etc.* (New York, 1858), iii.

17. William Goldhurst, "The New Revenge Tragedy: Comparative Treatments of the Beauchamp Case," *Southern Literary Journal* 22 (1989): 117–27; Robert D. Bamberg, *The Confession of Jereboam O. Beauchamp* (Philadelphia, 1966), 13–14.

18. L. J. Sharp, *Vindication of the Character of the Late Col. Solomon P. Sharp, from the Calumnies Published Against Him Since His Murder, by Patrick Darby and Jereboam O. Beauchamp* (Frankfort, 1827), 12, 13.

19. Mary Wollstonecraft, *A Vindication of the Rights of Woman,* 2nd ed. (New York, 1996), 61.

20. See G. J. Barker-Benfield, *The Culture of Sensibility: Sex and Society in Eighteenth-Century Britain* (Chicago, 1992), 312; Mark S. Phillips, *Society and Sentiment: Genres of Historical Writing in Britain, 1740–1820* (Princeton, 2000), 117; Kate Flint, *The Woman Reader, 1837–1914* (Oxford, Eng., 1993), 22–23.

21. Francis Wayland, *The Elements of Moral Science,* ed. Joseph L. Blau (Cambridge, Mass., 1963), 241.

22. [Francis Jenks], "National Literature," *Christian Examiner* 7 (1830), 278, 279; Catherine Kerrison, "The Novel as Teacher: Learning to Be Female in the Early American South," *Journal of Southern History* 69 (2003): 522; Richard L. Bushman, *The Refinement of America: Persons, Houses, Cities* (New York, 1992), 280, 286–87.

23. *North Star,* 28 April 1848; see Nina Baym, *Novels, Readers, and Reviewers: Responses to Fiction in Antebellum America* (Ithaca, 1984), 36–37.

24. "Fiction: A Dialogue," *Lowell Offering* 2 (1842), 251, 255, 261.

25. William P. Trent, *William Gilmore Simms* (1892; reprint, New York, 1968), 118.

26. William Gilmore Simms, *Beauchampe, or the Kentucky Tragedy,* 2 vols. (Philadelphia, 1842), 1:viii; see on this issue John Brewer, *A Sentimental Murder: Love and Madness in the Eighteenth Century* (New York, 2004), 172, 176.

27. William Gilmore Simms, *Charlemont* (Boston, n.d.), 97, 98.

28. *Godey's Lady's Book* 24 (1842), 288.

29. *Beauchamp, or the Murder of Col. Sharp. A Drama in Five Acts. Founded Upon*

*the Real Tragic Events and Facts, Which Transpired in Kentucky, Some Seven Years Hence* (n.p., 1833), 5, 11.

30. Loren J. Kallsen, ed., *The Kentucky Tragedy: A Problem in Romantic Attitudes* (Indianapolis, 1963), 120.

31. Kallsen, ed., *Kentucky Tragedy,* 155.

32. Sharp, *Vindication,* 12.

33. Edgar Allan Poe, *Politian: An Unfinished Tragedy,* ed. Thomas Olive Mabbott (Menasha, Wisc., 1923), 13.

34. Simms, *Charlemont,* 69.

35. Ibid., 84.

36. See, e.g., Lehuu, *Carnival on the Page,* 29; Mary Kelley, *Private Woman, Public Stage: Literary Domesticity in Nineteenth-Century America* (New York, 1984), 403; W. Gilmore, *Reading Becomes a Necessity,* 114.

37. Kerrison, "Novel as Teacher," 541.

38. Mary Kelley, *Private Woman,* 401, 415; Catherine E. Kelly, *In the New England Fashion: Reshaping Women's Lives in the Nineteenth Century* (Ithaca, 1999), 148.

39. *A Full and Complete Account of the Heberton Tragedy: To Which Is Added Beauchamp, or the Kentucky Tragedy* (New York, 1843), 48; *Life of Jereboam O. Beauchamp,* 6.

40. *Godey's Lady's Book* 14 (1837), 193.

41. *The Beauchamp Tragedy in Kentucky,* v.

42. Samuel Richardson, *Clarissa; or, The History of a Young Lady,* ed. Angus Ross (New York, 1985), 418.

43. Thomas Holley Chivers, *Conrad and Eudora; or, The Death of Alonzo. A Tragedy in Five Acts, Founded on the Murder of Sharpe, by Beauchamp, in Kentucky* (1834; reprint, Delmar, N.Y., 1978), 9.

44. William Gilmore Simms, *Beauchampe; or, The Kentucky Tragedy. A Sequel to Charlemont,* new and rev. ed. (1856; reprint, Chicago, 1890), 48.

45. Chivers, *Conrad,* 25; see Patricia Cline Cohen, *The Murder of Helen Jewett: The Life and Death of a Prostitute in Nineteenth-Century New York* (New York, 1998), 57.

46. S. Foster Damon, *Thomas Holley Chivers, Friend of Poe, With Selections from His Poems: A Strange Chapter in American Literary History* (New York, 1930), 75.

47. *A Full and Complete Account,* 23.

48. "The Sorrows of Amelia; or, Deluded Innocence—Founded on Fact," *Baltimore Weekly Magazine* (5 July 1800), 87; the story was reprinted in the *Ladies Museum* 1 (1825), 62–63, appearing at about the time of the Tragedy.

49. Mary E. MacMichael, "The Kentucky Tragedy," *Burton's Gentleman's Magazine* 2 (1838), 265.

50. R. F. Brissenden, *Virtue in Distress: Studies in the Novel of Sentiment from Richardson to Sade* (New York, 1974), 94; Barker-Benfield, *Culture of Sensibility,* 344–45.

51. Thomas Laquer, *Making Sex: Body and Gender from the Greeks to Freud* (Cambridge, Mass., 1990), 148; Nancy M. Theriot, *Mothers and Daughters in Nineteenth-Century America* (Lexington, 1996), 44; Nancy Cott, *Bonds of Womanhood: "Woman's Sphere" in New England, 1780–1835* (New Haven, 1977), 21.

52. "Feminology," *Godey's Lady's Book* 48 (1854), 273.

53. [Caleb Cushing], "The Social Condition of Women," *North American Review* 91 (1836): 513.

54. Catherine E. Kelly, *New England Fashion,* 156.

55. "Influence of Woman—Past and Present," *Ladies' Companion* 13 (1840), 245–46.

56. Nancy Isenberg, *Sex and Citizenship in Antebellum America* (Chapel Hill, 1998), 120.

57. Simms, *Charlemont,* 303.

58. Ibid., 318.

59. In Elizabeth Cady Stanton, Susan B. Anthony, and Matilda Joslyn Gage, *History of Woman Suffrage,* 3 vols. (1881–1886; reprint, New York, 1969), 1:75.

60. In Stanton et al., *History of Woman Suffrage,* 1:106.

61. Unknown to Joseph Desha, 2 July 1826, Joseph Desha papers, Kentucky Department for Libraries and Archives, Public Records Division, Frankfort.

62. Sarah Grimké, *Letters on the Equality of the Sexes and Other Essays,* ed. Elizabeth Ann Bartlett (New Haven, 1988), 87–88.

63. Kallsen, ed., *Kentucky Tragedy,* 11.

64. Chivers, *Conrad,* 24.

65. John Savage, *Sybil: A Tragedy in Five Acts* (New York, 1865), 27.

66. Kallsen, ed., *Kentucky Tragedy,* 159.

67. Chivers, *Conrad,* 26, 27.

68. See David Brion Davis, *Homicide in American Fiction, 1798–1860: A Study in Social Values* (Ithaca, 1957), 202.

69. Jan Lewis, "The Republican Wife: Virtue and Seduction in the Early Republic," *William and Mary Quarterly* 44 (1987): 689.

70. Vindex Veritatis, "Importance of Home Education," *Southern Ladies' Book* 2 (1840), 2.

71. Andrew Burstein, *Sentimental Democracy: The Evolution of America's Romantic Self-Image* (New York, 1999), 321.

72. Daniel Webster, "Influence of Woman," *Godey's Lady's Book* 44 (1852), 90.

73. "Fiction," 255.

74. "Feminology," 273.

75. *The Beauchamp Tragedy in Kentucky,* v, vi.

76. Patricia Cline Cohen, *Murder of Helen Jewett,* 184.

77. Elizabeth Barnes, *States of Sympathy: Seduction and Democracy in the American Novel* (New York, 1997), 103.

78. "Sporting with Female Affection," *Godey's Lady's Book* 2 (1831), 26.

79. Mary E. MacMichael, "A Chapter from My Old Diary," *Godey's Lady's Book* 12 (1836), 232.

80. Kallsen, ed., *Kentucky Tragedy,* 3.

81. There are many sources for an understanding of Southern honor. Among the most important are Kenneth Greenberg, *Honor and Slavery* (Princeton, 1996), and Bertram Wyatt-Brown, *Southern Honor: Ethics and Behavior in the Old South* (New York, 1982).

82. See Wyatt-Brown, *Southern Honor,* part 2.

83. Chivers, *Conrad,* 29.

84. Charlotte M. S. Barnes, "Octavia Bragaldi," in Barnes, *Plays, Prose and Poetry* (Philadelphia, 1848), 5.

85. Savage, *Sybil,* 82.

86. For useful summaries, see, e.g., David T. Courtwright, *Violent Land: Single Men and Social Disorder from the Frontier to the Inner City* (Cambridge, Mass., 1996), 10, 16–17; Leo Braudy, *From Chivalry to Terrorism: War and the Changing Nature of Masculinity* (New York, 2003), 11–12; and Eric H. Monkkonen, *Murder in New York City* (Berkeley, 2001), 58–59.

87. See Eugene D. Genovese, "The Chivalric Tradition in the Old South," *Sewanee Review* 108 (2000): 196; Braudy, *From Chivalry to Terrorism,* 203.

88. Chivers, *Conrad,* 24.

89. J. W. Cooke, "Portrait of a Murderess: Anna Cook(e) Beauchamp," *Filson Club Historical Quarterly* 65 (1991): 229–30.

90. Wyatt-Brown, *Southern Honor,* 33.

91. Chivers, *Conrad,* 59.

92. See, e.g., Dick Steward, *Duels and the Roots of Violence in Missouri* (Columbia, Mo., 2000), 37.

93. John Richardson, *Canadian Brothers,* 2:166.

94. Ibid.

95. "Woman," *Godey's Lady's Book* 4 (1832), 39; see Brewer, *Sentimental Murder,* 56; E. Anthony Rotundo, *American Manhood: Transformations in Masculinity from the Revolution to the Modern Era* (New York, 1993), 104–5.

96. William Gilmore Simms, *Charlemont* (Boston, n.d.), 312.

97. Rotundo, *American Manhood,* 3; David Leverenz, *Manhood and the American Renaissance* (Ithaca, 1989), 85; John Mayfield, "Being Shifty in a New Country: Southern Humor and the Masculine Ideal," in *Southern Manhood: Perspectives on Masculinity in the Old South,* ed. Craig Thompson Friend and Lorri Glover (Athens, Ga., 2004), 113–35.

98. Stephanie McCurry, *Masters of Small Worlds: Yeoman Households, Gender Relations, and the Political Culture of the Antebellum South Carolina Low Country* (New York, 1995), 132–34.

99. Charles Sellers, *The Market Revolution: Jacksonian America, 1815–46* (New York, 1991), 245–46.

100. Leverenz, *Manhood,* 5, 60.

101. Simms, *Beauchampe* (1856 ed.), 321.

102. Michel Chevalier, *Society, Manners, and Politics in the United States: Letters on North America,* ed. John William Ward (1961; reprint, Gloucester, Mass., 1967), 299.

103. Leverenz, *Manhood,* 74.

104. Mayfield, "Being Shifty," 115; see also Wells, *Origins,* 203. See also James Oakes, *The Ruling Race: A History of American Slaveholders* (1982; reprint, New York, 1998), 41, 58–65.

105. Karen Halttunen, *Confidence Men and Painted Women: A Study of Middle-Class Culture in America, 1830–1870* (New Haven, 1982), 34.

106. Eliza Leslie, *Miss Leslie's Behavior Book: A Guide and Manual for Young Ladies* (1859; reprint, New York, 1972), 187.

107. Halttunen, *Confidence Men,* 29–30.

108. "But He Is a Gentleman," *Godey's Lady's Book* 10 (1835), 158.

109. Chevalier, *Society,* 299.

## 4. THE MOST CERTAINLY HUMAN OF ALL LAWS

1. "Aunt Sally" to John C. Green, 3 July 1826 [*sic*], Green family papers, Filson Historical Society, Louisville, Ky.

2. George Pullen Jackson, *Spiritual Folk-Songs of Early America: Two Hundred and Fifty Tunes and Texts with an Introduction and Notes* (1937; reprint, New York, 1964), 151.

3. Dickson D. Bruce Jr., *And They All Sang Hallelujah: Plain-Folk Camp-Meeting Religion, 1800–1845* (Knoxville, 1974), 98–99, 113.

4. Dickson D. Bruce Jr., *Violence and Culture in the Antebellum South* (Austin, 1979), 11–12; Bertram Wyatt-Brown, *Southern Honor: Ethics and Behavior in the Old South* (New York, 1982), 27–29.

5. In Bruce, *Violence and Culture,* 70.

6. Ibid., 87–88.

7. Lawrence F. Kohl, *The Politics of Individualism: Parties and the American Character in the Jacksonian Era* (New York, 1989), 21–22.

8. Karen Halttunen, *Confidence Men and Painted Women: A Study of Middle-Class Culture in America, 1830–1870* (New Haven, 1982), 47; Kohl, *Politics of Individualism,* 25.

9. Ann Douglas, *The Feminization of American Culture* (New York, 1977), 124–27.

10. Halttunen, *Confidence Men,* 96.

11. Bruce, *Violence and Culture,* 39–41.

12. Kenneth Greenberg, *Honor and Slavery* (Princeton, 1996), 91.

13. Thomas Holley Chivers, *Conrad and Eudora; or, The Death of Alonzo. A Tragedy in Five Acts, Founded on the Murder of Sharpe, by Beauchamp, in Kentucky* (1834; reprint, Delmar, N.Y., 1978), 76.

14. Charlotte M. S. Barnes, "Octavia Bragaldi," in Barnes, *Plays, Prose and Poetry* (Philadelphia, 1848), 106.

15. Christopher Boehm, *Blood Revenge: The Anthropology of Feuding in Montenegro and Other Tribal Societies* (Lawrence, Kans., 1984), 89, 92, 110; see Bertram Wyatt-Brown, *The Shaping of Southern Culture: Honor, Grace, and War, 1760s–1880s* (Chapel Hill, 2001), 303.

16. Dick Steward, *Duels and the Roots of Violence in Missouri* (Columbia, Mo., 2000), 11.

17. Edward E. Baptist, *Creating an Old South: Middle Florida's Plantation Frontier Before the Civil War* (Chapel Hill, 2002), 107, 109.

18. Bruce, *Violence and Culture,* 36.

19. *The Beauchamp Tragedy in Kentucky, as Detailed in the Confession of Jereboam O. Beauchamp; to which is added a Biographical Sketch of Col. Solomon P. Sharp, and a Historical Account of the Old Court and New Court Party Controversy, etc.* (New York, 1858), ix.

20. William Gilmore Simms, *Beauchampe; or, The Kentucky Tragedy. A Sequel to Charlemont,* new and rev. ed. (1856; reprint, Chicago, 1890), 343.

21. *Beauchamp, or the Murder of Col. Sharp. A Drama in Five Acts. Founded Upon the Real Tragic Events and Facts, which Transpired in Kentucky, Some Seven Years Since* (n.p., 1833), 35.

22. Philip Fisher, *Vehement Passions* (Princeton, 2002), 173.

23. Charlotte M. S. Barnes, "Octavia Bragaldi," xii; see William Charvat, *The Origins of American Critical Thought* (1936; reprint, New York, 1961), 30–31; Nina Baym, *Novels, Readers, and Reviewers: Responses to Fiction in Antebellum America* (Ithaca, 1984), 90–91.

24. *The Beauchamp Tragedy in Kentucky,* iv.

25. Ibid.

26. Cynthia B. Herrup, *A House in Gross Disorder: Sex, Law and the 2nd Earl of Castlehaven* (New York, 1999), 144.

27. See Fisher, *Vehement Passions,* 26.

28. See Isabelle Lehuu, *Carnival on the Page: Popular Print Media in Antebellum America* (Chapel Hill, 2000), 56–57; Karen Halttunen, "Humanitarianism and the Pornography of Pain in Anglo-American Culture," *American Historical Review* 100 (1995): 332.

29. Roger Lane, *Murder in America: A History* (Columbus, Ohio, 1997), 82.

30. See David S. Reynolds, *Beneath the American Renaissance: The Subversive Imagination in the Age of Emerson and Melville* (New York, 1988), e.g., 85–86.

31. Karen Halttunen, *Murder Most Foul: The Killer and the American Gothic Imagination* (Cambridge, Mass., 1998), 34; David Brion Davis, *Homicide in American Fiction, 1798–1860: A Study in Social Values* (Ithaca, 1957), 11, 17.

32. Davis, *Homicide,* 62; Stuart Banner, *The Death Penalty: An American History* (Cambridge, Mass., 2002), 118–19.

33. Merle Curti, *Human Nature in American Thought: A History* (Madison, 1980), 90–91.

34. Stephen Kern, *A Cultural History of Causality: Science, Murder Novels, and Systems of Thought* (Princeton, 2004), 227–30; see also Helen Lefkowitz Horowitz, *Rereading Sex: Battles over Sexual Knowledge and Suppression in Nineteenth-Century America* (New York, 2002), 52.

35. Isaac Ray, *A Treatise on the Medical Jurisprudence of Insanity,* ed. Winfred Overholser (Cambridge, Mass., 1962), 115.

36. Ibid., 139.

37. Benjamin Rush, *Medical Inquiries and Observations,* 4 vols. (Philadelphia, 1815), 1:101–2.

38. Ray, *Treatise on Medical Jurisprudence,* 140.

39. Loren J. Kallsen, ed., *The Kentucky Tragedy: A Problem in Romantic Attitudes* (Indianapolis, 1963), 11.

40. Chivers, *Conrad,* 31.

41. Charlotte M. S. Barnes, "Octavia Bragaldi," 48, 49.

42. Chivers, *Conrad,* 53.

43. Davis, *Homicide,* 45–46.

44. Hendrik Hartog, "Lawyering, Husband's Rights, and 'the Unwritten Law' in Nineteenth-Century America," *Journal of American History* 84 (1997): 83–84.

45. Charlotte M. S. Barnes, "Octavia Bragaldi," 84.

46. Kallsen, ed., *Kentucky Tragedy,* 23.

47. Edgar Allan Poe, *Poetry and Tales,* ed. Patrick F. Quinn (New York, 1984), 555.

48. Bruce, *Violence and Culture,* 214–15; Bertram Wyatt-Brown, *Hearts of Darkness: Wellsprings of a Southern Literary Tradition* (Baton Rouge, 2003), 78–79.

49. William Gilmore Simms, *The Letters of William Gilmore Simms,* ed. Mary C. Simms Oliphant, Alfred Taylor Odell, and T. C. Duncan Eaves, 6 vols. (Columbia, S.C., 1952–1982), 2:225.

50. Mary E. MacMichael, "Woman's Revenge (Founded on Fact)," *Godey's Lady's Book* 12 (1836), 172.

51. Francis Wayland, *The Elements of Moral Science,* ed. Joseph L. Blau (Cambridge, Mass., 1963), 58.

52. Wayland, *Elements of Moral Science,* 95.

53. John Savage, *Sybil: A Tragedy in Five Acts* (New York, 1865), 34.

54. See Lisa Rodensky, *The Crime in Mind: Criminal Responsibility and the Victorian Novel* (New York, 2003), 149; Kern, *Cultural History,* 229–30.

55. Samuel Relf, *Infidelity; or,' the Victims of Sentiment. A Novel, in a Series of Letters* (Philadelphia, 1797), 65.

56. In John S. Hart, *Female Prose Writers of America,* new ed., rev. and enlarged (Philadelphia, 1855), 352.

57. Chivers, *Conrad,* 26.

58. *A Full and Complete Account of the Heberton Tragedy: To Which Is Added Beauchamp, or the Kentucky Tragedy* (New York, 1843), 49.

59. Charlotte M. S. Barnes, "Octavia Bragaldi," 37.

60. Henry St. Clair, *The United States Criminal Calendar: or, An Awful Warning to the Youth of America; Being an Account of the Most Horrid Murders, Piraces* [*sic*], *Highway Robberies, &c. &c.* (Boston, 1833), 289.

61. Charles Fenno Hoffman, *A Winter in the West. By a New Yorker,* 2 vols. (New York, 1835), 2:160.

62. William Gilmore Simms, *Charlemont* (Boston, n.d.), "Advertisement," no pp.

63. Reynolds, *Beneath the American Renaissance,* 448.

64. Bruce, *Violence and Culture,* 232.

65. Charlotte M. S. Barnes, "Octavia Bragaldi," 110.

66. See S. Foster Damon, *Thomas Holley Chivers, Friend of Poe, With Selections from His Poems: A Strange Chapter in American Literary History* (New York, 1930), 76; Charles M. Lombard, introduction to *The Unpublished Plays of Thomas Holley Chivers* (Delmar, N.Y., 1980), xxvi.

67. Charlotte M. S. Barnes, "Octavia Bragaldi," xii.

68. James Simpson, *Necessity of Popular Education, as a National Object; with Hints on the Treatment of Criminals and Observations on Homicidal Insanity* (Boston, 1834), 63.

69. Ibid., 73, 77–78; see Algirdas Julien Greimas and Jacques Fontanille, *The Semiotics of Passions: From States of Affairs to States of Feeling,* trans. Paul Perron and Frank Collins (Minneapolis, 1993), 48–49; Kern, *Cultural History,* 30–31.

70. Ray, *Treatise on Medical Jurisprudence,* 27; Wayland, *Elements of Moral Science,* 22–23.

71. Davis, *Homicide,* 150; see Ann Jessie Van Sant, *Eighteenth-Century Sensibility and the Novel: The Senses in Social Context* (Cambridge, Eng., 1993), 13–14; Roy Porter, *Flesh in the Age of Reason* (New York, 2004).

72. Curti, *Human Nature,* 164–65; Michael Sappol, *A Traffic of Dead Bodies: Anatomy and Embodied Social Identity in Nineteenth-Century America* (Princeton, 2002).

73. Damon, *Thomas Holley Chivers,* 153.

74. Robert Abzug, *Cosmos Crumbling: American Reformers and the Religious Imagination* (New York, 1994), 163–64.

75. Ann Douglas, *Feminization,* 205; Mary Louise Kete, *Sentimental Collaborations: Mourning and Middle-Class Identity in Nineteenth-Century America* (Durham, N.C., 2000), 64.

76. Halttunen, *Murder Most Foul,* 83–84.

77. Poe, *Poetry and Tales,* 842; Bruce, *Violence and Culture,* 238; see Amy Gilman Srebnick, *The Mysterious Death of Mary Rogers: Sex and Culture in Nineteenth-Century New York* (New York, 1995), 75.

78. Bruce Dain, *A Hideous Monster of the Mind: American Racial Theory in the Early Republic* (Cambridge, Mass., 2002), 83.

79. Sarah Grimké, *Letters on the Equality of the Sexes and Other Essays,* ed. Elizabeth Ann Bartlett (New Haven, 1988), 42. See G. J. Barker-Benfield, *The Horrors of the Half-Known Life: Male Attitudes Toward Women and Sexuality in Nineteenth-Century America* (New York, 1976), 83; Thomas Laquer, *Making Sex: Body and Gender from the Greeks to Freud* (Cambridge, Mass., 1990), 5–6, 155.

80. Curti, *Human Nature,* 160.

81. Simms, *Charlemont,* 252.

82. In Barker-Benfield, *Horrors,* 83.

83. See, e.g., Susan Edwards, *Female Sexuality and the Law: A Study of Constructs of Female Sexuality as They Inform Statute and Legal Procedure* (Oxford, Eng., 1981), 24; Laquer, *Making Sex,* 150.

84. Reynolds, *Beneath the American Renaissance,* 217; Horowitz, *Rereading Sex,* 32; see Michel Foucault, *The History of Sexuality,* vol. 1, *An Introduction,* trans. Robert Hurley (1978; reprint, New York, 1979), 35, 69, 71.

85. George Thompson, *Venus in Boston, and Other Tales of Nineteenth-Century City Life,* ed. David S. Reynolds and Kimberly R. Gladman (Amherst, Mass., 2002), 63.

86. Simpson, *Necessity for Popular Education,* 64.

87. Ruth Bloch, "Changing Conceptions of Sexuality and Romance in Eighteenth-Century America," *William and Mary Quarterly,* 60 (2003): 35; Thomas Laquer, *Solitary Sex: A Cultural History of Masturbation* (New York, 2003), 243–45.

88. Henry Home, Lord Kames, *Elements of Criticism, with Analyses, and Translations of Ancient and Foreign Illustrations,* ed. Abraham Mills (New York, 1845), 108.

89. *National Intelligencer,* 24 July 1826.

90. Simpson, *Necessity of Popular Education,* 64.

91. Simms, *Beauchampe* (1856 ed.), 342, italics in original; see Davis, *Homicide,* 42–43.

92. Adam Smith, *The Theory of Moral Sentiments* (1759; reprint, Indianapolis, 1976), 212.

93. Simpson, *Necessity of Popular Education,* 66–68.

94. Ibid., 64–65.

95. Cesare Beccaria, *An Essay on Crimes and Punishments, Translated from the Italian. With a Commentary Attributed to M. de Voltaire* (New York, 1809), 37.

## 5. ONE OBJECT—POWER!

1. Donald B. Cole, *A Jackson Man: Amos Kendall and the Rise of American Democracy* (Baton Rouge, 2004), 2; Edward C. Skeen, *1816: America Rising* (Lexington, 2003), 77.

2. Thomas Todd to Isaac Shelby, 7 June 1825, Isaac Shelby papers, Jacobs collection, Filson Historical Society, Louisville, Ky.

3. George Robertson, *Scrap Book on Law and Politics, Men and Times* (Lexington, 1855), 91.

4. Lucius P. Little, *Ben Hardin: His Times and Contemporaries, with Selections from His Speeches* (Louisville, 1887), 109.

5. *Niles' Weekly Register,* 3 December 1825.

6. Bray Hammond, *Banks and Politics in America from the Revolution to the Civil War* (Princeton, 1957), 283.

7. George Buckner to Thomas Buckner, 4 June 1826, Buckner family papers, Filson Historical Society, Louisville, Ky. On emigration, see Matthew Gerard Schoenbachler, "The Origins of Jacksonian Politics: Central Kentucky, 1790–1840" (Ph.D. diss., University of Kentucky, 1996), 234.

8. *Argus,* 22 March 1826.

9. *Patriot,* 3 April 1826, 22 May 1826.

10. *Spirit of '76,* 7 April 1826, 21 April 1826.

11. *Argus,* 11 January 1826.

12. Loren J. Kallsen, ed., *The Kentucky Tragedy: A Problem in Romantic Attitudes* (Indianapolis, 1963), 168.

13. William H. Hurst to William S. Bodley, 10 May 1825, Bodley-Clark papers, Filson Historical Society, Louisville, Ky.

14. Billie J. Hardin, "Amos Kendall and the 1824 Relief Controversy," *Register of the Kentucky Historical Society* 64 (1966): 203.

15. Robert V. Remini, *Henry Clay: Statesman for the Union* (New York, 1991), 276–77.

16. L. F. Johnson, *Famous Kentucky Tragedies and Trials: A Collection of Important and Interesting Tragedies and Criminal Trials which Have Taken Place in Kentucky* (Louisville, 1916), 38–39.

17. *Genius of Universal Emancipation,* 11 March 1826; *National Intelligencer,* 22 July 1826.

18. Francis Baker, "The Maidens of Mulberry Vale," *American Atheneum* 1 (1825), 34.

19. L. F. Johnson, *Famous Kentucky Tragedies,* 40; Arndt M. Stickles, *The Critical Court Struggle in Kentucky, 1819–1829* (Bloomington, 1929), 74; *Argus,* 27 June 1827; Sandra Frances VanBurkleo, "'That Our Pure Republican Principles Might Not Wither': Kentucky's Relief Crisis and the Pursuit of 'Moral Justice,' 1818–1826" (Ph.D. diss., University of Minnesota, 1988), 73–74.

20. Robt. S. Thomas and Geo. W. Williams, *A Statement of the Trial of Isaac B. Desha; Indicted for the Murder of Francis Baker, Late of Natchez, Mississippi; Held at Cynthiana, Kentucky, before the Hon. George Shannon* (Lexington, 1825), 161.

21. Henry Clay, *The Papers of Henry Clay,* ed. James F. Hopkins et al., 10 vols. (Lexington, 1959–1992), 4:603; Cole, *A Jackson Man,* 90–91.

22. *Spirit of '76,* 17 March 1826.

23. *Argus,* 27 June 1827.

24. *Kentucky Reporter,* 18 November 1828. See Jeannette H. McCarthy, "The Strange Case of Isaac Desha," *Register of the Kentucky Historical Society* 60 (1962): 293–303. It should be noted that the array of sources on the Desha case presents as confusing a picture as that of the Beauchamp-Sharp affair. The foregoing is an effort to provide as trustworthy an account as possible based on these often-conflicting sources.

25. *Spirit of '76,* 17 March 1826.

26. *Patriot,* 22 February 1826.

27. Kallsen, ed., *Kentucky Tragedy,* 48.

28. *Beauchamp, or the Murder of Col. Sharp. A Drama in Five Acts. Founded Upon the Real Tragic Events and Facts, which Transpired in Kentucky, Some Seven Years Since* (n.p., 1833), 21.

29. Thomas Holley Chivers, *Conrad and Eudora; or, The Death of Alonzo. A Tragedy in Five Acts, Founded on the Murder of Sharpe, by Beauchamp, in Kentucky* (1834; reprint, Delmar, N.Y., 1978), 51.

30. William Gilmore Simms, *Beauchampe; or, The Kentucky Tragedy. A Sequel to Charlemont,* new and rev. ed. (1856; reprint, Chicago, 1890), 348.

31. Drew Gilpin Faust, *A Sacred Circle: The Dilemma of the Intellectual in the Old South* (Baltimore, 1977), 105.

32. See Ronald P. Formisano, *The Transformation of Political Culture: Massachusetts Parties, 1790–1840* (New York, 1983), 84; Daniel Walker Howe, *The Political Culture of the American Whigs* (Chicago, 1979), 30; Anne C. Rose, *Voices of the Marketplace: American Thought and Culture, 1830–1860* (New York, 1995), 30.

33. *Patriot,* 20 March 1826.

34. *Spirit of ' 76,* 17 March 1826; see Bertram Wyatt-Brown, *The Shaping of Southern Culture: Honor, Grace, and War, 1760s–1880s* (Chapel Hill, 2001), 64.

35. Cole, *A Jackson Man,* 94, 97–101.

36. See Daniel Walker Howe, *Political Culture,* 51; Michael F. Holt, *The Rise and Fall of the American Whig Party: Jacksonian Politics and the Onset of the Civil War* (New York, 1999), 31; Jonathan Daniel Wells, *The Origins of the Southern Middle Class, 1800–1861* (Chapel Hill, 2004), 161.

37. The phrase is from Thomas W. Gallant, "Honor, Masculinity, and Ritual Knife Fighting in Nineteenth-Century Greece," *American Historical Review* 105 (2000): 375; see Jeffrey L. Pasley, *"The Tyranny of Printers": Newspaper Politics in the Early American Republic* (Charlottesville, 2001), 21.

38. Frederick Grimké, *The Nature and Tendency of Free Institutions,* ed. John William Ward (Cambridge, Mass., 1968), 185.

39. Ibid., 177.

40. In Elizabeth Barnes, *States of Sympathy: Seduction and Democracy in the American Novel* (New York, 1997), 41; see Paul Giles, *Transatlantic Insurrections:*

*British Culture and the Formation of American Literature* (Philadelphia, 2001), 75–76.

41. Kimberly K. Smith, *The Dominion of Voice: Riot, Reason, and Romance in Antebellum Politics* (Lawrence, Kans., 1999), 88.

42. "Political Responsibilities," *American Whig Review* 14 (1851): 366–67.

43. Chivers, *Conrad,* 8.

44. Formisano, *Transformation of Political Culture,* 23; Skeen, *1816,* 77.

45. Joan Wells Coward, *Kentucky in the New Republic: The Process of Constitution Making* (Lexington, 1979), e.g., 165; *Spirit of '76,* 19 May 1826; see Stephen Aron, *How the West Was Lost: The Transformation of Kentucky from Daniel Boone to Henry Clay* (Baltimore, 1996), 90–92. See also Matthew A. Crenson, *The Federal Machine: Beginnings of Bureaucracy in Jacksonian America* (Baltimore, 1975), 44–45.

46. Cole, *A Jackson Man,* 82–83.

47. Charles Sellers, *The Market Revolution: Jacksonian America, 1815–46* (New York, 1991), 63.

48. J. W. Cooke, "Pride and Depravity: A Preliminary Reexamination of the Beauchamp-Sharp Affair," *Border States* 6 (1987): 3; L. J. Sharp, *Vindication of the Character of the Late Col. Solomon P. Sharp, from the Calumnies Published Against Him Since His Murder, by Patrick Darby and Jereboam O. Beauchamp* (Frankfort, 1827), 46.

49. *Beauchamp, or the Murder of Col. Sharp,* 20.

50. John Savage, *Sybil: A Tragedy in Five Acts* (New York, 1865), 50.

51. Daniel Walker Howe, "The Political Psychology of *The Federalist,*" *William and Mary Quarterly* 44 (1987): 503.

52. In Dickson D. Bruce Jr., *The Rhetoric of Conservatism: The Virginia Convention of 1829–30 and the Conservative Tradition in the South* (San Marino, Calif., 1982), 115.

53. Wyatt-Brown, *Shaping of Southern Culture,* 65.

54. Chivers, *Conrad,* 51.

55. William Gilmore Simms, *Charlemont* (Boston, n.d.), 244.

56. Catherine E. Kelly, *In the New England Fashion: Reshaping Women's Lives in the Nineteenth Century* (Ithaca, 1999), 128–29, 145.

57. See Sellers, *Market Revolution,* 364.

58. Charlotte M. S. Barnes, "Octavia Bragaldi," in Barnes, *Plays, Prose and Poetry* (Philadelphia, 1848), 56.

59. Daniel Walker Howe, "Political Psychology," 486; Daniel Walker Howe, *Political Culture,* 28–29.

60. Professor Goodwin, "Civilization: American and European," *American Whig Review* 4 (1846): 29.

61. Horace Bushnell, "American Politics," *American National Preacher* 14 (1840): 196–97.

62. Ibid., 197.

63. Mary E. MacMichael, "Times as They Were, and Times as They Are," *Godey's Lady's Book* 12 (1836), 88.

64. Kallsen, ed., *Kentucky Tragedy,* 22.

65. For a classic statement, see Charles S. Sydnor, "The Southerner and the Laws,"

in *The Pursuit of Southern History: Presidential Addresses of the Southern Historical Association, 1935–1963*, ed. George Brown Tindall (Baton Rouge, 1964), 62–76.

66. Savage, *Sybil*, 95.

67. VanBurkleo, "'That Our Pure Republican Principles,'" 153.

68. Little, *Ben Hardin*, 133.

69. See Martin Van Buren, *Inquiry into the Origin and Course of Political Parties in the United States* (1867; reprint, New York, 1967), 325–27; Lawrence F. Kohl, *The Politics of Individualism: Parties and the American Character in the Jacksonian Era* (New York, 1989), 160–61.

70. Howe, *Political Culture*, 23–24, 34.

71. Kohl, *Politics of Individualism*, 39.

72. Dickson D. Bruce Jr., "Mrs. Henry's 'Solemn Promise' in Historical Perspective," in *In Search of Hannah Crafts: Critical Essays on The Bondwoman's Narrative*, ed. Henry Louis Gates Jr. and Hollis Robbins (New York, 2004), 135–41.

73. S. Foster Damon, *Thomas Holley Chivers, Friend of Poe, With Selections from His Poems: A Strange Chapter in American Literary History* (New York, 1930), 51.

74. Dickson D. Bruce Jr., *Violence and Culture in the Antebellum South* (Austin, 1979), 222.

75. Savage, *Sybil*, 85.

76. Simms, *Charlemont*, 244.

77. Alexis de Tocqueville, *Democracy in America*, trans. and ed. Harvey C. Mansfield and Delba Winthrop (Chicago, 2000), 244.

78. [Orestes Brownson], "Democracy," *Boston Quarterly Review* 1 (1838): 40.

79. Goodwin, "Civilization," 31.

80. [Brownson], "Democracy," 35.

81. Holt, *Rise and Fall*, 31.

82. Michel Chevalier, *Society, Manners, and Politics in the United States: Letters on North America*, ed. John William Ward (1961; reprint, Gloucester, Mass., 1967), 321.

83. Edmund S. Morgan, *American Slavery, American Freedom: The Ordeal of Colonial Virginia* (New York, 1975); Orlando Patterson, *Freedom: Freedom in the Making of Western Culture* (New York, 1991), 9.

84. Susan Neiman, *Evil in Modern Thought: An Alternative History of Philosophy* (Princeton, 2002), 68.

85. James E. Block, *A Nation of Agents: The American Path to a Modern Self and Society* (Cambridge, Mass., 2002), 316; Eric Foner, *The Story of American Freedom* (New York, 1998), 55.

86. William Leggett, *Democratick Editorials: Essays in Jacksonian Political Economy by William Leggett*, ed. Lawrence H. White (Indianapolis, 1984), 55.

87. Foner, *Story of American Freedom*, 54.

88. George Sidney Camp, *Democracy* (New York, 1841), 91; see Rush Welter, *The Mind of America, 1820–1860* (New York, 1975), 186–87.

89. [Orestes A. Brownson], "The American Democrat," *Boston Quarterly Review* 1 (1838): 365.

90. "Life and Speeches of John C. Calhoun," *Southern Quarterly Review* 9 (1846): 206–7.

91. Goodwin, "Civilization," 28–29.

92. Ralph Waldo Emerson, *The Selected Writings of Ralph Waldo Emerson,* ed. Brooks Atkinson (New York, 1950), 869; Russ Castronovo, *Necro Citizenship: Death, Eroticism, and the Public Sphere in the Nineteenth-Century United States* (Durham, N.C., 2001), 51; Jeffrey Sklansky, *The Soul's Economy: Market Society and Selfhood in American Thought, 1820–1920* (Chapel Hill, 2002), 37.

93. Kristen L. Hoganson, *Fighting for American Manhood: How Gender Politics Provoked the Spanish-American and Philippine-American Wars* (New Haven, 1998), 21–22; Nancy Isenberg, *Sex and Citizenship in Antebellum America* (Chapel Hill, 1998), e.g., 145.

94. Tocqueville, *Democracy,* 235.

95. H. W. Bellows, "Influence of the Trading Spirit Upon the Social and Moral Life of America," *American Whig Review* 1 (1845): 97.

96. See Block, *Nation of Agents,* 354; David Leverenz, *Manhood and the American Renaissance* (Ithaca, 1989), 12.

97. Karen Halttunen, *Murder Most Foul: The Killer and the American Gothic Imagination* (Cambridge, Mass., 1998), 87.

98. Frederick Douglass, *Autobiographies,* ed. Henry Louis Gates Jr. (New York, 1994), 65.

99. Leverenz, *Manhood,* 109, 115; Douglass, *Autobiographies,* 283.

100. Grimké, *Nature and Tendency,* 190.

101. Chevalier, *Society,* 184; see Andrew Burstein, *The Passions of Andrew Jackson* (New York, 2003), 183.

## CONCLUSION

1. Alexis de Tocqueville, *Democracy in America,* trans. and ed. Harvey C. Mansfield and Delba Winthrop (Chicago, 2000), e.g., 511–14.

2. See Charles Sellers, *The Market Revolution: Jacksonian America, 1815–46* (New York, 1991), 259; Thomas W. Laquer, *Solitary Sex: A Cultural History of Masturbation* (New York, 2003), e.g., 249.

3. For two especially useful discussions, see Lindon Barrett, "African American Slave Narratives: Literacy, the Body, Authority," *American Literary History* 7 (1995): 415–42; Karen Halttunen, "Humanitarianism and the Pornography of Pain in Anglo-American Culture," *American Historical Review* 100 (1995): 303–34.

# INDEX